Children, Families and Chr

Chronic childhood disease brings psychological challenges for families and carers as well as the children. In *Children, Families and Chronic Disease* Roger Bradford explores how they cope with these challenges, the psychological and social factors that influence outcomes, and the ways in which the delivery of services can be improved to promote adjustment.

The first part of the book discusses issues around definition and prevalence of chronic childhood disease, the problems it brings for children and their families, and the assumptions on which existing work has been based. The second part is based on the author's own studies into the effects of chronic disease and the factors that influence outcomes, using ideas from health psychology and systemic family therapy. In the third part of the book the author considers the implications of his studies for reassessing current theories of adjustment and suggests ways in which models of care could be extended. This in turn has implications for the organisation of services and highlights areas for future research.

Emphasising the integration of theory and practice, *Children, Families and Chronic Disease* demonstrates the need to develop a multi-level approach to delivery of care which takes into account the child, the family and the wider care system, with recognition of how they interrelate and influence each other.

Roger Bradford is a Consultant Clinical Psychologist in the NHS and Honorary Senior Lecturer at the University of Kent.

Children, Families and Chronic Disease

Psychological models and methods of care

Roger Bradford

London and New York

To my mother, father and Mary

First published 1997
by Routledge
11 New Fetter Lane, London EC4P 4EE

Simultaneously published in the USA and Canada by Routledge
29 West 35th Street, New York, NY 10001

Typeset in Times by Pure Tech India Ltd, Pondicherry
Printed and bound in Great Britain by TJ Press (Padstow) Ltd, Padstow,
Cornwall

British Library Cataloguing in Publication Data
A catalogue record for this book is available from the
British Library

Library of Congress Cataloguing in Publication Data
Bradford, Roger
Children, families, and chronic disease: psychological models
and methods of care/Roger Bradford.
p.   cm.
Includes bibliographical references and index.
1. Chronic diseases in children –Psychological aspects.
2. Adjustment (Psychology) in children.   3. Chronically ill children–
Family relationships. 4. Chronically ill children–
Services for.   I. Title.
RJ380. B73 1996
618.92'0001'9 –dc20   95–50973

ISBN 0–415–13146–4
      0–415–13147–2 (pbk)

Contents

Figures

Tables

Preface

I first became interested in the field of chronic illness and its effects on children and their families whilst training to be a clinical psychologist at Oxford. In my last year of the course, prompted by the fact that relatively little attention had been paid to this specific client group, I chose to do a research project on how children coped with medical procedures. Observing young children going through a routine investigation, I became fascinated by the following question: why was it that some children coped with the procedure, whilst others became highly distressed to the point of needing sedation or the procedure being abandoned?

This basic question has remained with me in my clinical work and underpins much of what is contained in this book. What can psychology tell us about why some children and their families cope whilst others with the same condition, or even one that is less serious, fare less well? What theories have been advanced and how well do they operate in practice? How might we better identify those at risk of poor coping so that scarce resources can be targeted more effectively? How might services be organised to promote patterns of adjustment and coping in children and their carers?

These questions underpin a series of studies that I have been involved in over the past ten years whilst working as a practising clinical psychologist in both hospital and community settings. The aim of my research has been to explore the psychological effects of chronic disease on the child patient and their parents, to highlight psychosocial factors that influence outcomes and to develop models that can help guide interventions. In the chapters that follow I will present my studies and draw out their implications for theory and practice. For me, investigating these issues has helped in thinking about what processes might be involved in adaptation to chronic childhood conditions, which in turn has helped in formulating ideas as to how we help children and families cope.

OUTLINE, PLAN AND A THEORETICAL APPROACH

This book is for a wide audience which includes students, clinicians, applied scientists and service managers. It is organised into three parts, with the first section providing an introduction to the area of chronic illness. In Chapter 1, I consider issues around definition, prevalence and classification and explore the challenges faced by children and their families in coping with a chronic disease. I then explore in Chapter 2 the assumptions made by researchers in studying the effects of disease and highlight the weaknesses of the models used.

In the second section of the book I present a series of studies that explore, either through experiments or through reflections on clinical practice, psychological factors that influence child and family adjustment. My own approach is to use ideas from health psychology and systemic therapy and to think about the connections between children, their parents and the system they find themselves in. Chapter 3 explores factors that influence children's behaviour during a routine X-ray procedure, and Chapter 4 considers influences on parental adjustment by investigating their experiences of the care system and whether health care staff identify their concerns. Influences on longer-term adjustment are explored in Chapter 5, whilst Chapter 6 considers the impact of new medical procedures, such as organ transplantation and the factors that influence adaptation. Family interaction and ways of intervening to promote coping and adjustment are considered in Chapter 7, and the role of community services in influencing outcomes is explored in Chapter 8.

In the final part of the book, I consider the implications of my studies by returning to the fundamental question that I started with, namely what might be some of the reasons why some children cope with their chronic condition, whilst others fare less well? In Chapter 9, I critically review the key theories that have been proposed, and then in Chapter 10 suggest ways in which they could be extended. In the final chapter, I look at the practical implications of how services might be organised to take into account these ideas, and highlight areas for future research.

Acknowledgements

Permission to reproduce the following figures is gratefully acknowledged: 9.2 Pless and Pinkerton, 1975; 9.3 Moos and Shaefer, 1984; 9.4 and 10.2 Rutter *et al.*, 1993; 9.5 Wallander *et al.*, 1989b; 10.1 Ley, 1988.

Part I

Introduction

Chapter 1

What is chronic disease?

INTRODUCTION

Susan: a case study

Susan is a 5-year-old who has a diagnosis of acute lymphoblastic leukaemia. Initially Mrs Wilkins coped well with the increased demands of having a child in hospital, but being a single mother meant that she had to give up her work to be with her daughter. The time Mrs Wilkins spent in hospital meant that Susan's younger brother saw less of his mother and he soon started to show behaviour problems.

By the time Susan was admitted for her next course of treatment, she appeared distressed and refused her injections. Susan told the nurse the treatment made her lose her hair and made her feel sick. For the first time Susan started to question why she had cancer and would she get better, because she had heard that another child with the same condition had died.

Mrs Wilkins was also finding the medical regime tiring. The anxiety about her daughter's condition, coupled with the children's constant demands, increasingly took an emotional toll. She felt that the ward staff and doctors were too busy to be interested in her problems and she became increasingly despondent.

Sam: a case study

Sam is a 6-year-old boy who has biliary atresia (a potentially life-threatening liver disease). He had an operation when he was a baby to correct his liver defect and whilst this was partially successful, he has recently developed oesophageal varices. This is a very distressing and frightening condition, where arteries in the windpipe can suddenly rupture, causing massive, uncontrolled bleeding. Sam has spent a large amount of time in hospital as a result of his liver disease, but despite this is remarkably well adjusted and copes well with his admissions. Both his parents are aware of their child's precarious health, but are able to maintain an optimistic outlook and actively take steps to make sure that Sam's and their own lives remain as normal as possible.

The case studies of Susan and Sam illustrate vividly many of the issues involved in coming to terms with the challenges of chronic childhood disease. There is the shock of diagnosis that has to be coped with, the treatment of the disease itself and then the ongoing disruptions and uncertainties which can have a knock-on effect on the whole family. Equally, the case study of Sam demonstrates that adjustment problems are not inevitable, even when a child and his or her family are faced with the most difficult of circumstances. This book is concerned with exploring the factors that influence how children and their families do come to terms with chronic disease and the processes that underlie this. Through exploring these issues, I hope to highlight ways in which families at risk of poor coping might be better identified and helped in their adjustment.

Modern health care can be said to have two main aims: to increase the life expectancy of the population and to improve the quality of people's lives (Kaplan *et al.*, 1989). Developments in paediatric medicine, which have included a growing emphasis on primary and secondary prevention, the widespread use of immunisation and screening programmes (Hall, 1992), improvements in neonatal care, surgical techniques and post-operative procedures (Zitelli *et al.*, 1986), coupled with the development of new medicines and treatments, have all served to ensure, on the one hand, the virtual eradication of some common childhood illnesses, and on the other, the survival of many more children with conditions that previously would have proved fatal.

As a consequence of these developments, 'chronic disease' has become a new illness that paediatricians and others must now treat. This new challenge has resulted in changes in the organisation of hospital and community services and in clinical practice, as professionals have had to develop their technical expertise to deal with the particular difficulties that this group of children can encounter. The Platt Report in 1959 recognised some of these challenges and, in doing so, set a blueprint for how hospital care should be provided, borrowing many of the concepts from theories of attachment that were being advanced at that time (Bowlby, 1971; Robertson, 1958). No longer were children expected to be isolated from their families during hospital admissions; rather, the care-taker was encouraged to stay with their child and to take an active role in preparing and helping their child cope with the experience (Sainsbury *et al.*, 1986). Pressure groups, such as the National Association for the Welfare of Children in Hospital (NAWCH), became a powerful lobbying force in ensuring that these changes were implemented and that the emotional care of children and families became as important as their medical management.

As a result of these collective pressures, paediatricians, nurses and others have had to develop an increasingly sophisticated understanding of the psychological needs of children and their families (Munson, 1986) and have had to develop communication skills to meet these (Ley, 1988). Whilst it is undoubtedly the case that significant progress has been achieved in helping children with chronic diseases and families cope and adjust, it is equally apparent that we still need to strive to ensure that the emotional needs of children and their parents are recognised and met.

DEFINITIONS

Perhaps one of the most difficult tasks in writing about chronic disease is to be clear what is meant by the term.

If one looks at the various studies that have attempted to map out how many children are affected by chronic diseases, it becomes very clear that a number of definitions have been used. For example, the Isle of Wight study considered children to have a chronic disease if their condition was associated with 'persisting or recurrent handicap of some kind [which] lasts for at least one year' (Rutter *et al.*, 1970: 275).

Others have suggested that chronic disease refers to 'a disorder with a protracted course which can be progressive and fatal, or associated with a relatively normal life span despite impaired physical or mental functioning' (Mattsson, 1972: 801). Pless and Pinkerton specified the following parameters in their definition of chronic disease: '[It is] a physical condition, usually non fatal condition, which lasts longer than three months in a given year, or necessitates a period of continuous hospitalisation of more than one month in a year' (Pless and Pinkerton, 1975: 90).

Eiser (1990) has defined chronic diseases as 'conditions that affect children for extended periods of time, often for life. These diseases can be "managed" to the extent that a degree of pain control or reduction in attacks, bleeding episodes or seizures can generally be achieved. However they cannot be cured' (Eiser, 1990: 3). Hobbs and Perrin (1985) argue that a chronic disorder is one 'that lasts for any substantial period of time, or has sequelae that are debilitating for a long period of time' (Hobbs and Perrin, 1985: 2). They note that such conditions 'persist for a number of years after onset and have a variable course with some improving, some remaining stable and some becoming progressively worse' (Hobbs and Perrin, 1985: 2).

These definitions highlight that whilst there is a general consensus as to what constitutes a chronic illness, namely that the condition is protracted and can result in a number of diverse and adverse outcomes, ranging from normal life expectancy to death, researchers have none the less placed differing emphases on certain aspects of the definition, particularly in relation to the issue of 'chronicity' and 'severity'.

The lack of agreed terminology has resulted in marked variations in how many children are thought to suffer from a chronic disease.

PREVALENCE

Research into the prevalence of chronic childhood disorders suggests a rate of approximately 10–15 per cent in the general population (Pless and Nolan, 1991), with 10 per cent (or 1–2 per cent of the total childhood population) having a condition that could be deemed severe (Pless and Roghmann, 1971). These figures represent an aggregate rate, as individual epidemiological studies have produced somewhat conflicting estimates, with prevalence rates ranging from 6 per cent (Rutter *et al.*, 1970) to 14 per cent (Cadman *et al.*, 1987) to 30 per cent (Mattsson, 1972).

The reasons for these discrepancies in prevalence are complex. As has been highlighted already, the exact definitions used to operationalise 'chronic disease' can significantly influence the number of children subsequently identified. Similarly, the methods of study employed to identify 'cases', for example, questionnaires in comparison to interviews, as well as the location where the research is carried out, contribute towards producing differing sample characteristics and hence differing prevalence rates (Gortmaker and Sappenfield, 1984). To take an example, in Rutter *et al.*'s (1970) study, prevalence figures are the result of investigating all children aged between 10–12 years on the Isle of Wight. Cases were identified initially on the basis of medical records held at schools and hospitals, and by parental screening questionnaire. Subsequently, those identified as having a possible disorder were followed up intensively, where a final diagnosis was made.

It is important to note that in using 'chronic physical handicap' as their criteria for case selection, Rutter *et al.* (1970) excluded other conditions that some researchers might have included (for example, obesity and chronic migraine). It is also apparent that Rutter *et al.* (1970) excluded 'milder' degrees of handicap from their final analysis (certain respiratory and sensory disorders). This has led some to suggest that the resulting prevalence rate of 6 per cent represents a 'conservative' estimate (Pless and Roghmann, 1971). In contrast, Mattsson (1972) included in his study all those conditions not studied by Rutter and colleagues, and indeed extended the definition of chronic childhood illness to encompass not only those with visual and hearing impairment, but also those with disorders of speech, learning and behaviour, as well. Given this wide-ranging definition, it is perhaps not surprising that a significantly higher prevalence rate of childhood 'disease' was obtained.

APPROACHES TO CLASSIFICATION

Clearly, there is less consensus as to what constitutes a chronic disease, and therefore its prevalence, than might have been expected. This lack of agreement extends also to the issue of whether it is possible to develop a system of classification within chronic diseases, in order to study, for example i) the impact of particular chronic childhood ii) conditions on psychological outcomes. If it is possible to arrive at a classification system, there is an ongoing debate as to how useful such schemes are. Such attempts at classification tend to fall into three main types: those that seek to group disorders on the grounds of their aetiology, their disease characteristics or their severity.

Aetiology

An example of this approach to classification is described by Fielding (1985), who amended Mattsson's (1972) original classification system. Fielding suggests that there are five main causes of disease and that the psychological effects of chronic disease should therefore be studied in relation to these categories:

- Diseases due to chromosomal aberrations: Down's, Klinefelter's and Turner's syndromes.
- Diseases as a result of abnormal heredity traits: sickle cell anaemia, cystic fibrosis, muscular dystrophy, diabetes myelitis.

- Diseases due to interuterine factors: damage caused by infections, for example rubella, and damage caused by other factors such as drugs or radiation exposure.
- Disorders resulting from perinatal traumatic and infectious events, including permanent damage to central nervous system and motor abilities.
- Diseases due to postnatal and childhood infections, neoplasms and other factors: meningitis, renal failure, physical injuries resulting in permanent handicaps, mental illness and mental retardation of organic aetiology.

(Fielding, 1985: 34)

This approach has the advantage that it mirrors closely the way in which paediatric medical services are organised, that is in terms of their sub-specialities. Thus, from a medical model, it may well make sense to think about the effects of chronic disease in terms of their impact on services and level and type of medical expertise required. However, it is less certain whether, and if so why, the psychosocial impact of chronic illness follows these diagnostic lines. For example, do children with abnormal hereditary traits differ psychologically as a group in comparison to children who suffer postnatal infections, and if so, why should that be the case?

If one looks at the research, the evidence to date is somewhat contradictory as to whether specific groups of disease are in fact associated with specific psychological outcomes. On the one hand, studies have suggested that certain factors within groups of conditions are linked to increased rates of psychopathology. For example, Rutter *et al.* (1970) identified an increased risk of emotional and behavioural problems in children who had neurological disorders.

On the other hand, Pless and Perrin (1985), in their review of the literature, conclude that studies that have sought to establish a link between specific diseases and particular psychosocial difficulties in the child have largely failed to demonstrate any significant association. As they see it, there is no such thing as a 'typical' psychological profile that applies to a specific disorder. Pless and Perrin (1985) argue that there is in fact far more evidence for the contention that 'common' reactions and problems occur, a point to which we will return shortly.

Disease characteristics

An alternative approach to classification advocated by Pless and Perrin (1985) is based on the hypothesis that psychological outcomes are mediated by specific disease factors. They suggest that diseases should be categorised in relation to whether they have an impact on

- the child's level of mobility–activity,
- whether the course of the disease is static or dynamic,
- the child's age when the disease process starts,
- whether the child's cognitive and sensory functioning is affected, and
- whether the condition is visible.

Pless and Perrin's (1985) argument is that the above dimensions may be important in teasing out the variable impact of 'chronic diseases' on children. For example, mobility–activity could be an important dimension, as many disorders that affect mobility require orthopaedic surgery as well as costly appliances and physical therapy for rehabilitation. Children requiring this level of support and intervention might experience, therefore, difficulties entering mainstream schooling and might, for example, find difficulty joining in with peers at recreation times. This might then have a knock-on effect to their development of self-esteem and social skills. Equally, diseases that affect mobility might increase the burden on mothers as the prime care giver, not to mention additional hardship, which could have indirect consequences on both maternal and child adjustment.

Whether the course of the illness is static (that is, a relatively fixed deficit such as a neurological impairment) or dynamic (changes over time) may also be important to distinguish. For example, whether the course of disease is predictable towards improvement or decline, or whether it is marked by exacerbations, with times when the child may be relatively healthy and others when he/she may be quite ill, could have important implications for adjustment. Equally, age of onset may have a differential effect on adaptation. For example, children with early onset problems (for example, liver and congenital heart disease) may have different developmental and service needs from those with later onset conditions (for example, diabetes or asthma). Similarly, children who have grown up with their disease might show differing patterns of adjustment in comparison to those who have been healthy and then acquire a disability later in childhood.

Whilst Pless and Perrin's (1985) overall hypothesis has face validity, it has not been subject to substantial empirical investigation. Where studies have explored individual dimensions of the model, such as the effect of disease visibility on adjustment, the results have proved rather inconclusive, with some studies finding an association, whilst others have failed to do so. For example, Mulhern *et al.* (1989) followed up long-term survivors of childhood cancer. They found that whilst the children showed subtle adjustment problems (four-fold increase in school problems and somatic complaints of unknown origin over the general population), it was the presence of functional disorders, not how visible the disease was, that increased the risk of experiencing these difficulties.

Severity

A final approach to classification to be considered here concerns disease severity. The issue of whether disease severity influences adjustment has attracted particular attention in the literature, as it would seem to be common sense that the more severe the condition the worse the psychological outcome, with the corollary being the milder the physical complaint, the less emotional distress experienced. However, it appears that the relationship may not be so simple. For example, MacLean *et al.* (1992) report a direct relationship between clinical severity of asthma and child adjustment. Thus, the worse the condition the poorer the child's adjustment. However, McAnarney *et al.* (1974) report that poor adaptation in children with arthritis was more likely in those children *without* disability than those with. Perrin *et al.* (1989), in exploring the impact of disease severity, found a curvilinear relationship, whereby children with moderate asthma were better adjusted than children with either mild or severe forms of the disease. Wallander *et al.* (1989a), on the other hand, have failed to establish *any* link between severity of disease in cerebral palsy and spina bifida and child maladjustment.

These studies highlight the fact that disease severity does not reliably predict how well a child will cope. One reason for the inconsistent relationship between severity and psychological outcomes lies in the fact that 'disease severity' can be difficult to translate into a clinically meaningful concept. For example, Hobbs and Perrin (1985) tied themselves up in linguistic knots when they proposed five criteria for assessing whether a disease is severe, based on its impact on psychosocial functioning. They argued that the following should be taken into account:

1. The illness places a large financial burden on the family.
2. The illness restricts significantly the child's physical development.

3. The illness impairs significantly the ability of the child to engage in accustomed and expected activities.
4. The illness contributes significantly to emotional problems for the child as expressed in maladaptive coping strategies.
5. The illness contributes significantly to the disruption of family life as evidenced, for example, in increased marital conflict and sibling behaviour disorder.

(Hobbs and Perrin, 1985: 2)

Hobbs and Perrin's frequent use of 'significant' in the above criteria does little to resolve the problem of objectively operationalising 'severity'; who, for example, should say whether the disorder significantly contributes to a given problem: the doctor, mother, father or child? Indeed there is some doubt as to how clinically meaningful the concept is. For example, a child either has cystic fibrosis or not, and the extent to which a child copes with the disease at any one particular point in time is as much a function of the services they receive and how the family copes with the various challenges, as it is of severity.

Overall, the balance of evidence tends to suggest that disease severity, as defined by physicians using 'objective criteria', is not a reliable predictor of subsequent adjustment (Walker *et al.*, 1987; Davis 1993).

Non-categorical approaches

Given the failure of classification approaches in reliably predicting psychological outcomes in children and their parents, researchers have turned increasingly to the argument that the tendency to look for differences between diseases has served to obscure the commonalities that exist. Perhaps, the argument goes, research should stop trying to find idiosyncratic consequences to conditions and concentrate more upon stresses and challenges that apply across conditions?

In 1982, Stein and Jessop advocated this approach when they called for a non-categorical approach to studying the effects of childhood chronic disease. They argued that the research had demonstrated convincingly that there were striking similarities in the challenges that childhood disease presented, regardless of the particular diagnosis, and that as a consequence, the search for idiosyncratic reactions to specific disorders was unwarranted.

As already highlighted, Pless and Perrin's review of the literature convinced them that a number of common challenges face children and their families and that these challenges cut across diagnostic considerations. They concluded:

> there are a limited number of difficulties frequently experienced by many, if not most, families who have a child with a chronic disorder. The difficulties vary only slightly from disorder to disorder or from family to family. If anything, the nature of the family, more than the nature of the disorder, is likely to determine the frequency with which certain problems are experienced.
>
> (Pless and Perrin, 1985: 49)

Varni and Wallander (1988), in a more recent commentary, have reached a similar conclusion, citing as evidence their own as well as others' research. For example, Wallander *et al.* (1988) investigated the hypothesis that child adjustment would vary as a function of the child's diagnostic condition. They asked mothers of 270 chronically ill and handicapped children aged 4–16 to complete the Child Behaviour Checklist (Achenback and Edelbrock, 1983), a screening tool for emotional and behavioural difficulties. Children had a diagnosis of either juvenile diabetes, spina bifida, juvenile rheumatoid arthritis, haemophilia, chronic obesity or cerebral palsy.

Analysis of the completed Child Behaviour Checklists demonstrated that, as a group, the children did have higher behavioural and social competence problems in comparison to a normative sample of healthy peers (10 per cent versus 2 per cent). However, the children's adjustment problems did not vary in relation to their particular diagnosis. Thus children with spina bifida had the same rate and type of difficulties as, for example, children with diabetes.

If these arguments for a non-categorical approach have some justification, what might some of the common issues be that children and families face in adjusting to a chronic disease?

CHALLENGES FACED BY CHILDREN AND FAMILIES

Challenges faced by children

Chronically ill children face the same developmental tasks and challenges as healthy children. However, mastery of these tasks and successful coping with the common stresses of childhood are made more difficult by the continuing presence of a disease that can significantly alter the child's physical and mental functioning, as well as interactions with the environment (Garrison and McQuiston, 1989). Over and above the 'normal' tasks of childhood, children with a chronic disease face a number of specific challenges (Fielding, 1985). Initially, there are the unpleasant and painful symptoms that may be associated with the disease itself. For example, children with sickle cell anaemia can experience excruciatingly painful attacks, known as 'crises', which can afflict hands and feet, arms or legs and sometimes the abdomen, all of which can last for several days (West, 1991).

Following the identification of a problem, the child is likely to undergo assessment and treatment procedures, which in themselves can be both worrying and painful and which may produce side-effects in their own right. For example, children with leukaemia may experience highly invasive assessments, such as bone marrow aspirations (Katz *et al.*, 1980; Jay *et al.*, 1985) and medical treatments including radiotherapy and drugs which can result in the child vomiting, having mouth ulcers, constipation and suffering hair loss. Treatment may also involve repeated hospital admissions, which can be highly disruptive to the development of the child's sense of security (Platt Report, 1959). There may be separations from loved ones and from normal family life, as well as possible disruption to school attendance and to academic progress (Klein *et al.*, 1984; Perrin and MacLean, 1988).

Children with a chronic condition face the task as they grow older of needing to foster independence not only from their parents, but also from the medical and nursing professions. In some diseases, for example diabetes, the child will need to take increasing responsibility for their own medical management. A further challenge is the development of effective coping mechanisms. The course of the disease may be characterised by periods of uncertainty as the symptoms wax and wane, and the child is likely to face numerous assessment and treatment procedures (Moos and Shaefer, 1984) all of which need to be mastered. The child's coping mechanisms can also be tested by the restrictions imposed (Worchel *et al.*, 1988), either as the direct result of the disease process and its medical management, or as a consequence of indirect influences, such as parents becoming over-protective.

Challenges faced by parents

The challenges that parents face are no less significant. Parents will need to adjust to the news that their child has a condition that potentially will affect the child for his or her lifetime (Tew and Laurence, 1973). Whether the child has been born with a chronic condition, or develops an illness later in life, parents will be confronted with the reality that their plans and expectations will have to be adjusted to take into account the limitations imposed by the child's condition. The fact that the nature and extent of those limitations can be hard to predict adds to the strains as parents struggle to come to grips with the uncertainty of their child's future.

A second stress that confronts parents is dealing with medical services and the 'doctor–patient' relationship. While the child is in hospital, parents are faced with the necessity of handing over certain aspects of their child's care to doctors or nurses. Yet at the same time they need to retain a central role in helping their child cope with the procedures, and even to take on some of the responsibility for the medical management of the child by, for example, providing physiotherapy in the case of cystic fibrosis, or giving insulin injections if the child has diabetes. A related stress is the need to monitor the child's illness and to decide when medication or intervention is required.

Caring for the child at home can also create problems. The more routine aspects of caring for a child can become more complicated, time consuming and emotionally laden (Eiser, 1990). For example, feeding problems in infancy are a relatively common feature of normal development (Skuse, 1994). However, when they occur within the context of a chronic disease, particularly one that is life threatening, the significance the feeding difficulty can take on is vastly heightened and can result in battles of will between parent and child (Drotar and Strum, 1988). Equally, tensions can develop between parents as to whose responsibility it is to meet the demands of care giving.

A fourth major stress for parents is coping with the disruption to normal family life. The demands of attending frequent hospital appointments and the need to ensure that medications are given on time mean that the potential exists for family life to revolve increasingly around the sick child, at the expense of other family members (Minuchin *et al.*, 1975). Equally, the burden of balancing these demands can place new or additional strains on the marital relationship (Sabbeth and Leventhal, 1984), which can be further complicated by the frequent financial pressures associated with looking after an ill child. For example parents may need to give up work to look after their child (Breslau *et al.*, 1982), and incur extra expense as a result of travelling long distances to hospital or as a consequence of needing to obtain special equipment, provide special diets or adaptations to the home (Fielding, 1985). Studies of doctor–patient communication highlight that parents are often dissatisfied with their medical consultations

(Ley, 1988), which in turn increases all the stresses associated with looking after an ill child.

Challenges faced by siblings

The impact of chronic disorders on healthy siblings is a sadly neglected area. What evidence is available tends to suggest that brothers and sisters of ill children experience a number of psychological problems, including mood changes, attention-seeking behaviour, changes in academic performance, withdrawal, somatic complaints and other regressed behaviours (Drotar and Crawford, 1985). The reasons why healthy siblings might show such reactions include the hypothesis that at the time of diagnosis parents inevitably focus their energies on the affected child and as a consequence other children in the family have to cope with the parents being less available, both emotionally and practically. At such times it is easy to see that brothers and sisters might develop a sense that there is a 'special' relationship between the sick child and the parents that to some extent excludes them. The reality is that parents will feel drained by the emotional roller coaster they are on in coming to terms with the diagnosis of a serious problem and as a result may feel that they lack the resources to recognise and meet fully the needs of their other children. The realisation of this can of course induce more guilt at a time when the parents are already feeling vulnerable.

Healthy siblings may also suffer a degree of isolation. This can be a consequence of the family physically needing to protect the sick child from common childhood infections, which means that opportunities to have friends around are reduced. Equally, there is evidence to suggest that a number of parents actively decide not to discuss the issue of illness at home, for fear this might upset the sick child's brothers and sisters. The effect of this can be for the non-affected children to feel inhibited to ask questions, as if the subject was taboo. Over time, this 'collusion of silence' can become so entrenched that parents might interpret the child's lack of inquiry as disinterest.

The little research that has been conducted suggests that healthy siblings often harbour feelings that parents either fail to recognise or, where they are identified, tend to underestimate (Walker, 1988). This mismatch, between what siblings feel and parental estimates of the impact of having a sick brother or sister, is to some extent compounded by the hospital system, as the focus of medical and nursing teams is invariably upon the dyads of mother–sick child, father–sick child and parents–sick child. For example, Stewart *et al.* (1992) interviewed ten healthy siblings, each with a brother or sister with a terminal illness. They found that none of the children had ever had the opportunity to discuss their siblings' illness with a doctor.

The extent of difficulties experienced by siblings has been clarified by Cadman *et al.* (1988). They surveyed 3,294 children between the ages of 4–16 years who had a sibling with a chronic disease or disorder. Compared to the general population, Cadman *et al.* (1988) found that their sample experienced a two-fold increase in emotional disorders, such as depression and anxiety. Whilst this is an important finding, particularly in highlighting that siblings have needs that require attending to, the study none the less illustrates an overall tendency within research to seek out 'pathological' reactions to a chronic condition, a point that will be developed more fully in the next section.

It is important not to lose sight of the fact that adverse reactions are not inevitable and indeed there is some limited research to suggest that an over-emphasis on pathology is misleading. For example, Horowitz and Kazak (1990) found that chronic illness affords the opportunity for siblings to develop prosocial skills, in the form of children showing more affection, consideration, helping and praising, in comparison to children from families where there is no chronic disease.

CRITIQUE OF PSYCHOLOGICAL APPROACHES

In the light of the challenges faced by the child patient and their family, it is perhaps not surprising that researchers have become increasingly interested in exploring the psychological sequelae of chronic illness. The early research into the psychosocial effects of chronic disease was largely based on the assumption that chronic disease would inevitably have an adverse effect on the patient and on those who looked after him or her (for example, Knowles, 1971; Mattsson, 1972; Gayton *et al.*, 1977). As a consequence, the research has tended to emphasise the pathology surrounding the way in which families, and in particular mothers, coped with the diagnosis and subsequent management of the sick child. These early studies have been criticised on the grounds that many of the studies were in fact largely anecdotal in nature, with little attempt being made to go beyond subjective evaluations and uncontrolled investigations (Fielding, 1985). As such, much of the research was descriptive and barely represented an adequate test of the hypothesis that families often failed to cope.

Research that followed was arguably more rigorous, as more qualitative and quantitative approaches were introduced, based largely upon semi-structured interviews and paper and pen measures. Whilst these developments in research design addressed some of the earlier criticisms, these studies still rarely questioned the underlying assumption that chronic disease was a significant factor in inducing psychopathology and maladjustment, with successful coping in children and their families being unusual, and poor coping the norm (for example, Kroll and Jacobs, 1995). The researcher's task was, therefore, to calibrate the extent of the difficulties, albeit using the more 'objective' tools that had been generated in mainstream psychology, such as intelligence tests, personality questionnaires and assessments of mental health (Tavormina *et al.*, 1976; Bedell *et al.*, 1977; Kellerman *et al.*, 1980). These studies have been in turn subject to criticism. For example, the underlying theoretical assumptions of pathology have been found inadequate, as more recent research has failed to confirm that adverse effects on child and family functioning are inevitable. Indeed there is some evidence to suggest that positive effects can result from the diagnosis of a problem. Hauser *et al.* (1986), for example, found that following a diagnosis of diabetes in a child, families tended to show more 'enabling behaviours', for example, acceptance, empathy and problem-solving activities.

Equally, the notion that chronic disease is a unitary phenomenon, which can be said to have a similar impact on children and families, has not been borne out (Fielding, 1985). Clinical experience shows that the reactions of families vary greatly, with some being devastated, whilst others appear to cope well. It is becoming clear that inconsistent results that have been reported concerning the psychosocial effects of chronic disease are often the consequence of researchers failing to put the child's illness into context. For example, studies have neglected variables such as the child's age at diagnosis, aspects of the disease, complexity of the medical regimen and how these relate to the child and family's adjustment. As Fielding (1985) has argued, it is inappropriate to assume, in a group study, that all children will be similar in terms of their illness; some will be in remission and others in relapse, yet this has not always been taken into account.

The methods and measures used to determine 'adjustment' have also attracted criticism. Eiser (1990) argues, for example, that in selecting certain measures, most researchers pay little attention to whether they have any theoretical relevance to the child's adjustment. A related point is made by Perrin *et al.* (1991) when they review the frequent use of the Child Behaviour Check List (CBCL) (Achenbach and Edelbock, 1983) in studies of child adjustment to chronic disease. This measure has come to dominate the field (12 out of 20 studies in America published between 1987–1989 relied upon the measure), yet Perrin *et al.* (1991) highlight three key problems in its use. Firstly, scores can be artificially inflated, because the scale includes several items that directly tap physical health problems ('child has asthma', 'stomach-aches', 'constipated', 'wets self', etc). Clearly a child with a chronic disease is highly likely to experience a number of physical symptoms and therefore their scores on the CBCL will be elevated in comparison to their healthy peers, thereby giving the possibly spurious impression that they experience more psychological problems. Interestingly, the same criticism can be made of the Rutter A questionnaire (Rutter *et al.*, 1970), which has dominated research in the UK, as it too includes physical health items in its screening for psychiatric disorders.

A second limitation highlighted by Perrin *et al.* (1991) concerns the CBCL's insensitivity to mild adjustment problems. The CBCL was designed to identify children with significant emotional and behavioural disorders, and as such it may well fail to identify children whose difficulties do not reach such intensity, yet which may still be of concern to the child themselves and their family. A related point is that, given the original rationale for the development of the measure, it understandably fails to sample behaviours of particular relevance to children coping with chronic disease, such as compliance with medication or distress during medical procedures. Arguably such items are of theoretical importance in defining child 'adjustment', and their absence from the CBCL calls into question the relevance of the measure with this particular population.

Thirdly, the CBCL provides a score not only for emotional/behavioural difficulties but also for 'social competence'. Perrin *et al.* (1991) argue that this latter scale is incomplete and potentially misleading as it focuses on the child's accomplishment and participation in activities. The presence of a chronic disorder, however, often means the child may have restricted opportunities to join such activities (for example, sports and membership of clubs) as the illness itself or the need to attend hospital can have both direct and indirect effects. It has been concluded, rightly, that 'the fact that some children with a chronic illness are unable to participate in certain social activities solely because of their condition does not mean they are less socially competent' (Perrin *et al.*, 1991: 416).

Taken as a whole, a criticism that can be levelled at much of the research to date is its failure to be driven by conceptual or theoretical models, and an over-reliance on measures derived from the broader mental health field to capture the intricacies of family relationships and interactions in relation to chronic disease. This is not to say that such measures do not have a place, but their use needs to be carefully considered in the light of their appropriateness and relevance to the particular issues faced by children with a chronic condition and their families.

In the next chapter I will explore how these criticisms might be addressed through the development of new models and methods of investigation.

SUMMARY

The main points of this chapter can be summarised as follows.

- Many more children are surviving illnesses that previously would have proved fatal. This has a number of implications for the development of paediatric services and for the training of staff. Equally, we need to acknowledge that Chronic childhood problems require skilled intervention involving both medical and psychological approaches.

- Epidemiological studies point to between 6–30 per cent of children having a chronic disorder. Whilst surveys have not always agreed as to what constitutes a 'chronic illness', it is clear that there are many children and families who have to cope with a condition that is incurable and that has significant implications for the child's development and life expectancy.

- Attempts to study psychological outcomes in relation to the child's particular disorder, specific disease characteristics or disease severity have produced inconsistent and often contradictory results.

- As a consequence, 'non-categorical' approaches are now being advocated, with the emphasis on identification of common stresses and challenges faced by the child patient, siblings and parents.

- Historically, psychological research has been dominated by studies that have measured the adverse effects that result from a chronic disease. Underlying these studies is the assumption that psychopathology in both the child and their carers is inevitable. Much of this research can be criticised for adopting an overly simplistic approach and for relying on research designs of questionable relevance.

Chapter 2

Old and new approaches

Clinical experience confirms time and again that the idea of children and parents inevitably developing psychological problems in coping with a chronic disease does not stand up to close scrutiny.

OLD APPROACHES

In Chapter 1, I suggested that psychological research has become overly focused on what can be described as a 'pathological' model, the underlying assumption being that psychological problems, or 'pathology', are common and therefore the researcher's task is to calibrate the extent of difficulties encountered. There are probably two main reasons why psychological research has pursued this particular line of enquiry. In getting to grips with any 'new' problem area, there is an understandable desire to map out the size of the territory. Not only does this provide useful information in terms of drawing attention to the extent of difficulties experienced but such research can also have implications for the development of new services to meet the problems identified. Thus, having identified a certain number of children as suffering from a chronic disease and delineated the psychological problems that result, it is possible to argue for resources to be allocated to meet likely demand.

A second reason for research following a pathological model is the fact that until recently, there have been very few measures available to address any other type of question. Our conceptualisation and definition of mental health have been such that we have seen child and family 'adjustment' or 'adaptation' or 'coping' as being the absence of mental health difficulties, and these in turn have been defined as the individual not experiencing certain symptoms (anxiety, depression, conduct disorders and the like). Psychological measures have been developed within this context, their aim being to classify an individual correctly as to their mental health.

These old approaches highlight a major limitation: if adjustment is conceived as being the absence of mental health difficulties, then it is not surprising that mental health measures will be employed to investigate the issue. Clearly, such measures allow the researcher to explore problems that families might have using reliable and valid procedures. The major drawback to this approach, however, is that it can often be unhelpful or inappropriate to think about a child's adjustment to chronic disease simply in terms of mental health categories. For example, children will face both painful and invasive procedures in the investigation and treatment of their disease, but the definition of whether a child was able to cope with the procedure in terms of their mental health status would not be a very sensitive or appropriate way to proceed. Rather it would be more desirable to take, for example, a developmental perspective by considering how children of a similar age cope and what factors influence the strategies used.

The pathological model can also be criticised for overly focusing on difficulties, failures and deviations from the 'normal'. Not only is the approach inherently pessimistic, it also fails to explain the more recent findings that psychological outcomes in chronic childhood disease are not inevitably negative. For example, the assumption that marital breakdown is common in families where a child has a chronic disease is not supported by the evidence, which in fact indicates the divorce rate is no higher in comparison to those parents with healthy children (Sabbeth and Leventhal, 1984; Cadman *et al.*, 1991). Indeed, there is some research that suggests the presence of a chronic disease may actually bring families closer together (for example, Barbarin *et al.*, 1985) and have a positive effect on sibling relationships. Horowitz and Kazak (1990), for example, report that following the diagnosis of cancer, siblings showed advanced development (in comparison to age-matched controls) in prosocial behaviours, such as being more considerate, sharing and showing affection and generally being more helpful.

Pathological models have failed also to address the fundamental question, posed by researcher and clinician alike, as to why some children and their families cope successfully with the challenges they face in adjusting to a chronic disease, whilst others with the same condition fare less well. This in many ways is the central question that needs to be addressed, as gaining insight into this would help develop our understanding of the pathways that underpin adaptation and lead to the better targeting of resources.

These arguments against the pathological model point to a need to reappraise how child adjustment is understood and investigated as well as to a need to reconceptualise the psychological impact of chronic disorders on the child patient and their families. We also need to develop measures that are more sensitive to the specific issues and challenges engendered by chronic disease.

NEW APPROACHES

In addressing these issues, I believe there are two promising new approaches that we could follow. These are paediatric health psychology and systems theory.

Paediatric health psychology

With the emergence of paediatric health psychology as a distinct discipline in the last ten years, there is a growing potential for new ways to investigate, intervene in and understand the psychological sequelae of chronic disease. Paediatric health psychology can be described as:

> the aggregate of the specific educational, scientific, and professional contributions of the discipline of psychology to the promotion and maintenance of health, the prevention and treatment of illness, and related dysfunctions, and to the analysis and improvement of the health care system and health policy formation.
>
> (Division of Health Psychology, quoted by Roberts, 1986: 5)

At the heart of the approach is the conceptualisation of chronic diseases as creating particular stresses and strains which families then react to with a range of responses and coping behaviours (Wallander, 1990). Under this paradigm, the focus of interest shifts away from measuring pathology per se to enquiring into questions such as:

- which families or family members are vulnerable to the stress engendered by a chronic disorder
- which aspects of caring are particularly difficult
- which psychosocial variables contribute to poor coping
- what are the unmet service needs of families
- which families adapt to the potential stresses and how do they do so?

These are compelling questions, because their answers could have direct implications for theory, policy and practice, and might result in new ideas as to how families at risk of poor coping and adjustment could be identified. Furthermore, research into this area might suggest ways of how best to organise services so that family adaptation is enhanced. Equally, such a change in emphasis might have implications for clinicians in developing new ways of working with children and their families by, for example, highlighting factors in doctor–patient interaction that influence the process of adaptation in their child patients. Within the context of modern health care, arriving at some answer to the above issues is increasingly a priority, as the matching of resources to identified need becomes more imperative, for both financial and clinical reasons.

Systems theory

To study families is to take an inherently integrative and complex view of adjustment (Kazak, 1989). 'Systemic' approaches provide a framework in which we can start to explore the impact of chronic disease on children and their families and factors that influence this process. According to Hoffman (1981), the key principles underlying the 'systemic' approach are:

a) systems are composed of interrelated parts
b) change in one part is associated with change in all others
c) systems maintain a regular state of balance (homeostasis)
d) systems maintain a balance between periods of change and stability.

In the context of chronic illness, the focus of a systems approach is to see the way in which people behave and the problems they have as being related to their family structure and organisation, which in turn is influenced by the wider environment. A family's structure, or functioning, develops in response to the tasks it has to fulfil or achieve. Epstein *et al.* (1978) identify three sets of tasks:

1. Basic tasks – these fall into two types: instrumental and affective. Examples of the former include the provision of food and shelter, whilst provision of nurturance, affection and support are examples of the latter.
2. Developmental tasks – again there are broadly two types. Firstly, there are actions directed at ensuring the healthy develop-

ment of the individual by, for example, ensuring there is appropriate respect for each person's individuality. Secondly, there are tasks that relate to family stages, ensuring the family unit is flexible to new demands.

3.   Hazardous events – crises that occur in association with illness, accidents, unemployment and the like.

(Will and Wrate, 1985)

The diagnosis of a chronic illness or disorder clearly represents a 'hazardous event', with the family needing to establish a new balance to cope with the challenges it will face. From a systems perspective, a problem in any member of a family (such as a chronic disease) has an effect on all other members, and changes in behaviour in any one element of the system (for example, the parents becoming protective) affect all others. Thus, a chronic illness has ramifications for all those involved.

A THEORETICAL APPROACH

The overall purpose of this book is to explore how adjustment varies, to highlight some of the causal pathways underlying adjustment and to draw out the implications of these findings for theory, policy and practice in the development and delivery of hospital and community services. In pursuing these questions, the approach I have taken is to link ideas from health psychology and systems theory and to explore through experiments and reflections on clinical practice how child and family adjustment is influenced by risk factors. The variables that I focus upon particularly are those relating to the individual (for example, temperament and health beliefs), the family (for example, family functioning and communication) and characteristics of the social context that the child and family find themselves in (for example, hospital and wider care system).

The overview of the literature provided in Chapter 1 highlighted a number of methodological criticisms in the research to date, in particular an over-emphasis and reliance on pen and paper measures of questionable relevance to the population under study and an over-emphasis on mother and child adjustment at the expense of family dynamics. In addressing these criticisms, the focus of my research programme is to use, where appropriate, observational methodologies, that systematically assess the patterns of interaction both within families and between family members and the health care system, and to use assessment tools that are sensitive to the issues involved in chronic childhood disease. Rather than seeing children and parents as functioning in isolation from each other, the emphasis is placed on the interdependence between children, their families and the context in which they find themselves.

In exploring the challenges that children and families face, my approach is consistent with what has been termed an 'applicable research' model. The essential characteristic of this approach is 'a strong orientation towards a practical problem [with] the goal of making convincing recommendations for its solution' (Watts, 1984: 41).

MAP OF THE RESEARCH PROGRAMME

In Part II of the book nine studies will be presented which either directly test influences on adjustment, or highlight important factors indirectly, through reflections on clinical practice and the organisation of services. I start by exploring risk factors to child distress during a routine assessment procedure in Chapter 3 and then assess influences on parental adjustment by investigating parents' experiences of the care system and whether health care staff identify their concerns (Chapter 4.) Influences on longer-term adjustment are explored in Chapter 5, whilst Chapter 6 considers the impact of new medical procedures, such as organ transplantation, and the factors that influence adaptation. Family interaction and ways of intervening to promote coping and adjustment are considered in Chapter 7 and the role of community services in influencing outcomes is explored in Chapter 8. The arrangement of these studies is such that we start with the child and family as outpatients, then move on to their inpatient stay, culminating in discharge and return to local services.

SUMMARY

The key points of the chapter can be summarised as follows:

- To date, most research has tended to follow a pathological model in studying the effects of chronic illness and disease. Such models emphasise the difficulties and failures that children and families experience as a consequence of a chronic condition.
- This approach is increasingly subject to criticism. With the advent of more sophisticated studies, evidence has started to emerge that indicates that psychological problems are not inevitable and that

many families in fact adapt successfully to the challenges they face. The current picture suggests that significant psychological disturbance or maladjustment is not inevitable, rather that children with a chronic disease and their families are a group who are at increased risk of developing difficulties.

- Not only has there been criticism of the assumptions that have underpinned much of the research, but it is also increasingly recognised that the measures used to assess adjustment have a number of limitations and that the focus on mother–child dyads has been overly restrictive.

- In the light of these criticisms, new models have started to emerge that do not assume that chronic illness inevitably leads to failures, problems and deviation from the norm. Research has also started to take a wider focus, with the family and care system becoming areas for investigation. Equally, researchers have recognised that assessment tools from the wider mental health field may not be appropriate to use in studying chronic disease, and more 'ecologically valid' tools are now in the process of being developed.

- Models from health psychology and systemic family therapy hold particular promise in aiding our understanding of the effects of chronic conditions and ways in which we might start to intervene to promote patterns of adjustment. It is in the light of these models that a series of studies will be described in Part II of the book, which attempt to explore psychological factors that influence adaptation.

Part II

Psychological studies

Chapter 3

Child distress

INTRODUCTION

Anecdotal evidence suggests that medical assessment procedures are made difficult by children's distressed reactions to them. Surprisingly, little research has attempted to describe, quantify or account for these problems in a systematic way. In particular, there is a lack of information concerning the procedures that children find upsetting and whether certain children are more 'at risk' of distressed reactions than others.

To date, research has concentrated on gaining reliable descriptions of child distress (Hyson, 1981; Katz et al., 1980; Jay et al., 1983) and investigating psychosocial variables in relation to this. Studies have highlighted a number of child variables associated with distress, including age (Hyson, 1981; Katz et al., 1980), sex (Katz et al., 1980), typical preference for information (Peterson and Toler, 1986) and coping style (Burnstein and Meichenbaum, 1979). Maternal variables including anxiety (Johnson and Baldwin, 1968; Jay et al., 1983), responsiveness (Venham et al., 1979), discipline style (Zabin and Melamed, 1980), interaction (Bush et al., 1986) and presence or absence during the procedure (Gross et al., 1983; Shaw and Routh, 1982) have also been found to influence rates of child distress, as have procedural variables such as whether the child had experienced the investigation before (Jay et al., 1983), whether this had been aversive (Dahlquist et al., 1986) and the degree to which the child had a sense of control (Kavanagh, 1983; Melamed and Ridley-Johnson, 1988).

The above vulnerability factors have been identified in relation to children typically undergoing moderately to highly painful medical procedures, such as surgery and bone marrow aspirations. Little attention has been directed, however, at routine, relatively non-invasive or painful procedures that children frequently have to cope with. The purpose of this study was to explore rates of child distress during a routine medical procedure and to identify psychosocial factors associated with this (Bradford, 1990a). Attendance at an X-ray department was selected, as evidence suggests that this is a common experience for children (Gyll, 1977) and that many adults (Wilson-Barnett, 1978) and children (Bradford, 1986) can find the experience distressing. Where child upset becomes marked this can have clinical implications not only in increasing the likelihood of a child developing a phobic reaction (Klein, 1994) but also there may be a need to repeat the procedure and/or sedate the child, both of which carry their own risks.

DESIGN

The study was carried out at an X-ray department at a hospital in Oxford. The X-ray room itself contained two large X-ray machines, with a glassed cubicle at one corner of the room where the radiographer and myself stood whilst the procedure was completed. Mothers were encouraged to remain in the room with their child, providing there were no medical contra-indications, for example, pregnancy. Whilst the X-ray room was not specifically designed for child patients, the radiographers had made some attempts to make the environment more 'child-centred' by, for example, having pictures on the walls and toys available to play with.

Children entered the X-ray room, either carried by the parent or walking freely depending on their age and/or distress, and had their top clothes removed by the attending parent who, in the majority of cases, was the mother. The child patient was then placed in front of an X-ray machine and either held by the parent or left standing free. The actual chest X-ray procedure involved two X-rays being taken, a frontal and a lateral view, with the child patient lying or standing according to age. Between the two X-rays being taken, the child was given a barium meal solution to drink, which acted as a contrast to highlight the development of the heart, lung and liver. Typically, the whole procedure took under five minutes, and on completion the child would be re-clothed by the parent. The radiographer developed the film in another room and made the ratings of behavioural distress.

One of the interesting things to note about studies concerned with child distress during medical procedures is that many focus on children over 5 years of age. Most staff will tell you, however, that it is children younger than this who create most difficulties. In this study, therefore, I decided to recruit children who were most likely to be distressed, namely those between 1 and 4 years of age . In order to gain a relatively homogeneous group, all the children had to be accompanied by at least one of their parents and had been referred by a paediatric cardiac consultant for a standard assessment of possible congenital heart disease or for follow-up after a diagnosis had been made.

Parents were recruited to the study in two ways: direct contact by me after the procedure or by letter if I had not been present. Consent for the study was obtained after the procedure had been completed in order to minimise the possibility of the parent/child changing their behaviour as a consequence of being observed by a psychologist interested in child distress.

Forty-eight families met the selection criteria during the time of the study (five months), with ten declining to participate. The final sample of 38 children included 22 boys and 16 girls, with the sexes proportionately distributed among three age groups (group 1: 12–23 months; group 2: 24–35 months; group 3: 36–47 months). Age group 1 contained 13 boys and 9 girls; age group 2 contained 5 boys and 4 girls; age group 3 contained 5 boys and 2 girls. For 10 children this was their first X-ray, 5 had had one previously, 7 had experienced between two to five and 16 had attended for X-rays on six or more occasions.

In order to test whether the families who agreed to take part in the study differed from those who declined, the two groups were compared in relation to the child's age, sex and level of distress shown. Analyses revealed no significant differences between the two groups. Thus it is possible to say that the group of children included in the study were a fairly representative group.

Families who agreed to take part in the study were followed up at their homes within a two-week period, where the child's stranger sociability was assessed, followed by the parental interview and the completion of the questionnaires.

MEASURES

Distress

Ratings of behavioural distress were made by one of five radiographers who worked in the department. In order to ensure acceptable inter-rater reliability, all received training in the use of the scales prior to their actual use. Rating of distress had to be brief and 'user friendly' so as to fit into the everyday practice of the department. Two ratings were requested:

- Completion of a 9-point Likert scale with the end points anchored 'Not at all' and 'High Distress'.
- Completion of an amended version of the Observational Scale of Behaviour Distress (OSBD) (Jay *et al.*, 1983).

Table 3.1   Amended Observational Scale of Behavioural Distress

Date	Name of child Age	Procedure	Rating of distress
What was the nature of the distress? Please tick the appropriate boxes.		1	9
		Not at all	High distress

BEHAVIOUR	DEFINITION	LARGE EXTENT	OCCASIONALLY	ABSENT
Crying	Tears in eyes or running down face			
Clinging	Physically holds on to parent or radiographer			
Fear (verbal)	Says 'I'm afraid' or 'I'm scared' etc.			
Pain	Says 'ow', 'ouch', etc.			
Screams	No tears, raises voice			
Carry	Has to be carried into the room or put on table			
Flail	Random movement of limbs; intention to make aggressive contact			
Refusal	Does not follow instructions			
Position	Re. body placement on table/in front of X-ray machine			
Restrain	Has to be held down owing to lack of cooperation			
Muscular rigidity	Any of the following: clenched fist, white knuckles, gritted teeth, eyes clenched shut, body stiffness			
Emotional support	Seeks reassurance either verbally or non-verbally			

Source: Bradford, 1990a: 982

With reference to the OSBD (Jay *et al.*, 1983), when I carried out some initial piloting, I found that several items needed to be substituted, as either they did not occur ('Information Seeking'), or were difficult to rate reliably ('Nervous Behaviour'). In their place I selected three more clinically relevant items from the Procedural Rating Scale of Behavioural Distress (Katz *et al.*, 1980). The final scale used is detailed in Table 3.1.

For the purpose of analysis, the Likert scale was divided into two groupings: 'Not Distressed' (a score of three or below) and 'Distressed' (a score of four and above). For the amended OSBD, each individual behaviour was scored according to its frequency (absent $= 0$, occasional $= 1$, large extent $= 2$). During their training in the use of the scale, several radiographers raised the point that not all the eleven items were of equal importance, and so weightings (a value of 2) were added to specific behaviours ('Restrain', 'Scream', 'Flail' and 'Muscular rigidity'.

The weighting system was arrived at by asking the radiographers to rank order all eleven behaviours in terms of which were most indicative of distress. The total OSBD score was the sum of all the behavioural ratings.

Scores on the OSBD were then categorised into 'Not distressed' and 'Distressed' on the basis of correlational analyses with the Likert scale. This analysis highlighted that a score of four and below on the amended OSBD was highly associated with the Likert groupings of 'Not Distressed' ($r = 0.93$, p <0.0001). Cross tabulations of the two Likert categories and by the two OSBD groupings also confirmed that the cut-off scores resulted in good discrimination (see Table 3.2).

Table 3.2   Cross-tabulation of amended OSBD by Likert groupings

	Likert Not Distressed	Likert Distressed
OSBD Not Distressed	17	1
OSBD Distressed	2	18

Source: Bradford, 1990a: 975

PSYCHOSOCIAL VARIABLES INVESTIGATED IN RELATION TO DISTRESS

Having established that the two measures of distress were largely in agreement, it is possible to use 'child distress' as the dependent variable to which other factors can then be compared to see whether they influence the rates of distress shown by the children. There were seven factors that I was particularly keen to investigate.

It is possible that distress might be related to developmental issues such as how confident a child feels in a novel situation or with a stranger. To test this idea I completed a standardised assessment of the child's *Stranger Sociability* when I visited the child at home on follow-up. Thompson and Lamb (1982) have detailed one way in which stranger sociability can be assessed, which in essence involves a series of social overtures of gradually increasing intrusiveness conducted by a stranger in the mother's presence. The initial social bids occur while the infant is seated on the mother's lap; first an interesting toy is offered the child and then the stranger attempts to initiate a give-and-take exchange. Following this, the infant is placed on the floor and the child's initial response to floor freedom observed. The stranger then moves to the floor, again offers the child a toy and initiates a turn-taking exchange. After a few moments of play, the stranger attempts to pick up the infant. The child's reaction to these overtures is scored on a sliding scale of 'stranger sociability', as is the child's reaction when the stranger leaves the room.

I was also interested to explore whether other factors in the child's background such as medical history and psychosocial development might influence distress. Equally, it could be that the parents' own medical history might be of importance, as possibly parents who had 'bad' experiences themselves at hospital might be more worried and this might then be communicated to the child. To explore these aspects, a structured interview was developed which sought information on four areas:

1   General background information: data about the child's age, sex and the family structure.
2   The child's medical history: complications at birth, age on reaching developmental milestones, data on illnesses, hospitalisation, previous reactions to X-rays and frequency of contact with GP in the preceding year.
3   Psychosocial development: reactions to strangers, frequency of contact with other children and adults, experience of separation and attendance at playgroup, toddlers groups or any similar agency, based upon a scale developed by Stacey *et al.* (1971).
4   The parents' own medical history: their experiences of hospitals, their attitude towards them and concerns about both the appointment at the X-ray department and their behaviour in the setting.

The data generated from the structured interview was of four types: frequency counts of behaviour (for example, number of hospitalisations), scores from Likert scales (for example, parental concern about the X-ray), categorical data (for example, 'yes' or 'no') and responses to open-ended questions, which were translated by the researcher subsequently into categorical data. On the basis of summing up the relevant scores, three scales were generated: the child's *medical* score, *social development* score and a *parental concern* score.

Finally, I was interested to explore whether parental knowledge might be important in understanding child distress; those parents who had a clear idea as to what would happen might be better able to prepare and support their child, whereas those who were unsure might not have been. Alternatively, it might be that child distress in the hospital was nothing to do with the procedure *per se*, but was simply a reflection of how the child behaved in a number of settings, which in turn might be related to the parental style of managing problem behaviours. To explore these questions, parents were asked to complete three questionnaires:

Parental knowledge   A questionnaire was developed for the study covering parental understanding of the reason for the X-ray, what the different procedures involved, whether the child was allowed to eat or drink before/after the procedure and beliefs about side-effects of the X-ray and barium meal.

Parental discipline   Zabin and Melamed (1980) have developed a questionnaire to assess disciplinary style. It poses fourteen situations that children may encounter in growing up and presents five forced-choice alternatives as to how the parent would help their child to cope. The options cover a range of parental disciplinary techniques: positive reinforcement, modelling, reassurance, force and reinforcement of dependency. Evidence suggests that the first three styles are 'positive', in that they help the child cope with a stressful experience, whereas the last two are 'negative', demonstrating an association with child distress (Zabin and Melamed, 1980). This dichotomy between styles was employed in the study.

Behaviour problems   Jenkins *et al.*'s (1980) semi-structured interview was used to establish the presence of child behaviour problems. The interview assesses the parents' perception of the presence/absence of developmental problems such as feeding, sleep, toileting, management difficulties and the mother's perceived ability to cope with them.

RESULTS

Inter-rater reliability

To what extent did the radiographers agree in their ratings of child distress?

To assess this, twenty-one children going through the X-ray procedure were randomly chosen. The radiographer on duty that day and myself both completed the amended OSBD on the children, blind to each other's ratings. Scores were subjected to Pearson Product Moment correlations, results indicating an overall agreement rate of 0.79 ($p < 0.001$).

Rater and parental agreement

Does 'child distress' mean the same thing for radiographers and parents?

Support for the validity of the measure comes from a comparison of both parent's and my ratings of distress on the 9-point Likert scale, with radiographer ratings of distress on the OSBD. Parental estimates of their child's level of distress during the X-ray showed a strong association with radiographer ratings ($r = 0.55$, $p < 0.001$), as did the researcher's estimate ($r = 0.82$, $p < 0.0001$).

Behaviours shown by the children

What types of behaviour were shown by the children?

The 'Not Distressed' group contained eighteen children (47 per cent of the sample), with the remaining twenty falling in the 'Distressed' group. A visual inspection of the data suggested that the children in the 'Not Distressed' group fell into two broad types: those who demonstrated none of the distress behaviours sampled on the amended OSBD (eight children) and those who tended to display 'reassurance-type' behaviours, such as close physical contact with the mother and seeking emotional support, but who remained generally cooperative during the procedure.

The 'Distressed' children also fell into two broad types: those who demonstrated 'reassurance-type' behaviours as described above, in addition to being more demanding and clingy. These children tended to cry, were slightly defiant and required a small amount of restraint. Overt motoric distress, for example rigidity or flailing, was rare, as was the child screaming.

The remaining children demonstrated a wider range of distressed behaviours and to a much more intense degree. A central core of behaviours common to these children included screaming, flailing, becoming rigid, showing resistance to the procedure and requiring restraint. Table 3.3 illustrates the frequencies of each of the eleven behaviours on the amended OSBD.

As can be seen, the overt expression of both pain and fear was rare, which would be consistent with the nature of the non-invasive/painless procedure undergone. Most children required some degree of emotional support during the X-ray and approximately half needed to be carried or were clingy to the mother. Overt motoric distress (flail, refusal of position, restraint and rigidity) was more common than emotional distress (cry and scream).

Table 3.3   Frequencies of behaviour observed on the amended OSBD

| Behaviour | Numbers of children in each category | | |
	Absent	Occasional	Large extent
Cry	24	9	5
Cling	21	10	7
Fear	35	2	1
Pain	35	2	1
Scream	26	5	7
Carry	19	8	11
Flail	23	10	5
Refuse	19	9	10
Restraint	19	12	7
Rigidity	23	10	5
Emotional support	15	13	10

Source: Bradford 1990a: 977

Overall, these results do convey a sense of what we often see in outpatient departments: a number of children who cope well, a number who are wary but can be reassured easily and a number who are apprehensive and require a lot of support. Finally, there is the group of children who are distressed, uncooperative and difficult to soothe.

What factors might influence which group a child falls into?

Influence of age and gender

Does distress vary in relation to the child's age or gender?

A three (age) x two (sex) analysis of variance was carried out on the eleven behaviours of the amended OSBD to highlight age and sex differences in the expression of distress. No significant main effects were found on any of the behaviours. In other words, levels of child distress were not influenced by the child's age or gender.

Influence of psychosocial variables

What factors were associated with child distress?

Scores for each of the seven psychosocial variables were subjected to a two (amended OSBD distress grouping) by two (sex) analysis of variance, with age as covariate. In order to control for Type I errors (the danger of saying that a result is significant when it is not) that are inherent in the repeated ANOVA design, the conventional 0.05 level of significance was adjusted by the Bonferroni Inequality, yielding a revised significance level of 0.007 (Stevens, 1986).

Two factors were significantly differentiated by the child's rates of distress. Firstly, the child's stranger sociability assessment, which reflects the child's ability to tolerate and interact with a stranger, was associated with the child's category of distress $F (1, 38) = 18.9, p < 0.0001$. Thus, children who had low stranger sociability tended to show more distress as demonstrated by higher scores on the amended OSBD. No interactional effect was found for either the child's age or sex. A second factor, the parent's discipline style, was also correlated significantly with the child's distress rating $F (1, 38) = 9.9, p < 0.003$. Thus parents who typically use 'negative' discipline styles in helping their child cope with stressful events tended to have children who were distressed during the X-ray. Again, no interactional effects were found for age or sex.

Child distress was not differentiated by the remaining five psychosocial variables, although the child's social development score did reach significance at .01 level ($F (1, 38) = 7.1, p < 0.01$), indicating a trend in the data. Overall, the results indicate that a child's stranger sociability and the parent's discipline style, but none of the other factors investigated, were associated with high rates of distress.

DISCUSSION

The above results supported the hypothesis that psychosocial factors play an important part in understanding child distress during routine medical assessment procedures. The association found in this study between parental discipline style and child distress is important as it highlights the need to take into account the wider context, in this case the child's temperament and their family, in understanding why a child might behave in a particular way (Bush *et al.*, 1986; Greenbaum *et al.*, 1988; Jay *et al.*, 1983; Venham *et al.*, 1979; Zabin and Melamed, 1980). Interestingly, the finding concerning the child's stranger sociability and distress during medical procedures has not been demonstrated previously and as such it underlines the importance of not only the wider context, but also the role of individual differences in explaining child distress.

The origins of individual differences in stranger sociability remain poorly understood. Wariness of strangers may be influenced by an infant's prior experiences, constitutionally based aspects of temperament (Thompson and Lamb, 1979), the quality of the care-giving environment (Stephenson and Lamb, 1979), security of attachment (Main, 1973) and parenting styles (Ainsworth *et al.*, 1978; Bowlby, 1971). There is evidence to suggest that wariness follows clear developmental paths (Greenberg and Marvin, 1982), although in this study no age effects on distress were found, possibly as a result of the small sample size and the age distribution.

From the literature (Byng-Hall, 1995) it would seem that there is a probable interactional effect between a child's sense of security, ability to tolerate novel environments and strangers, and the parents' style of discipline. In this context, it may be important to consider the child's social development score which, whilst being insufficiently strong to meet the revised level set by the Bonferroni Inequality, was significant at 0.01 level, suggesting a trend in the data. Results on this variable indicated that those children who were rated by their parents as having limited social experiences were rarely left alone, reacted poorly to strangers and separation experiences, and tended to be the same children who gained high scores on the amended OSBD. The association between social development and coping has been noted previously by Stacey *et al.* (1971) when they noted that children who were cohesively involved in family interaction, to the exclusion of outsiders, were the group who were most distressed during a hospital admission for minor surgery.

On the basis of these results, it seems that children who are wary of interacting with a stranger and whose parents typically use 'negative' discipline styles, may be a group particularly at risk of distressed reactions. Further, these children may have limited social experiences, which possibly reflects either the parents' unwillingness to expose them to such contacts, or the child's own inability to cope with the experience. The direction of causation is important, although no

attempt was made in the study to investigate this in a systematic way.
An important trend noted from the structured interview was that some
parents in the study described themselves as being 'over-protective'
and this appeared to be a pattern that occurred in families that had
suffered a miscarriage or where the child patient was perceived as
being seriously ill. Research by Forrest and Standish (1985) has highlighted the frequent over-protectiveness of parents to siblings who are
born following a miscarriage and ample evidence exists concerning
the effect that illness can have on the parents' perception of the child
and subsequent management (for example, Minuchin *et al.*, 1975).

The above hypothesis concerning vulnerability to distressed reactions is clearly limited by the fact that the sample was small and contained only children with a query of, or definite diagnosis of,
congenital heart disease. It may also be that the results are specific to
the population studied. Linde *et al.* (1966) have reported that parents
of the children with congenital heart disease tended to be over-protec-

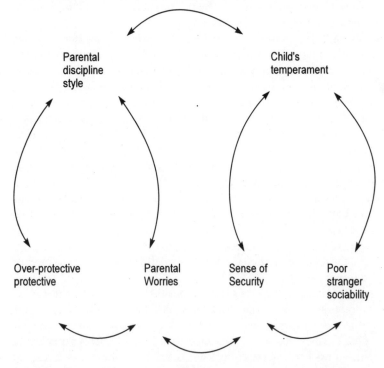

Figure 3.1   An aetiological model of child distress during medical assessment
procedures

tive and 'pamper' their children and that the 'pampered' child was frequently 'discontented, frustrated and unhappy'. In addition, they were said to be dependent on the family, fearful of separation, needed constant reassurance of being loved, were aggressively demanding of attention and had difficulty in establishing rapport with adults and peers. The descriptions of children with congenital heart disease made by Linde *et al.* (1966) and by Kramer *et al.* (1989) have several similarities to some of the children's behaviour observed in the X-ray room, which may suggest that such conditions may be associated with particular patterns of interaction developing in affected families.

Pulling these various strands together, it is possible to see a model emerging that explains how child distress during medical procedures might come about. This is illustrated in Figure 3.1.

In the next chapter, I want to expand these ideas by exploring factors that impact on how well parents are able to support their child. If parental discipline styles do impact on child distress, what issues influence the behaviour shown by parents?

SUMMARY

- Thirty-eight children, aged 1–4 years with a query or definite diagnosis of congenital heart disease, were observed during an X-ray procedure and their behaviour rated on an amended version of the Observational Scale of Behavioural Distress.
- Families were followed up after their outpatient appointment and assessed on a number of psychosocial variables. High rates of behavioural distress were found to be associated with children's low stranger sociability and negative parental style of discipline.
- Child distress did not vary in relation to the child's age, sex, previous medical history, pre-existing behaviour problems, nor was it related to parental knowledge about the procedure, or worries. There was a trend for the child's social development being related to rates of distress.
- It appears that child distress is best understood within a developmental and interactional context. Possible patterns of interaction between children and their families may be particularly important in understanding children's coping behaviours during medical procedures.
- Developing assessment measures that tap specific behaviours involved in coping with chronic disease or its treatment is essential in being able to unravel pathways underlying successful adjustment.

Chapter 4

Parental distress and staff effectiveness

INTRODUCTION

There has been much research into how parents, and in particular mothers, cope with the diagnosis of a chronic illness in their child (Cunningham, 1979; Drotar *et al.*, 1975; Emede and Brown, 1978; Kennedy, 1970). The approach adopted in most studies is to see the child's diagnosis as being similar to a bereavement for parents, producing grief reactions, followed by the stages of shock and disbelief, denial, anger, adaptation and adjustment (Raphael, 1984).

Whether or not parents do in fact go through discrete stages in their adjustment is a matter of some debate; it has been suggested that a more appropriate model recognises that parents suffer from 'chronic sorrow' (Olshansky, 1962), which is characterised by periods of coping punctuated by periods of mourning, the latter most frequently brought on by particular life stages, such as the child leaving school, when the handicap and its implications for all are thrown most clearly into relief and result in the reawakening of old feelings of loss.

If grief is a normal part of coping with a child with a chronic illness, what influence can health care professionals have on easing the process? Are there common patterns of communication between parents and staff that can either help or hinder adjustment, and if so, what lesson can be learnt in order to improve the running of services to meet the needs of parents? In this chapter, two studies will be presented that explore these issues. The first (Bradford, 1990b) is concerned with detailing factors that influence parents' satisfaction with the care they receive whilst looking after their child. The study seeks to highlight what are, from a parent's point of view, the important dimensions that influence their coping. In the second, interlinked study (Bradford, 1991a) I assess the extent to which paediatric staff from a variety of backgrounds identify accurately the worries and concerns of parents. This latter aspect is particularly important to explore, as clearly if staff do not appreciate the nature and extent of parental distress they are less likely to be effective in helping parents cope, which may well have wider implications for the adjustment of the child, parent and family as a whole.

STUDY 1: PARENTS' EXPERIENCES OF CARE

Parents of chronically ill children are frequent users of hospital services. Research has shown consistently that both the child patient and their family are at increased risk of developing emotional and adjustment problems (Drotar *et al.*, 1981; Koocher *et al.*, 1980). The factors that mediate between successful and unsuccessful adjustment remain poorly understood, although a number of variables relating to the child, parent and family functioning have started to emerge (Wallander *et al.*, 1989b).

The relationship between parent satisfaction with hospital services and subsequent psychological adjustment is an area that has received little attention, although there are good reasons for assuming that the interface is important. For example, research has demonstrated an association between parental dissatisfaction and services being poorly used (Becker *et al.*, 1979) and decreases in compliance with medical advice (Korsch and Negrete, 1972). Furthermore, ongoing parental dissatisfaction is likely to exacerbate stresses surrounding any hospital contact and parents who are highly stressed may well then have difficulty supporting their child (Wolfer and Visintainer, 1975). There is also some evidence to suggest that parental views about the way in which they are told about their child's illness can have profound effects on their own adjustment and their early treatment of their child (Svarstad and Lipton, 1977; Springer and Steele, 1980).

Satisfaction can be seen as having four key elements: the extent to which patients receive, understand and recall information (Ley, 1988) whether expectations and concerns are elicited (Korsch *et al.*, 1968); whether an opportunity is given to discuss emotional aspects to the illness (Dare and Hemsley, 1986) and whether the service correctly identifies and manages the medical aspects of the condition. Measuring parental satisfaction is problematic as there are few assessment tools available. Many studies have relied on unstructured interviews (Reddihough *et al.*, 1977) or questionnaires developed by researchers (Deisher *et al.*, 1965), which may not be directly relevant to the parents' concerns (Johnson, 1982). Often, only one feature of care is assessed, for example satisfaction with information (Nugent, 1987) and at only one point in the child's care, for example during a hospital admission (Robinson, 1968). In addition, samples surveyed are usually parents of non-chronically ill children (for example, Korsch *et al.*, 1968).

The aim of the first current study described here was to follow up a group of parents who have a chronically ill child and assess their experiences of the care received, at a number of points, from the time of initial identification of a problem, to referral on for specialist assessment and treatment, to discharge.

DESIGN

The study was carried out in the children's liver unit at a London teaching hospital. Families were invited to take part in the study if they had been inpatients, or had attended outpatients (having had a previous admission to the hospital) during a four-month sampling period. Parents whose child had died during or subsequent to the admission/attending outpatients were not included in the sample. Ninety-two families met the above inclusion criteria.

MEASURE

The Expanded Survey of Parental Satisfaction (ESPS) (Bradford, 1991a) was used to assess parents' experiences of care and their levels of satisfaction. The ESPS is a questionnaire designed specifically to identify emotional distress and its causes in parents of children with liver disease. The measure was originally developed by Dare and Hemsley (1986) who carried out semi-structured interviews with parents of children with liver disorders to identify common concerns. The measure was subsequently refined into a questionnaire format that could be administered by a member of staff or completed by the parents themselves. The authors report good reliability in its use as a self- completed questionnaire.

In this study the measure was amended by the addition of several new items and simplification of the scoring system. In addition, the wording of some items was clarified in order to facilitate its use as a postal questionnaire. The Expanded Survey of Parental Satisfaction (ESPS) consists of thirty-five items, covering parental satisfaction with information and emotional support, medical management and opportunity to discuss concerns throughout the child's care. The sections and areas surveyed are summarised in Table 4.1.

Table 4.1   The Expanded Survey of Parental Satisfaction

Sections	Areas investigated
1 Contact with services prior to admission	Satisfaction with speed of referral on, information, emotional support, empathy. Whether parent given chance to discuss feelings/emotional impact and whether this was wanted.
2 Inpatient experience	Satisfaction with medical care. Information, its clarity, repetition, whether given written information, degree of conflicting information; felt able to ask questions. Emotional support, whether upset noticed and responded to. Discussion of worries, child's prognosis, impact on daily life, emotional problems of parents, siblings. Financial strain experienced, how understanding employer was, whether employment was ever put at risk through time off.
3 Outpatient experience	Satisfaction with physical and emotional care. Amount of information and contact with other agencies/families.

Source: Bradford, 1990b: 45

RESULTS

Ninety-two families were sent the ESPS with a covering letter and a prepaid return envelope. Follow up letters were sent to families who had not returned their questionnaire within a one-month period. In total, fifty-four parents (58 per cent of the available sample) completed the measure. The characteristics of the sample in terms of the child patients' age, sex, diagnosis and whether the liver disease was progressive or not are detailed in Table 4.2.

In the light of the response rate, which is typical for this type of study, it was important to establish whether the sample differed significantly from those parents who did not complete the ESPS. Chi-square analyses were performed comparing the children in relation to their age and sex. As the sample size was not large enough to permit separation into diagnostic groups for statistical analysis, a comparison was made as to whether the liver disease was progressive or not, which provided a rough measure of severity. Results indicated no significant differences between the two groups on these variables.

Table 4.2   Sample characteristics of children in satisfaction study

		Number	%
Sex	Male	25	46
	Female	29	54
Age	Less than 1 year	9	17
	1 to 5 years	25	46
	5 years and older	20	37
Diagnosis			
	Neonatal hepatitis	6	11
	Biliary atresia	21	39
	Budd Chiari	1	2
	Alpha 1 antitrypsin deficiency	11	20
	Hepatitis non-A/non-B	3	6
	Portal vein thrombosis	3	6
	Cryptogenic	1	2
	Perforated bile duct	1	2
	Alagilles syndrome	1	2
	Metabolic	2	4
	Choledochal cyst	4	7
Cirrhotic		25	46
Non-cirrhotic		29	54

Source: Bradford, 1990b: 46

PARENTS' CONCERNS AND SATISFACTION

The levels of parental satisfaction with their child's medical management, information, emotional support and opportunity to discuss worries are summarised in Table 4.3.

Table 4.3   Summary of overall parental satisfaction

	Prior to admission %	Stage Admission %	Discharge %
Medical management	70	86	92
Information	42	77	66
Emotional support	46	56	60
Discussion of worries	38	52	48

Source: Bradford, 1990b: 46

Pre-admission

Prior to their admission to the liver unit, parents reported being ill-prepared by their referral agency, be that their GP or another hospital.

Parents expressed concerns about the paucity of information as well as the way in which it was given. Fifty-eight per cent reported receiving either none or only a small amount concerning areas such as their child's illness, investigations to be undergone, or the likely length of their admission.

Perceived lack of information was strongly associated with parental dissatisfaction (x^2 = 10.84, p <0.001). Where parents were given information, over a quarter (26 per cent) felt that this had been handled insensitively. Again, perceived lack of empathy was an important factor in the parents' overall rating of satisfaction: 67.5 per cent who considered the doctor to have been sensitive, expressed satisfaction with the support given. This was in comparison to only 8 per cent satisfaction rate when the doctor was considered to have been insensitive (x^2 = 11.65, p <0.003).

Sixty-two per cent of parents reported that they were not given an opportunity to discuss their feelings and concerns about their child's illness, despite 89 per cent indicating on the questionnaire that they had wanted the chance to do so. These factors emerged as being important in determining parental satisfaction; where parents wanted and were given the chance to discuss their worries, 95 per cent were satisfied with their emotional support, whereas only 16 per cent of parents were satisfied when no such opportunity was available (x^2 = 28.09, p <0.001). Overall, 54 per cent of parents were dissatisfied with the emotional support provided at this stage.

Admission to the paediatric unit

Eighty-one per cent of the samples' initial contact was as inpatients. Parents had a wide range of reactions to their child's admission, from relief to apprehension. The majority experienced a mixture of anxiety, fearfulness coupled with a sense of confusion and feeling 'lost' (60 per cent). A small number described panic reactions, feeling depressed and resentful, coupled with guilt (11 per cent). A third of parents experienced a sense of relief on their admission (29 per cent).

Medical management

The large majority of parents expressed satisfaction with their child's medical management at the unit (86 per cent).

Information

Fifty-three per cent of the sample felt that the amount of information given to them during their admission was 'just right'. Twenty-six per cent felt they had received too little, 8 per cent too much; 79 per cent considered that the information had been given in a clear, understandable way and for 91 per cent the information was repeated at a later stage. Just over half were given a written booklet about liver disease which was found useful by 83 per cent who received it. The amount of information ($x^2 = 3.74$, p <0.05) and the extent to which it was understandable ($x^2 = 10.5$, p <0.001) were significantly related to overall satisfaction with information.

Parents identified two particular areas of dissatisfaction. Firstly, only 47 per cent were able to report that they never received conflicting information about their child's illness. Secondly, 36 per cent felt unable to ask the questions they wanted.

Emotional support

A major determinant of providing emotional support is whether emotional distress is recognised. Just under a quarter of parents (22 per cent) reported that their distress was never/rarely recognised, with a further 31 per cent only sometimes having their upset noticed. Thus just under half the parents (47 per cent) had their distress reliably identified by staff. A second determinant is that once distress is noticed, some appropriate response is made. For 21 per cent of parents, their perception was that staff avoided approaching them when they were upset. Once distress was identified and responded to by staff, 85 per cent of parents found this helpful/very helpful.

Discussion of worries

The outlook for a child's future is a major concern for parents of ill children, yet 49 per cent reported that this topic was not addressed. When asked whether they wanted this topic discussed, only 10 per cent said they had not wanted a specific chance to do so. Sixty-four per cent of parents also expressed dissatisfaction with lack of discussion concerning the effect of the liver disease on their child's everyday life, a topic that 91 per cent wanted to talk about. As a result of the perceived lack of discussion, parents reported feeling ill-prepared for the extent of the impact of their child's liver disease on themselves, other children and the wider family.

Seventy-five per cent of the liver children had siblings of whom 55 per cent were described by parents as experiencing emotional or behavioural problems. Common reactions included jealousy, resentment, siblings becoming over-protective or fearful for the child and signs of regressed behaviour such as withdrawal, speech and general behavioural problems. The majority of parents (87 per cent) reported that they received little or no help with these difficulties. Parents experienced high rates of marital disharmony and tension (58 per cent) associated with their child's illness, although only one parent reported that this actually resulted in divorce. The existence of marital tensions was significantly correlated with siblings demonstrating emotional and behavioural problems at home ($r = 0.39$, $p < 0.01$).

In most cases, relationship problems were poorly recognised (85 per cent) by the unit, with the extended family being the people most likely to be aware of the difficulties (50 per cent). Unfortunately, the adequacy of response from the family was rated as 'little help' by 40 per cent of parents. When asked whether they would have liked the opportunity to discuss their difficulties with appropriate hospital personnel, 64 per cent indicated affirmatively, 10 per cent negatively, with the remainder failing to respond.

Fifty-five per cent of parents reported financial difficulties as a result of their child's illness and hospitalisation. Fifty-eight per cent had to arrange annual leave in order to be with their child, 4 per cent had a GP willing to write a covering letter to the employer and 13 per cent were given compassionate leave from work. Over a third experienced problems with their employer's willingness to allow time off work and 32 per cent of families reported that at least one member had given up work in order to look after the ill child. Parents rarely felt that these practical problems were appreciated by the unit.

Discharge

Most families (49 per cent) attended outpatients on a six-monthly basis, with 9 per cent attending monthly, 32 per cent every third month, and 19 per cent yearly. Sixty-six per cent rated the information given as adequate, with 34 per cent dissatisfied that they were not told enough; no parent complained of being given too much. Sixty-three per cent considered the information was given in a clear way, although 28 per cent failed to ask all the questions they wanted. Interestingly, doctors failing to enquire about the family's coping was correlated with families not receiving help for marital disharmony and problems shown by siblings ($r = 0.70$, p <0.001), indicating that families rarely present their concerns and thereby receive help, unless the doctor takes the initiative for asking. Furthermore, whether the doctor enquired about the child's overall development and discussed the impact of the child's illness on the family was highly associated with parental satisfaction ($r = 0.63$, p <0.001). Forty per cent of families were dissatisfied with the emotional support they were given by the unit.

OVERVIEW

This study focused on parents' subjective experiences of care received, as evidence suggests that parental level of dissatisfaction is a factor in predicting family adjustment to chronic, life-threatening diseases (Wells and Schwebel, 1987; Murray and Callan, 1988). Whilst the study can be criticised on the grounds of the small sample size, lack of control group and subjective nature of parents' accounts, which do not necessarily reflect the 'reality' of what took place, the picture that emerges merits some attention.

The results highlighted a number of areas where parents reported that services failed to meet their needs. The survey highlighted that at admission, parents need basic information about what procedures are likely to be carried out, why and how long the admission will last. Whilst it may be unreasonable to expect referring agencies to know the answer to all of these questions, it does demonstrate a need for parents to be given detailed information on their admission to hospital and for staff not to assume that parents are informed about their child's illness. In addition, there is a need to provide emotional support and a chance to 'talk through' their experiences with hospital staff, as again this appeared to be an area where parents had unrecognised needs.

The use of books to supplement the discussions with staff was clearly appreciated, suggesting that this may be an important aspect to build into the running of paediatric units. Parents also identified the need for information to be given at a pace and time that suited them, rather than the medical team, a finding that has been highlighted in another context (Woolley *et al.*, 1989a). This mismatch may account for the small percentage of parents who felt that they were given too much information. Evidence suggests that in coping with 'bad news', patients may erect defences in order not to be overwhelmed (Krantz *et al.*, 1980). If this coping style is not recognised, patients may be forced inadvertently to hear more information than they are able to accept. Clearly, in imparting information it is essential to pace and tailor what is said to the parental coping style. In addition, it is important to develop a system through multidisciplinary teams whereby parents can receive emotional support around particular stress points (Wolfer and Visintainer, 1975) so that information imparted can be accepted and 'worked through'.

In summary, the use of survey questionnaires is recommended as an important method in auditing paediatric services to ensure that parental concerns are identified and changes in hospital practice targeted. It is said that paediatric medicine should have three goals: to treat the disease; to prevent it interfering with the child's general development; and to prevent the disease adversely affecting the family. The questionnaire data reported here is one method of evaluating the extent to which a service achieves this third goal.

In terms of the wider implications of the results, it seems reasonable to suggest that parents' adjustment and the behaviour they show towards their sick child may well be influenced by the nature and adequacy of support received from health care professionals. This hypothesis is explored further in the next study.

STUDY 2: STAFF ACCURACY IN PREDICTING PARENTAL CONCERNS

Perhaps one of the most salutary messages from the first study was that staff did not appear to be available to address parental worries and concerns. Why might this have been the case?

Surprisingly, little research has been carried out in relation to how accurate staff are at identifying the concerns of parents. In the adult field, there are numerous studies that have explored how well general practitioners, hospital staff and others diagnose emotional and psychiatric problems, with the evidence suggesting that such difficulties are vastly under-identified (Bridges and Goldberg, 1984; Maguire, 1974; Wilkinson, 1987). The consequence of this can be that patients fail to receive the help they need (Hardman, 1989) and continue to experience psychological distress even after discharge from hospital (Mayou, 1988).

A number of explanations have been advanced for the poor detection of psychological morbidity. It has been suggested that failures in identifying patients' worries stem from lack of time (Rosser and Maguire, 1982), poor interviewing skills (Maguire and Rutter, 1976), assumption that the patient will disclose the problem and hence there is no need to enquire actively (Hardman *et al.*, 1989) and professionals' avoidance of awkward questions and strong emotions (Maguire, 1984). The purpose of this next study was to investigate, firstly, whether paediatric staff were as inaccurate in estimating the concerns of parents caring for a chronically ill child as their colleagues in adult services appeared to be, and secondly, to assess what role staff awareness and level of contact with parents had on subsequent accuracy.

DESIGN

This study was also carried out at the liver unit at a London teaching hospital. Six groups of paediatric staff who currently or had worked on the liver unit were asked to take part. The six groups were: ward doctors (n = 7, including senior house officers, registrars and senior registrars); ward rurses (n = 9, including sisters and staff nurses); liver team (n = 7, including consultants, lecturer, dietician, nurse specialist and researchers); psychiatric staff (n = 7, including consultants and senior registrars, social workers and a psychologist); student nurses (n = 18, all first-year trainees) and medical students (n = 15, all first-year clinical on paediatric training placement).

MEASURE

The six groups separately completed a shortened form of eight items from the ESPS, which were selected on the basis of being typical of parental concerns. The items used are summarised in Table 4.4. Staff in each group were requested to estimate what had been the average parental response to each item.

Staff estimates on each item were deemed accurate if they fell within ±10 per cent of the actual average frequency reported by parents in this study. To test for significance of difference between parental responses and staff estimates, Kruskal Wallis' one-way analysis of variance was carried out. Where a difference was found between staff groups in accuracy, this was further investigated using Mann Whitney tests.

RESULTS

Rate of agreement between staff

To what extent did the staff groups agree in their estimates of parental concerns?

Table 4.4   Items selected from The Expanded Survey of Parental Satisfaction

1   To what extent were parents satisfied with the amount of information they received whilst staying with their child in hospital?
2   To what extent were parents satisfied with the emotional support they received during their child's admission?
3   What percentage of parents had the opportunity to discuss their child's prognosis/outlook?
4   What percentage of parents had the opportunity to discuss the impact of liver disease on family daily life?
5   What percentage of parents had financial problems/hardship as a consequence of their child having liver disease?
6   What percentage of parents had marital difficulties/tensions?
7   What percentage of parents reported that the child's siblings had emotional problems?
8   What percentage of parents kept in contact with other families who had children with similar liver diseases?

The results of this question are graphically demonstrated in Figure 4.1.

As can be seen, for each item from the ESPS, a surprisingly wide range of responses was given by the six staff groups. In other words, there was little agreement between them and they showed little ability to gauge parental concerns accurately! Thus, on item 1, 'To what extent were parents satisfied with the information they received whilst staying with their child in hospital?', ward doctors, the liver team, ward nurses and student nurses achieved a scatter of scores between 15 to 30 per cent accuracy, with one staff group failing to estimate correctly at all (psychiatric staff) whilst medical students gained the highest accuracy rate of 60 per cent. Similarly, on item 5, 'To what extent did parents report financial hardship as a consequence of having a child with liver disease?', no group achieved higher than 40 per cent accuracy, with the liver team, ward nurses and medical students only being on average 10 per cent accurate. Data on mean, standard deviation and range per item from the ESPS are summarised in Table 4.5.

Accuracy of each staff group

Were some staff groups more 'accurate' than others?

In order to test for the effect of group membership on accuracy, Kruskal Wallis' one-way analyses of variance were computed for, firstly, staff accuracy on each item and, secondly, overall staff accuracy on the eight items combined.

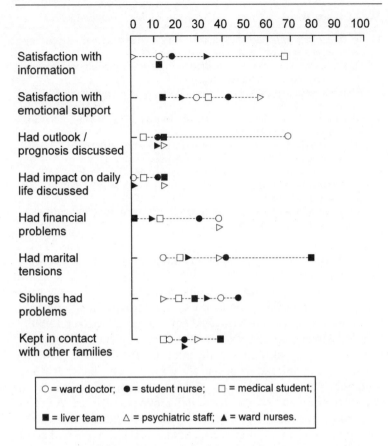

Figure 4.1 Staff estimates of parental responses – percentage accuracy rate
Source: Bradford, 1991a: 43

With reference to the first set of analyses, it was found that significant differences in group accuracy for individual items were found for only two items (see Table 4.6). In other words, accuracy on items 4 and 6 were influenced by being a member of a particular staff group. Further analysis using Mann Whitney tests demonstrated that ward doctors were significantly more inaccurate on item 4 ($Z = 4.06$, $p < 0.0001$) in comparison to other staff groups. Conversely, the liver team were significantly more accurate on item 6 ($Z = 3.07$, $p < 0.002$) than any other group.

Investigation of whether any one group of staff was more likely to be inaccurate overall on all items from the ESPS revealed that accuracy did not vary as a function of group membership ($x^2 = 5.89$, p <0.32). Thus, professional training and background did not influence whether parental concerns were accurately gauged.

Table 4.5 Staff accuracy in estimating parental responses

Item	Ward drs	Student nurses	Medical students	Liver team	Psych. staff	Ward nurses
1 Mean estimate	56.4	56.0	56.5	50.7	51.4	60.6
SD	15.5	12.8	16.7	16.9	21.2	25.2
Range	40–80	40–80	20–80	40–80	30–80	6–95
2 Mean estimate	45.7	53.5	46.0	33.3	40.0	59.4
SD	12.7	15.4	19.9	10.1	16.3	21.9
Range	30–70	25–80	20–90	20–50	20–60	20–80
3 Mean estimate	57.1	81.1	78.3	62.9	76.7	76.1
SD	15.0	15.3	11.3	26.1	24.8	18.7
Range	30–80	50–100	60–100	60–90	35–100	40–90
4 Mean estimate	92.9	51.6	31.8	30.7	40.7	63.8
SD	18.9	25.0	20.4	11.0	20.9	20.1
Range	50–100	15–90	10–70	20–50	20–70	20–80
5 Mean estimate	45.7	58.5	45.5	60.0	60.0	60.6
SD	16.2	18.9	21.8	21.0	14.1	22.0
Range	20–60	20–90	7–80	40–90	40–80	30–90
6 Mean estimate	45.7	50.0	42.3	55.0	41.4	54.2
SD	11.3	17.1	14.3	7.6	16.5	31.9
Range	30–60	20–85	20–70	50–70	25–70	8–100
7 Mean estimate	40.0	57.1	46.3	47.1	37.9	45.5
SD	10.0	15.8	26.7	17.0	18.9	23.5
Range	30–50	20–80	15–90	30–80	15–70	4–85
8 Mean estimate	46.4	34.8	17.7	38.6	22.9	48.3
SD	32.0	27.2	16.4	18.6	13.8	20.0
Range	5–100	2–100	5–60	20–60	10–40	30–95

Source: Bradford, 1991a: 44

Table 4.6 Significance of differences in group accuracy on each item

	Item	Chi-square	Significance
1	Satisfaction with information	8.4	N.S.
2	Satisfaction with emotional support	6.54	N.S.
3	Had outlook/prognosis discussed	8.55	N.S.
4	Had impact on daily life discussed	17.91	.005
5	Had financial problems	4.52	N.S.
6	Had marital tensions	11.88	.05
7	Siblings had problems	4.95	N.S.
8	Kept in contact with other families	4.08	N.S.

Source: Bradford, 1991a: 45

Direction of inaccuracy

Was staff inaccuracy the result of over- or under-estimating parental concerns?

Staff's tendency to over- or under-estimate parental concerns was also investigated. Inspection of the data demonstrated that inaccuracies in estimating the extent of financial, marital and sibling difficulties all resulted from the groups under-estimating the magnitude of problems. Errors in accuracy on item 3 (discussion of prognosis) occurred owing to all staff over-estimating the number of parents who were given this opportunity. Furthermore, ward doctors and nurses over-estimated how many families had an opportunity to discuss the general impact that liver disease would have, and, in combination with the liver team, they also over-estimated the number of families who kept in contact with other families post-discharge.

Overall, results pointed to staff from a variety of backgrounds tending to under-estimate the impact of liver disease whilst over-estimating parents' opportunities to discuss their concerns. Interestingly, all staff under-estimated parental satisfaction with information and all, excepting nurses (who over-estimated), believed that parents would be more dissatisfied with their emotional support during hospitalisation than they actually were. Tests for significance of difference in groups' tendency to over-/under-estimate are summarised in Table 4.7. Mann Whitney tests showed that the differences on item 2 were accounted for by the liver and psychiatric teams' under-estimations ($Z = 3.07$, p <0.002); on item 4, by ward doctors' over-estimation ($Z = 3.16$, p <0.0001), and on item 7, by ward doctors' and nurses' over-estimations ($Z = 3.16$, p <0.002).

Table 4.7   Significance of difference in group under-/over-estimation on each item

	Item	Chi-square	Significance
1	Satisfaction with information	3.14	N.S.
2	Satisfaction with emotional support	12.57	.05
3	Had outlook/prognosis discussed	9.33	N.S.
4	Had impact on daily life discussed	24.99	.0001
5	Had financial problems	7.27	N.S.
6	Had marital tensions	4.32	N.S.
7	Siblings had problems	12.52	.05
8	Kept in contact with other families	4.08	N.S.

Source: Bradford, 1991a: 45

Influence of contact

Did frequency of contact with families influence staff accuracy?

The question of whether staff level of contact with affected families influenced accuracy was also investigated. It was hypothesised that ward doctors, nurses and the liver team would be more accurate in their estimates than other groups. Analysis indicated that level of contact made no difference in staff accuracy, except on item 4, where those having less contact with families were more accurate in their estimates ($Z = 1.94$, p <0.05).

DISCUSSION

The identification of psychological problems and worries in adult medical consultations is known to be poor. This study suggests that the parents of children with chronic, life-threatening disorders similarly fail to have concerns identified. This appeared to be related to medical, paramedical and nursing staff under-estimating the psychological impact of the disorder, whilst over-estimating the opportunities available for parents to discuss worries.

Given the small number of parents involved in the study, could it be that the sample was in some way biased and perhaps unrepresentative of other families who might have a child with liver disease or another chronic condition? Might the group of parents, for example, be unduly negative (or positive) about their experiences which, therefore, would make it particularly problematic for staff to predict accurately the responses that were made to the ESPS?

Comparing the parents of children sampled with the typical range of liver disorders seen on the unit failed to reveal any systematic bias in, for example, type of disease suffered by the child. It did not appear, therefore, that the sample was different or unrepresentative of children generally attending the unit. Comparisons were also made between the rates of satisfaction/dissatisfaction reported in the first study using the ESPS to Dare and Hemsley's (1986) original sample. Again, no significant differences were found in the type of responses made by the parents. Whilst this is a salutary lesson, that is, despite five years separating the two studies, parents still reported that their needs were not always met. In relation to the current results it seems that the group of parents studied were not significantly different from other parents who had attended the unit in the recent or distant past.

Perhaps parents of children with liver disease are a particularly unhappy and needy group and therefore high rates of dissatisfaction are inevitable. Whilst there may well be disease-specific stresses for families looking after a child with liver disease (these are explored further in the next chapter), an analysis of studies concerned with other illness groups suggests strikingly similar frequencies of both distress (Koocher *et al.*, 1980) and dissatisfaction with non-medical aspects of paediatric care (Reddihough, 1977; Quine and Rutter, 1994). It is difficult to see, therefore, that the failures of staff in this study to predict parental response accurately on the ESPS can be attributed simply to sample bias, unrepresentative responses or disease-specific issues.

This study suggests that professionals' lack of awareness of the problems experienced by parents and consequent under-estimation of emotional distress may be significant. It is perhaps not surprising, in the first study's analysis of the responses of parents to the ESPS, that many parents failed to receive the help they wanted. Clearly, if staff do not expect parents to experience significant psychological morbidity, or to seek help from their social network, they are less likely to enquire into problems and initiate appropriate referrals.

The results of this study point to the need to have teaching for staff so that they become more aware of the psychological challenges children and families face, the types of concerns they have and risk factors that might make adjustment problems more likely (Bradford, 1990b). In addition, training in interview and counselling skills is needed to help staff recognise problems and provide them with the skills to feel able to respond to families' concerns (Davis, 1993; Evans *et al.*, 1987; Hardman *et al.*, 1989). Whilst there are often problems of attempting to integrate psychological approaches into hospital settings (Nichols, 1985), the amelioration of parental distress in caring for a chronically ill child is clearly an essential goal in promoting successful adjustment for the whole family (Bradford and Singer, 1991; Bradford and Spinks, 1992).

In conclusion, the two studies highlight that as outpatients, during admission and following discharge, parents often fail to have their psychological needs identified and met. This appears to be influenced, at least in part, by staff expectations and behaviour. It seems that if children are to cope optimally with illness and its treatment, then the people most intimately involved in aiding this process – the child's parents – need to be supported adequately themselves. Where the care system fails to attend to such issues, or does so in an unhelpful way, it is reasonable to predict that the likelihood of families developing psychological problems is correspondingly increased.

This notion will be explored further in the next chapter, where I investigate the extent to which psychological problems persist where a child has a chronic disease, and the factors that influence psychological outcomes.

SUMMARY

- Parental adjustment is influenced by the way in which hospital services manage not only the medical aspects of their child's care, but also by the degree to which they have their psychological needs met.

- The use of screening measures to assess emotional distress and levels of satisfaction with help offered is one practical way in which this latter aspect can be audited and areas for improvement identified.

- Fifty-eight parents of a child with liver disease completed The Expanded Survey of Parental Satisfaction (Dare and Hemsley, 1986; Bradford, 1991a). Prior to admission to hospital, many parents expressed dissatisfaction with their emotional care, the information given, and speed of referral on. As inpatients, parental dissatisfaction was associated with distress not being noticed or responded to, lack of discussion of the child's prognosis and development, inadequate recognition of pressures imposed on marriages and the emotional/behavioural problems shown by siblings. As outpatients, 40 per cent were dissatisfied with the emotional care given and 36 per cent with the amount of information provided.

- The results highlight a number of areas where changes in hospital procedures could help reduce parental distress. These include:
  - detailed information made available at the time of admission, including written information;
  - opportunity at particular stress points to talk through the information imparted and its emotional implications;
  - information tailored to parental coping style and paced to the needs of parents and not to the needs of the hospital.

- Research suggests that parents may fail to have their emotional needs met owing to a combination of staffs' lack of time, avoidance of awkward questions and strong emotions, poor interviewing skills and an assumption that the patient will take the lead in disclosing a problem. In exploring this further, comparisons were made between the views and experiences of parents and medical, paramedical and nursing staffs' estimates of the same problems.

Results demonstrated a large variability both within and between staff groups in their accuracy coupled with a tendency to under-estimate the extent of emotional problems experienced, whilst over-estimating parents'opportunities to discuss concerns.

- The results highlighted the need for staff training to increase both awareness and accuracy in identifying psychological morbidity as well as increasing interviewing and counselling skills.

Chapter 5

Longer-term adjustment

INTRODUCTION

Identifying and meeting the psychological needs of children and their families can often be a time-consuming process. Whilst inpatient admissions potentially allow time for staff to be able to assess a situation and mobilise the necessary supports, the picture is much more complicated when families are managed on an outpatient basis following discharge. Busy outpatient clinics often seem like the last place where troubled families might feel able to raise concerns. This, coupled with the fact that there is undeniably great time pressures on doctors and others to get though their patient lists, can contribute to a sense of fragmented care, with the psychological challenges of looking after a sick child over-shadowed by physical investigations.

Parents often complain that they feel uneasy about raising psychological concerns in the context of what can appear a purely 'medical' consultation. This raises the issue of how well families adjust once they have left the intense atmosphere of the ward and the social support it can provide, through meeting others going through similar difficulties, and opportunities to talk to staff. Once discharged, do parents succeed in getting back to 'a normal life'; to what extent do emotional problems persist; and what factors are important in predicting outcomes?

In the following study (Bradford, 1994a) I explored these issues by following up a group of parents who had been through the paediatric liver unit at a hospital in London. They had all had to cope with their child being given a diagnosis of a terminal illness, in this case a liver disease known as biliary atresia. This condition is the most common hepatobiliary disorder in childhood, with an incidence of approximately 1 in 14,000 to 1 in 22,000 births (McClement *et al.*, 1985), and if left undiagnosed or untreated, death from liver failure typically occurs within two years. Whilst the cause of the disease is unknown, it is thought to occur as the result of an inflammatory process that destroys part of the biliary tree, resulting in obstructive jaundice. Surgical intervention in the form of portoenterostomy (or the 'Kasai procedure', as named after its originator in 1959) can successfully restore bile drainage in approximately 50 per cent of cases. Where the procedure is unsuccessful, most children go on to become candidates for liver transplantation (Vergani *et al.*, 1989).

It is well established that children who have a chronic disease are a population at risk of developing emotional and behavioural problems, with a two- to three-fold increased rate of psychological difficulties in comparison to their healthy peers (Pless and Nolan, 1991). It is equally apparent, however, that not all children experience problems in adjustment (Bradford, 1990a), which raises the important questions of how best to identify children and families at risk of developing psychological problems and why some children and their families cope with the challenges created by their condition, whilst others fare less well.

Wallander *et al.* (1989b) have proposed a conceptual model that attempts to answer these two questions. Wallander *et al.* suggest that adaptation to chronic disease and disability is determined by the interplay of risk and resistance factors. They identify three 'risk' factors: *disease and disability variables* (for example, disease severity, visibility, associated medical problems); the child's *level of functional independence*; and *psychosocial stressors* which relate to the disease as well as other life events and 'daily hassles'. Three sets of resistance factors are also suggested. These relate to *intrapersonal* variables (for example, temperament, problem-solving ability); *social-ecological* (for example, family environment, social support, utilitarian resources); and *stress processing abilities* (cognitive appraisal and coping strategies). Wallander *et al.*'s argument is that adaptation to disease can be predicted by exploring the relative balance of risk and resistance factors.

Wallander and colleagues have carried out a series of studies to test their model (Wallander *et al.*, 1988; 1989a; 1989b; 1989c; 1990). One area that they have focused upon in particular is the extent to which disease parameters, and specifically severity of the child's disease, influences adaptation. The evidence from their own research and others' reveals a somewhat contradictory picture. One reason for this lies in the fact that severity is a difficult concept to operationalise, as already discussed in Chapter 1, and it may well mean differing things in different conditions. This raises the issue of whether seeking to establish perceptions of severity may not be of greater use. To date, most studies have limited themselves to measuring the child's 'objective' health status (for example, spinal cord lesion level, presence of a shunt, bladder control, etc) and its effect on adjustment, rather than exploring the parent's perception of their child's health status. Evidence is starting to emerge that these 'subjective' beliefs may be more important in understanding the relationship between disease parameters and adjustment (Walker *et al.*, 1987; Perrin *et al.*, 1989), than 'objective' indices alone.

In the light of Wallander *et al.*'s (1989b) model, and my interest in exploring how families coped once they were discharged from the ward, the aims of this study were largely two-fold: firstly to explore the longer-term adjustment of children and their families, and secondly to investigate the influence of disease severity on outcomes. The hypotheses tested were, firstly, that children and their mothers would demonstrate high levels of adjustment problems and, secondly, that maternal perceptions of their child's health would prove to be more important than objective indices in predicting the child's adaptation.

DESIGN

The study was carried out at a London teaching hospital. In order to be included in the study, children had to have had a diagnosis of biliary atresia, had undergone corrective surgery (portoenterostomy) in the past, had not undergone liver transplantation, were currently in the age range 2 years 6 months to 16 years of age and had attended the outpatient department at the hospital in the last five months. This resulted in a sample of fifty-three children.

Families were asked to take part in the study when they attended outpatients and were then sent a detailed questionnaire with an accompanying letter from the paediatric surgeon and psychologist, explaining that the unit was seeking to assess the psychological impact of biliary atresia on children and their families.

MEASURE

The questionnaire sent to families consisted of the following five sections.

Background information

This concerned the child's age, sex and age at portoenterostomy. This latter item was included as some evidence suggests that age at surgery is a significant factor in successful surgical outcome (Vergani *et al.*, 1989); children operated on before 8 weeks of age have been found to have a significantly better medical outcome than those operated after this time. Given the specificity of age at surgery, medical records were also checked to establish the child's precise age when operated on, as it was possible that some parents might have difficulty recalling this particular piece of information with precise accuracy. Age at porto-enterostomy was subsequently scored as a dichotomous variable, i.e., 'under 8 weeks' or 'over 8 weeks'.

Ratings of child's objective health

Data was gathered on: number of hospital admissions experienced by child, number of days spent in hospital, frequency of outpatient appointments, and number of medications taken by child. Similar parameters have been used in previous studies to determine children's health status (for example, Perrin *et al.*, 1989; DeMaso *et al.*, 1991). For each item, the parent responded on a 4-point scale ('none', 'one', 'two to five', 'six or more'), with a score of 0 to 3 allocated to their answers. The child's 'objective health' score was the sum total of these items.

Ratings of child's subjective health

Mothers completed three 4-point scales that have been developed by Lewis *et al.* (1989) to assess perceptions of a child's health. In addition, this scale was supplemented by eight items that previous research (Bradford, 1990b) as well as clinical experience have suggested are important dimensions in coping with liver disease. The eleven items are detailed in Table 5.1.

Rating of child's psychological adjustment

For children aged 2 years 6 months to 4 years 11 months, mothers completed the Behaviour Check List (BCL) (Richman, 1987). This is a widely used measure employed to assess the occurrence of childhood behavioural difficulties, with good reliability and validity data having been reported (Richman, 1987). For children over 5 years of age, the Rutter A Scale (Rutter *et al.*, 1970) was completed. This measure has been used widely to identify emotional and behavioural disorders in childhood and adolescence, with acceptable reliability and validity data reported. On both questionnaires, mothers were also asked to indicate their attribution as to the cause of the problem behaviours. To determine whether the children's scores fell within a clinical range on the BCL and Rutter A Scale, i.e. at a level indicating the presence of an emotional and/or behavioural problem, criteria recommended by the respective authors were used.

Table 5.1 Items used to explore mother's subjective ratings of their child's health

1	In general would you say your child's health is excellent, good, fair or poor?
2	During the last *3 months* how much have you worried about your child's health?
3	Over the last *3 months* how much distress has your child's health caused him/her?
4	As a result of illness, do you think that your child misses out on things he/she would like to do?
5	Would you say that health problems are making him/her more dependent on others?
6	To what extent do health problems interfere with your child's ability to lead a normal life?
7	Compared to others in a similar situation, how well do you think you are coping?
8	To what extent do the health problems interfere with your ability to lead a normal life?
9	How much do you worry about your child's future?
10	How much do you worry about becoming over-protective of your child?
11	How much do you worry about the side effects of medication?

Maternal ratings of own adjustment

Mothers completed the twelve-item version of the General Health Questionnaire (GHQ) (Goldberg, 1972). Recent research indicates that this version is as reliable as the original sixty-item questionnaire, which has been employed extensively as a screening measure for psychiatric disorders. Caseness was scored according to the criteria specified by the authors.

ANALYSIS

In order to test the two hypotheses, data was analysed initially to determine frequencies of psychological problems in children and their mothers. Pearson correlations were computed to explore the relationship between the occurrence of behaviour problems and mother's attributions as to the cause of these. Subsequently, data from the Rutter A and BCL were transformed into standardised scores, thereby creating a single scale which was defined as 'child adjustment'. A multiple regression analysis was then performed using the subject/ variable ratio recommended by Clarke and Cook (1992). 'Child adjustment' was treated as the dependent variable with the predictor variables being: 'child's objective health', 'child's subjective health' and 'maternal GHQ score'. Items were entered into the equation using the stepwise procedure, with the significance level set at 0.05.

RESULTS

Forty-five questionnaires were completed, representing a response rate of 85 per cent. Statistical comparisons between responders/non-responders were not possible, owing to the small numbers involved, although inspection of the medical records of those who failed to return the measure did not reveal any consistent differences. The mean age for the portoenterostomy operation was 9.48 weeks (SD 3.56 weeks, Range 3–21 weeks) and the average age of the children at follow-up was 5 years 9 months (SD 2 years 9 months, Range 2.5–14 years). The distribution of children in the sample was thirteen males (29 per cent) and thirty-two females (71 per cent). Eleven per cent of families were single parents.

Children's current health status

The health profile of the children at follow-up is summarised in Table 5.2. Thirty-one per cent of the sample had not been inpatients in the preceding year, whilst 40 per cent had been admitted once, 25 per cent on two to five occasions and 4 per cent on six or more occasions.

Table 5.2   Children's objective health status

	None	One	Two–five	Six or more
Number of admissions	14 (31%)	18 (40%)	11 (25%)	2 (4%)
Number of days in hospital	15 (33%)	0 (–)	17 (38%)	13 (29%)
Number of outpatient appointments	0 (–)	4 (9%)	27 (60%)	14 (31%)
Number of medications	5 (11%)	3 (7%)	22 (49%)	15 (33%)

Source: Bradford, 1994a: 399

Where an admission had taken place, this was typically for between two to five days, although for a significant percentage (29 per cent), their stay lasted for over six days. All the children had attended outpatients in the preceding year, with the majority having visited two to five times and all the children were on some form of drug therapy to help counteract the effects of liver disease. The mean score on the scale was 6.9 (SD. 2.47, Range 2–12).

Maternal perceptions of their child's current health

Results from this scale are summarised in Table 5.3.

Table 5.3   Mother's perception of their child's 'subjective health' status

Item	0	1	2	3
1 Health at the moment	15 (33)	19 (42)	10 (22)	1 (2)
2 Amount of worry caused	10 (22)	18 (40)	6 (13)	11 (24)
3 Extent of pain/distress	26 (58)	11 (24)	4 (9)	4 (9)
4 Impact on child's life	31 (69)	10 (22)	4 (9)	
5 Parental coping	33 (73)	11 (24)	1 (2)	
6 Impact on parent's life	26 (58)	14 (31)	5 (11)	
7 Worry about future	6 (13)	15 (33)	24 (53)	
8 Worry about over-protecting	18 (40)	16 (36)	11 (24)	
9 Worry about medication	21 (47)	11 (24)	13 (29)	
10 Extent to which child misses out	30 (68)	14 (32)		
11 Extent to which child dependent	27 (67)	13 (33)		

Items 1–3 are scored on a 4-point scale; items 4–9 on a 3-point scale and items 10–11 on a 2-point scale. Higher scores per item are indicative of increased perception of a poor outcome in child. Numbers in brackets are percentages.

Source: Bradford, 1994a: 400

For the majority of mothers (75 per cent), their perception was that their child's health was either excellent or good; only one parent rated their child's health as poor. Despite this, many indicated that they were still worried about their child's health. These concerns were largely related to the child's future, side-effects of medication and the parent becoming over-protective. A third of mothers indicated that their child was more dependent and missed out on normal activities.

Ratings of child's adjustment

Twenty-four children were rated on the Behaviour Check List (BCL). The average score on the BCL was 11.54, SD 7.9, Range 2–33. Eleven children (46 per cent) scored above the recommended cut-off. In exploring the child's adjustment in greater detail, Table 5.4 illustrates the nature of emotional and behavioural problems experienced in children aged between 2 years 6 months to 4 years 11 months.

Table 5.4   Behaviour Check List: frequency of items endorsed by mothers

Item	No problem (%)	Slight problem (%)	Definite problem (%)	Attribution of problem to liver disease (%)
Appetite	54	25	21	92
Faddy	29	50	21	42
Wets night	50	17	33	66
Wets day	71	8	21	71
Soils	75	12	13	83
Settle	50	33	17	92
Wake night	38	29	33	67
Go through	42	38	21	50
Activity	13	33	54	43
Concentration	58	29	13	70
Clingy	75	25	(–)	67
Independent	50	42	8	42
Control	50	46	4	50
Temper tantrums	38	58	4	33
Miserable	79	8	13	60
Worries	75	17	8	50
Fears	58	33	8	50
Sib. relations	83	17	(–)	0
Peer relations	75	21	4	16
Three words	96	4	(–)	100
Clear speech	88	8	4	33

Source: Bradford, 1994a: 401

Twenty-one children were rated by their mothers on the Rutter A scale. The mean score was 14.05, SD 10.26, Range 0–35, with nine children (43 per cent) scoring above the cut-off. In total, twenty children (44 per cent of the sample) were rated as having adjustment problems. Table 5.5 details the results for children over 5 years of age.

Maternal beliefs as to the cause of adjustment problems

The association between the child's adjustment and mother's attribution as to the cause of problems was explored by correlating the child's total BCL and Rutter A scores with the mother's overall judgement as

Table 5.5   Rutter A Scale: frequency of items endorsed by mothers

Item	No problem (%)	Slight problem (%)	Definite problem (%)	Attribution of problem to liver disease (%)
Headaches	38	62	(−)	23
Stomach-ache	43	47	10	25
Biliousness	71	24	5	33
Wets bed/pants	71	10	19	50
Soils	66	24	10	29
Temper tantrums	38	43	19	23
School tears	86	14	(−)	33
Truants	95	(−)	5	0
Stammer/stutter	86	14	(−)	67
Speech problem	100	(−)	(−)	0
Steals	85	10	5	33
Eating problem	43	43	14	42
Sleep problem	48	48	5	55
Restless	38	24	38	23
Squirmy	48	33	19	46
Destroys	81	(−)	19	50
Fights	62	28	10	25
Not liked	81	14	5	0
Worries	62	14	24	25
Solitary	57	29	14	33
Irritable	47	29	24	9
Miserable	66	24	10	14
Twitches	85	10	5	67
Sucks thumb	90	10	(−)	0
Bites nails	62	28	10	13
Disobedient	43	38	19	33
Fearful	57	29	14	33
Fussy	76	19	5	40
Lies	71	19	10	50
Concentration	52	24	24	30
Bullies	85	10	5	0

Source: Bradford, 1994a: 402

to whether difficulties were related to liver disease. Results for children under 5 years of age indicated a strong positive correlation ($r = 0.86$, $p < 0.001$). Inspection of the individual items on the BCL highlighted that the child's appetite, difficulties in settling at night, encopresis, enuresis and concentration span in particular were attributed by the parent to the child's disease. On one item (three words), the finding that this was always linked to liver disease was a function of only one child experiencing a language delay which the parent then attributed to the disease.

Results for the Rutter A also indicated a significant overall association between adjustment problems and maternal attribution to liver disease (r = 0.59, p <0.01). The problems of enuresis, articulation difficulties, twitching, lying and destructiveness were all perceived by the mother to be particularly related to the child's disease.

Maternal ratings of their own adjustment

Of the respondents, forty-four mothers (98 per cent) completed the GHQ-12. Sixteen scored above the cut-off (36 per cent), with the average score being 2.27, SD 3.22, Range 0–10.

Factors associated with child adjustment

To explore the relative influence of the child's objective health status, maternal perceptions of the impact of liver disease and maternal GHQ scores on the child's adjustment scores, I completed a stepwise multiple regression. This is a statistical procedure which weighs the relative importance of each variable in relation to the factor one is most interested in, in this case child adjustment. The results of this analysis are summarised in Table 5.6.

Table 5.6 Stepwise regression analysis to predict child adjustment

	B	t	Sig.
Subjective health	.64	5.39	.0001
GHQ	.76	1.89	.07
Objective health	.84	1.16	.25

Dependent variable = Child adjustment score, which was derived from scores from the Behaviour Check List and Rutter A scales, which were transformed into standardised scores.

Source: Bradford, 1994a: 403

The results shown in Table 5.6 mean that neither maternal GHQ scores (how depressed mothers felt) nor the child's objective health score (how often the child was in hospital, etc.) were significantly associated with child adjustment problems. However, the mothers' perceptions of their child's health (extent to which child misses out, etc.) were significantly associated with the child's psychological adjustment score (b = 0.64, t = 5.4, p <0.0001). In total, 40 per cent of the overall variance in child adjustment was explained by this single factor.

DISCUSSION

The results reported here describe the nature and prevalence of emotional and behavioural problems in children with liver disease. The finding that 44 per cent of children and 36 per cent of mothers scored over the cut-off for 'caseness' on standardised psychological assessments supported the original hypothesis that adjustment problems would be common. These results indicate that many children with liver disease not only experience delays in their development, as has been demonstrated in previous studies, but also suffer from emotional and behavioural problems. The incidence of problems is comparable to other diseases that are inborn and potentially fatal. Thompson *et al.* (1992a), for example, found that 60 per cent of children with cystic fibrosis and 34 per cent of their mothers (Thompson *et al.*, 1992b) had problems in adjustment. The similarity in findings lends support for the notion that potentially life-threatening disorders impose particular strains on children and their carers.

In exploring the underlying influences on adjustment, the study supported the second hypothesis that mothers' perceptions of their child's health status were better predictors of the child's adjustment than objective health parameters. The study builds on the previous attempts to explore these relationships (Perrin *et al.*, 1989; Walker *et al.*, 1987: Thompson *et al.*, 1992a) in that perceptions of severity were operationalised using eleven items. Other studies, for example DeMaso *et al.* (1991), have tended to assess perceptions on the basis of single items, for example 'how severe is your child's heart condition?'. The current study employed the items developed by Lewis *et al.* (1989), and supplemented these with additional questions. This approach arguably provides a more realistic assessment of beliefs and perceptions of illness. This scale appeared to be a valuable adjunct to Lewis *et al.*'s (1989) scale.

The study also explored mothers' attributions as to the cause of their child's adjustment difficulties. Surprisingly, this issue has been relatively neglected in the literature to date. Results indicated that many mothers did consider the disease process to be a major cause of specific emotional and behavioural problems in their child. This finding draws attention to the importance of doctors and others actively enquiring into parental health beliefs concerning their child's illness. This is an important area as clearly health beliefs have relevance for how the disease process is construed by parents and has implications for how doctors should communicate with patients and how mental health workers should attempt to intervene in addressing the psychological sequelae of chronic disease.

It has been noted that many families fail to access mental health services that might be of benefit to them (Garrison and McQuiston, 1989). This failure has been linked to poor doctor–patient communication (Bradford, 1990b), inaccuracies in identifying concerns (Bradford, 1991a), parents not raising issues (Cadman *et al.*, 1987) and a lack of availability of services (Drotar and Bush, 1985). The current results suggest that health beliefs may also be an important factor. For example, if a mother believes that their child's sleep problem is caused by liver disease, she may not be impressed by the paediatrician referring her on to a psychologist for advice.

From a theoretical point of view, the findings of the study fit several of the predictions that Wallander *et al.*'s (1989b) model would make. Firstly, as the incidence of adjustment problems in children and their mothers was similar to that reported in relation to other conditions, a 'non-categorical' approach to investigating the psychological sequelae of chronic diseases is supported. Secondly, the model proposes that cognitive appraisal is a key mediating factor in understanding adjustment. This feature is confirmed by parental perceptions and beliefs emerging as important in predicting child adjustment. Wallander *et al.*'s (1989b) model is not supported, however, in its contention that disease severity *per se* would be predictive of adaptation, as objective health indices did not explain child adjustment.

In considering these findings, several limitations in the design of the study should be borne in mind. Firstly, the sample size was small, as a consequence of the condition under study being rare. This may raise an issue of how generalisable the results are. Equally, the study relied heavily on maternal reports of their child's health and development. This aspect of the study could have been strengthened if multiple respondents had been used by, for example, including fathers, playgroups and schools. Finally, it is possible that if different criteria had been used to operationalise the child's objective health status, such as liver function tests, this variable might have been more significantly associated with child adjustment. Balanced against this, however, is the fact that other studies that have included this type of data have failed to establish a consistent relationship between severity and psychological outcome in child patients (for example, Mullins *et al.*, 1991; Wallander *et al.*, 1989c).

Bearing these limitations in mind, the results highlight the importance of doctors and others screening for emotional and behavioural problems in their child patients. Reliable and valid tools are now widely available, which can be completed by the parent in a relatively short period of time. This study suggests that if doctors screened for the occurrence of behaviour problems and enquired into the parents' perceptions and beliefs concerning the child's illness and its impact, families at risk of poor adjustment could be identified and appropriate support organised. Parental attribution as to the cause of the emotional/behavioural problem, and therefore the appropriateness of referral on to mental health services, needs to be actively explored at this stage, as this study suggests that health beliefs may well play an important role in how well families engage subsequently with psychological treatments. The reliance upon objective health indices alone would not seem to be an effective way to identify children and families in need.

The key message is that we need to be able to engage more effectively with children and families and that we can only start to do this when we have a sophisticated appreciation of the challenges they face. In the next chapter, I will develop this theme by exploring some of the issues that can arise when medical advances exceed our understanding of the psychological consequences of the treatment offered. This situation can create real problems for medical, nursing and other staff in trying to support children and families.

SUMMARY

- Mothers of forty-five children with a liver disease (biliary atresia) completed a questionnaire concerned with their child's health status and psychological adjustment. Emotional and behavioural problems were found to be common; 46 per cent of children under five and 43 per cent over 5 years of age scored above the cut-off on standardised measures of adjustment. Maternal mental health difficulties were present in 36 per cent of the sample.

- Results indicated that maternal perception of their child's health was the single best predictor of child adjustment, with 40 per cent of the variance in children's psychological adjustment being accounted for by this factor.

- Contrary to the expectations of some theoretical models that have been proposed (for example, Wallander *et al.*'s 1989 model of adaptation), neither maternal mental health, nor objective parameters of the child's health status contributed significantly to child adjustment.

- We need to be far more sensitive to parental beliefs about their child's condition, as this would seem to be an important way to target families in need. Equally, parental theories of illness causation, and how they relate to psychological problems the child might show, need to be carefully explored to ensure that services offered match parental expectations wherever possible.

Chapter 6

Medical advances

INTRODUCTION

In evaluating the effectiveness of any intervention, it is necessary to look at a number of parameters, including physical, psychological and social aspects to patient functioning. This is particularly true where a new form of treatment is developed.

Organ transplantation represents a good example of how rapid advances in one sphere – in this case, medical progress – can quickly outstrip our understanding in other areas, for example psychological and social outcomes. When this imbalance persists, dilemmas can frequently result for patients and doctors as there is a lack of information or 'hard data' upon which to make informed decisions. For example, as organ transplantation becomes more successful, demand for suitable organs inevitably outstrips supply. This raises the dilemma of who should receive the available organ. Should it be the person at the top of the waiting list (who by definition is the most ill and whose longer-term quality of life might already be compromised) or someone who is not so acutely ill? Equally, what role should patient compliance play in medical teams' decision making and what weight should be applied to the vexed issue of 'healthy' verses 'unhealthy' lifestyles?

When parents are faced with the 'choice' of allowing their child to have an organ transplant, discussions inevitably focus on medical outcomes, and in particular survival rates. Should this be the only index? As media attention focuses on the plight of those who desperately wait for the chance of life that an organ transplant can represent, do we lose sight of what happens once a donor is identified? What are the stresses that families face and what is the long-term adjustment of survivors?

To draw out some of the answers and issues involved, I will review the literature on the psychosocial impact of transplantation in relation to one group of children – namely those awaiting liver transplantation (Bradford, 1991b). As this is a relatively new procedure, it highlights many of the important issues involved. Having considered the psychosocial impact of liver transplantation on children and their families, I will then go on to consider ways in which services could be organised to promote successful coping. With a colleague, Laura Tomlinson at St. Thomas' Hospital in London, we have developed some 'guidelines for good practice' for children undergoing transplantation for a variety of diseases (Bradford and Tomlinson, 1990).

LIVER TRANSPLANTATION

Liver transplantation is now the treatment of choice for a variety of advanced child hepatic disorders (Tarter *et al.*, 1988), the majority of which are either biliary atresia or other diseases initially presenting with conjugated hyperbilirubinaemia in infancy. Whilst liver transplantation has become a more common procedure, with several centres around the country carrying out the operation, the early history of paediatric liver transplantation in the United Kingdom was not promising. Only seven transplants were carried out on children under 16 by 1983 and none survived longer than seven weeks (Pett *et al.*, 1987).

The picture since then has been transformed dramatically, with survival rates at one year now reported to be over 80 per cent (Salt *et al.*, 1992). The advent of cyclosporin (an anti-rejection drug used following transplantation), coupled with advances made in surgical technique and post-operative care, account for many of the changes in survival rates (Zitelli *et al.*, 1986).

Health care is said to have two main aims: to increase life expectancy and to improve the quality of life during the years that people are alive (Kaplan *et al.*, 1989). Liver transplantation has achieved the first goal, but there is less evidence as to its impact on the second. As medical audit becomes increasingly important in the allocation of resources, transplant teams and others will need to show success in enhancing not only the physical, but also psychological and social aspects of the child's functioning (Lewis, 1989).

Pre-transplant developmental status

Anecdotally, it has been noted that many children with chronic liver diseases show signs of general developmental delay at the time of assessment for transplantation (Penn *et al.*, 1971). Surprisingly, few studies have attempted to delineate the exact nature of these delays. Alagille *et al.* (1975) reported a group of patients whose clinical, biochemical and histological features differentiated them from other varieties of biliary disease. As part of this syndrome, it was noted that 'mild to moderate mental handicap' was evident in 60 per cent of patients.

Burgess *et al.* (1982) and Stewart *et al.* (1987) have reported on the developmental status of children with biliary atresia. This disease is the most common hepatobiliary disorder in childhood, with an incidence of approximately one in 14,000 to one in 22,000 births (McClement *et al.*, 1985). The results of Burgess *et al.*'s (1982) and Stewart *et al.*'s (1987) investigations showed that children with biliary atresia frequently had significant delays in their cognitive, motor and social abilities. Studies of other liver disease groups (Stewart *et al.*, 1988) conclude that children with alpha 1 antitrypsin deficiency, idiopathic cirrhosis and neonatal hepatitis are all at risk of significant developmental delays. Wilson's disease, which most often presents in late childhood or early adolescence, similarly has psychological concomitants (Wilson, 1912; Carr and McDonnell, 1986). Common sequelae include dysarthria, poor coordination, mood changes and poor school performance (Mowat, 1987).

Investigation of factors associated with developmental delay in biliary atresia point to growth variables, serum vitamin E levels, age of onset of disease and age at portoenterostomy as being predictive of the extent of delay (Stewart *et al.*, 1987; 1989). The degree of intellectual deterioration of Wilson's disease appears to relate to the duration that the disease remains untreated (David and Goldstein, 1974; Kneher and Bearn, 1956).

On the basis of these studies it would appear that there is a need to monitor the developmental and cognitive status of children awaiting liver transplantation. The timing of the transplant also needs to be carefully weighed, because allowing the disease to progress to significant hepatic compromise and even 'near death' conditions may severely limit the quality of the eventual clinical outcome (Stewart *et al.*, 1988). On the research front, further elucidation of the nature and extent of developmental delays in liver diseases needs to be carried out, as well as investigating factors associated with increased risk.

Pre-transplant psychological functioning

As a result of their jaundice, ascites, muscle wasting and short stature, children with liver diseases have been noted to be frequent 'targets of ridicule' (House *et al.*, 1983). In interviewing children and families prior to liver transplantation, researchers have found that up to 50 per cent of children have psychological difficulties. Particular problems noted included: regression, belligerence, apprehension and fear, difficulties with important relationships, persistent fear of death, feelings of rejection, helplessness, suicidal thoughts and worries over receiving someone else's liver (House *et al.*, 1983). In comparing this population with children waiting for a renal transplant, the authors conclude that children prior to liver transplantation show more psychopathology than other groups of patients. They argue that this finding is due to the parental anxiety surrounding the lack of alternative interventions for end-stage liver disease and the fact that should the procedure be unsuccessful, the only treatment option remains further transplantation.

There is a need for further studies to substantiate these findings as this is the only study to date that reports on pre-operative psychological functioning.

Pre-transplant family functioning

A common pattern of interaction that has been noted frequently in families waiting for transplant centres upon parent–child protection and dependency. Several authors have commented upon the parents', particularly the mothers', need to protect the child, which can be shown by the family becoming isolated and inward-looking, at the same time infantilising and over-indulging the child (Penn *et al.*, 1971; House *et al.*, 1983; Zitelli *et al.*, 1988). The child is said to be often dependent, demanding and difficult to comfort. The combination of parental over-protection and child dependency is commonly associated with family discord and child emotional/behavioural problems. Similar family styles of interaction have been described in other transplant groups (Klein *et al.*, 1984) as well as in families where a child has congenital heart disease (Bradford, 1990a) and other chronic conditions (Minuchin *et al.*, 1975).

Gold *et al.* (1986) have identified two particular stressors that families have to contend with. Firstly, there is the need to maintain the child's fragile health and to ensure that a target weight of 10 kilos is achieved. Evidence has shown that children under this weight fare significantly worse during and post- liver transplantation. Secondly, parents have to come to terms with the paradox that whilst keeping their child healthy, it is those who are most ill who are likely to be transplanted first. This inevitably engenders feelings of competition, guilt, a sense of being forgotten by the hospital and ambivalence about whether their child should go through a procedure that at the same time is both life-saving and threatening.

It is not surprising, in the light of the above, that many families when psychiatrically assessed prior to transplant, are found to have significant morbidity. The problem is what sense to make of this finding. As with the research on child functioning, it is not clear what is causal, or indeed whether assessments are valid (Serrano *et al.*, 1987). Frequently, an assumption of pathology is made, when in fact patterns of interaction could be adaptive (Valesco De Parra *et al.*, 1973). For example, in ensuring that a child remains relatively infection free, it may be appropriate for families to become insular. Further, given the child's compromised liver function, poor nutritional status and the need to ensure weight gain, it is possible to see the enmeshed mother–child relationship as being adaptive in enhancing survival. The 'pathology' only arises when the threat no longer exists, yet these patterns of behaviour become entrenched.

Child and family adjustment post-transplant

Many families experience a sense of euphoria following successful transplantation (Gold *et al.*, 1986). The constant need to keep the child healthy whilst on the waiting list can now be relinquished to intensive care staff. This 'cease-fire period' (Gold *et al.*, 1986) is soon shattered by the first episode of infection and rejection. Ninety per cent of patients on the Cambridge–King's transplant programme experience these problems within two weeks of their operation (Bhaduri, 1990, pers. comm.). This heralds the start of a 'roller coaster' period (Gold *et al.*, 1986), where the emotional state of both parent and child closely follows the course of the medical condition. This continuous raising of hopes matched by periods of disillusionment can result in conflicts developing and becoming overt, expression of anger and even distancing from the patient (Bradford and Tomlinson, 1990).

It has been found that those children who were well-adjusted pre-transplant continued to progress psychologically, whilst those with difficulties pre-transplant showed increased patterns of dependency or 'a severely adverse reaction to hospital' (Penn *et al.*, 1971). Reports of child anxiety and depression are common (Mowat, 1987), whilst a sense of hopelessness is a frequent problem for parents (Krener, 1987). Emotional reactions brought on by frustration at not being 'cured' are common in both parent and child. Accepting the limitations of the transplant, that it does not represent a cure but is another form of illness which may be easier to manage, presents a major challenge. Some researchers have suggested that children experience psychological difficulties accepting and integrating the new organ as a result (Penn *et al.*, 1971; Serrano *et al.*, 1987). Whilst examples of individual cases do occur, overall there is little firm evidence to suggest that integrating the new organ is a pervasive problem (Bradford and Tomlinson, 1990).

Longer-term quality of life

It has been rightly concluded that 'the true value of any procedure is gauged by its ability to return its recipient to a normal life' (Andrews, 1987). The evidence to date concerning liver transplantation is not wholly conclusive.

Zitelli *et al.* (1987; 1988) evaluated the changes in lifestyle in sixty-five patients, on average 37 months after transplant. Comparing each child's pre- and post-transplant profile, it was found that children experienced significantly fewer admissions, number of days in hospital and medications. Fifty-one per cent of the sample were in age-appropriate education (although two were found subsequently to have a learning disability), 26 per cent were one year behind, 12 per cent were two years behind and 9 per cent were in special education. Formal assessments of each child's cognitive abilities pre- and post-transplant showed no significant group difference. Measures of the child's psychological development suggested improvements in motor and social skills. Parental perceptions were also that their child was less dependent, complaining and demanding and they as parents were more consistent in their discipline, less infantilising. Thirty-two per cent of the children were found to be enuretic in the absence of any physical cause, with several children being described as defiant and aggressive. Nine of fifty-nine couples separated.

Other studies have not reached the same conclusions as Zitelli. For example, cognitive changes following transplant have been investigated in two studies (Stewart *et al.*, 1989; Andrews, 1987). Both concluded that, as a group, liver transplant patients do not show significant changes in IQ after the operation. The importance of these studies is in recalling that many children pre-transplant are found to be developmentally delayed. Thus liver transplantation does not appear to help in ameliorating cognitive impairments for the majority of children. Indeed, a significant minority experience neurological complications post-transplant (Paradis, Freese and Sharp, 1988) and a small number of children suffer a deterioration in their cognitive abilities.

Changes in motor and social skills have also been subject to further evaluation (Stewart *et al.*, 1989). The authors report that no significant changes in motor skills were evident following transplant and changes in social abilities occurred only in children over 4 years of age. Improvements were related to skill in sporting activity, greater responsibility at home and more frequent peer contacts. In contrast, none of the children showed a significant improvement in the number of close friends or in behaviour with family or friends. Other researchers report that no significant changes in frequency or duration of hospital admissions occur and that the significant impact of drug side-effects (for example, hirsutism, hypertension, oedema, cushingoid appearance) is associated with mild emotional lability in a third of patients (Colonna *et al.*, 1988).

The long-term problems of families have also been studied. It is reported that many families experience problems in adjusting back into a 'normal' life (Weichler and Hakos, 1989) and that many mothers abandon work in order to care for their child, creating further financial hardships (Boutsen and Gilbert, 1987). Emotional problems have been found to continue for several years (Zitelli *et al.*, 1988; Gold *et al.*, 1988), with families being hypervigilant for signs of rejection, experiencing difficulties in 'letting go' of the hospital and readjusting their role, as shown by a need for constant fund raising, tensions in whether to keep in contact with other liver transplant families for fear of bad news and worries over side-effects to medications.

CONCLUSION

The majority of the studies reviewed in this newly developing area have important methodological limitations. Many base their assessments on impressions of adjustment or parental reports. Whilst these are undoubtedly important sources of information, they are open to the criticism of lacking objectivity and replicability. Assessments are also often carried out in the period immediately before transplant, which may bias the results. Furthermore, the number of children evaluated is often small and follow-up periods following liver transplantation short. Thus it is not clear how valid the results are and whether they would be different with a larger sample followed up for a longer period. In addition, it is not clear to what extent results from the USA, where the majority of reports originate from, are applicable to a British population. Studies can also be criticised on theoretical grounds. Little attempt is made to relate psychological functioning to the child's medical status, and few studies use objective standardised assessment measures to evaluate the extent to which individual differences in psychological functioning pre-transplant influence postoperative adjustment. Similarly, there is a lack of information concerning the reactions of siblings to the inevitable upheaval of transplantation, despite the well-documented evidence that they are a group at risk of developing problems (Breslau *et al.*, 1981). These limitations need to be addressed in future studies so that medical teams can evaluate the effect of treatments and provide parents with the necessary information to make informed decisions concerning transplantation. The integration of psychosocial evaluations into medical practice is a major goal in assessing children's health status and evaluating the impact of surgical interventions.

This review demonstrates that children who are candidates for liver transplantation face particular challenges which carry implications for their adjustment. In the next part of this chapter I will explore what could be done to help these and other children and their families facing organ transplantation.

GUIDELINES FOR PRACTICE

Discussing transplantation

The focus so far has been on paediatric liver transplantation, but there are many common issues that cut across transplant groups in terms of how best to help children and families cope with the procedure. Whether one is working with children who require kidney transplantation, which is one of the most well-established procedures (survival rates are more than 79 per cent fourteen years after the operation, Rigden *et al.*, 1989), or in an area that is only starting to develop (for example, paediatric heart and lung transplantation), there is mounting evidence as to how best to manage child and family care from a psychological point of view.

In the vast majority of cases, it is possible to plan and discuss the likely need for transplantation with the family. Whilst there are a number of occasions where transplantation has to be performed without prior preparation, increasing technical skill in the management of children means that it is becoming possible to take psychosocial factors into consideration when planning the optimal time for the operation, thereby maximising the quality of life for both child and family. The balancing of medical and psychosocial factors to make the operation as successful as possible is likely to become an important goal for all teams.

Gold *et al.* (1986) identified two ways in which parents may react to the information about transplantation that can present problems for teams. The first entails being highly assertive, and is often reflected in having difficulties in relinquishing control of their child's management, seeking detailed information about the procedures to be undergone, and requesting second opinions. Medical and nursing teams alike can find this both over-demanding and undermining, and it gives the families the appearance of being emotionally detached in their relentless pursuit of information. It is often at this time that mental health workers are asked to become involved because of worries that the family may be denying the inevitability of their child's condition.

Despite the tensions that this style of coping sometimes produces, it is often one of the most successful ways of dealing with what might otherwise be an overwhelming situation (Mattsson, 1972). The pitfall for the medical team occurs when tensions become heightened to the extent that communication breaks down between them and the families. It is important that such families are recognised early on so that strenuous efforts can be made to form a working alliance by regular consultations, thereby promoting trust and confidence, and by keeping the parents as fully informed and involved as possible. It is essential also that the team nominates a key person, usually a senior member of staff, through whom communication with the family is filtered. This reduces the likelihood of friction occurring between members of the team and the family.

An alternative way of dealing with the news about transplantation is for families to become 'under-organised'. Because of their apparent compliance, these parents seem to present no overt concerns for medical teams. The pitfall is the assumption that the family have a clear understanding of the procedure and its implications. In general, patients' knowledge of body systems is poor. For example, fewer than half of adult patients know the location of important organs (Boyle, 1970), and many have misconceptions about their functions and how treatment relates to them (Roth *et al.*, 1962). In addition, their understanding of medical terms in common use is often confused (Ley, 1988) and families frequently have questions that they feel too inhibited to ask. Bradford (1990b) found, for example, that a third of patients on a liver unit failed to ask the questions that they wanted. A common misconception for families is the anticipation that following transplantation their child will be 'as new', and as a result they minimise the continuing need for drugs and visits to hospital. It is only in discussing transplantation with the family, and through eliciting information rather than just imparting it, that the lack of knowledge and the misconceptions that they harbour become clear.

An issue that often confronts transplant teams is how much and in what way children should be informed of their illness and forthcoming operation. Evidence from paediatric oncologists suggests that the knowledge children have of their illness and the way it is acquired is associated with psychological adjustment in later life (Slavin *et al.*, 1982). Children who were informed of their diagnosis directly and at an early stage – that is, within a year of diagnosis or by the age of 6 years – were better adjusted than those who were not told or who acquired the information through indirect channels such as by overhearing. Similarly, parents often want to know what they should tell the other children in the family. By studying the siblings of children who had died it was found that keeping the child informed of a brother or sister's diagnosis and prognosis was an important protective factor in later adjustment (Pettle-Michaels and Lansdown, 1986). Transplantation has a profound effect on every member of the family and efforts should be made to help parents recognise the need for open communication, which should clearly include discussion with their other children.

The way in which children should be told of transplantation needs to take into account both their emotional and cognitive development, as a child's knowledge of the body, its functioning and the causes and prevention of illness and treatment are closely related to their developmental stage. Pre-school children tend to think that illness has a magical explanation or alternatively as being a result of their behaviour, usually a wrongdoing (Bibace and Walsh, 1980). Consequently, treatment is often seen as a form of punishment. Primary school children think that illness is caused by germs or contamination (Bibace and Walsh, 1980). Thus, these children are likely to understand procedures such as barrier nursing but may fail to understand the need for immunosuppressant treatment and frequent blood tests. It is not until the teenage years that a clear concept of the body as a functioning system emerges (Eiser, 1990).

In addition to taking into account the child's developmental level, research evidence highlights the fact that from an early age children develop 'scripts' or stories in their minds about everyday events (Nelson, 1986). The importance of this is that children who have been exposed, for example, to frequent hospital procedures may well develop quite a clear appreciation of the sequence of events involved in treatment. It is wise not to assume, therefore, that a child's developmental level is the only important factor that influences knowledge acquisition; both social context and experience appear to have a role as well.

Surprisingly, research on doctor–patient interaction suggests that paediatricians often fail to speak directly to their child patients to explore their understanding of the illness and its treatment (Pantell *et al.*, 1982). It would seem, therefore, that doctors need to communicate more, particularly to reassure the pre-school age group about the causes of their admissions to hospital and illnesses, to discuss anxieties about treatment with the primary school age children, and to hold open, frank consultations with older children. Equally, consultations are not simply about imparting information, but they should also actively explore misconceptions that a child and family might have.

The prospect of a transplant obviously provokes anxiety. There is a need, therefore, to help children and their families discuss and cope with the forthcoming admission and procedure, and in particular to identify those who are most likely to adjust badly (Bradford, 1990b). Factors that increase vulnerability include: poor maternal mental health, poor communication and lack of cohesion within the family, lack of social supports and a previous psychiatric history in the child patient (Wallander *et al.*, 1989a).

Psychological interventions help to reduce distress for both child and parents, reduce the need for drugs, speed up discharge, and improve adjustment back to home life (Visintainer and Wolfer, 1975). A number of techniques can be used to facilitate coping: visits before admission (Azarnoff and Woody, 1981); videos of actors demonstrating modelling and mastery techniques. (Melamed and Siegel, 1975); play therapy (Cassel and Paul, 1967), and providing information and emotional support for parents (Visintainer and Wolfer, 1975). Careful preparation before admission is clearly vital for transplant patients, many of whom will enter hospital at very short notice. It is important that these families are made familiar early on with the ward and with the staff who will support them throughout their stay, but also that they should be prepared for the procedures, sights and sounds they will experience. Scrapbooks and photograph albums of other children during various stages of treatment can be invaluable aids that are relatively easy and inexpensive to provide. It may also be helpful to offer written advice about what practical steps need to be taken to prepare for admission.

During this period the team will want to foster a positive attitude in the family about the forthcoming operation, whilst not denying the reality that some procedures are unsuccessful. The team needs to be aware of and plan for the support the family will require if the operation fails and the child dies, as well as the profound effect that such an event has on staff and other families on the unit. The bereaved family will often look for support during this period to those members of staff whom they already know. It is important to recognise that a main source of stress among staff is the sense of impotence that they feel when they are unable to relieve the distress of parents who have lost a child. Wooley *et al.* (1989b) identified particular issues of staff finding parental anger, as part of the grief response, difficult to cope with. It is advisable, therefore, that all members of the team, including the most junior, should be familiar with the processes of grief, and know what to do when faced by grieving parents and siblings (Raphael, 1984). In our experience it is important that the members of the unit have the opportunity to explore their own feelings about the loss of a child. Where this is seen as too threatening or inappropriate, it is possible to approach the topic by offering a structured session on the psychology of death and grieving. This usually opens out into a discussion of events on the unit and allows staff to deal with their own feelings at their own pace.

After the operation

After transplantation, children will spend variable amounts of time in the intensive care unit. Though there is little evidence about the emotional effects of being in an intensive care unit on children, there have been a number of studies of parents' reactions. Specific areas of parental concern include the sights and sounds associated with the physical environment, such as monitor alarms, equipment and seeing other ill children. They are worried about the child's appearance, mood changes in older children, procedures carried out on their child, such as the taking of blood, the insertion of catheters and cannulas, and physiotherapy treatment. Parents are also concerned about other aspects, such as staff behaviour and communications (including the use of jargon, levity and apparent remoteness); how they should behave in relation to their child and the lack of a clear role; and the child's behaviour, when this included confusional states, demanding behaviour or inactivity. Miles and Carter (1982) advocate the need for clear communication about what to expect and what the parents' role is.

A common complication immediately after the operation is infection and the need for barrier nursing. The isolation associated with this form of treatment can lead to the child reacting with anger towards staff and parents, poor compliance and tearfulness. Structuring the child's day so that boredom and loneliness are minimised, as well as ensuring that the child can communicate, is an essential part of nursing care. This can include incorporating free play periods with nursing staff who may otherwise have limited contact other than during aversive procedures, the creative use of video and television to give the child access to what is happening outside the room, and communication with peers by audio tapes.

A number of psychological techniques have been developed to help children cope with specific medical procedures. These include giving the child clear signals and advanced warning that a procedure will take place by, for example, explaining that blood will only be taken when the nurse wears a red badge; helping the child to take part in the actual intervention (Kavanagh, 1983); teaching relaxation by using breathing exercises and imagining pleasant scenes (Hilgard and LeBarron, 1984); modelling effective coping and positive self-talk (Zastowny *et al.*, 1986) and using the child's ability to imagine their favourite television characters dealing appropriately with such circumstances. In addition, staff can increase the child's compliance by rewarding effective coping during procedures with star charts, bravery certificates and badges (Jay *et al.*, 1985).

In the weeks after transplantation it is not uncommon for children to experience changes in mood, including unhappiness, crying and mild depression, which in most cases reach a peak about a month after the operation (Korsch *et al.*, 1971). Parents should be warned of this, both to ameliorate the child's distress and to decrease their own anxiety. It may also help parents to achieve an appropriate balance in their approach to their child. A particular concern at this stage of the child's recovery is that of infection. For patients who have received liver transplants this is a common complication that serves to highlight for both child and parent their continuing vulnerability. It can also arise in patients who have received kidney transplants and who, despite previous information, regard the failure of the graft to provide adequate function immediately as an ominous sign. The emotional state of both parent and child is usually closely related to the course of the medical condition, with disturbance being associated with periods of infection, rejection and poor functioning of the graft. This continuous raising of hopes matched by periods of disillusionment can result in conflicts developing and becoming overt, expressions of anger, and even distancing from the child patient. This process may be mirrored within the team treating the child, with staff adopting polarised positions in relation to the child's continuing treatment. Ideally these conflicts need to be acknowledged and steps taken to reach a consensus. The reality is often more complex because of the differing burdens of professional responsibility.

Discharge

As the child's medical condition becomes more stable, the team increasingly becomes aware of the need to help the child back into a more normal pattern of life. Of particular concern for both parents and children are problems of losing contact with peer groups, falling behind with school work and the types of restrictions that may be imposed on the child's physical recreation. Brookes (1983) reported that the child's return to school after the operation is often most stressful and clearly this needs to be planned in advance. In addition to children and parents, this process should include teaching staff from both hospital and school, as well as doctors, to provide accurate information on the child's needs and abilities and to dispel myths and reduce anxieties about the child's vulnerability. Over-protection by others is a common problem for children with chronic disorders, and this is also true for children with transplanted organs (Korsch et al., 1971; House et al., 1983).

It is important, therefore, that medical staff actively inquire about the child's acquisition of an appropriate degree of independence when seen for follow-up (Bradford, 1990b). Where it is possible for teams to work in a multidisciplinary fashion, much of this kind of follow-up is appropriately carried out by other, non-medical, members of the team such as teachers, who may be able to approach the child's school to get a wider picture. If the team do have concerns about the adequacy of the child's development, training in particular skills and graded behavioural programmes, like those developed for adolescents (Magrab and Jacobstein, 1984), can be helpful, as well as family treatments.

Long-term management

Long-term success of organ transplantation depends on adherence to medical regimes and treatment plans over extended periods of time.

Non-compliance can be a considerable problem, particularly in young teenage recipients. Fine (1989) reported that three-quarters of the recipients of renal transplants who admitted to not taking their drugs subsequently lost their graft.

Much work has been done on this problem of non-compliance, and factors to consider are:

- *Characteristics of the treatment regime* – side-effects, duration, complexity
- *Doctor–patient relationship* – dissatisfaction with consultation, long waiting time
- *Family functioning* – family instability or discord, poor communication, lack of support from family members, maternal mood, poor maternal understanding of treatment, lack of supervision
- *Individual characteristics* – age (adolescence), sex (female), poor understanding, health belief system (perceived vulnerability and effectiveness of treatment), psychological problems prior to treatment.

A number of approaches aimed at increasing compliance have been described (Ley, 1988). It is worthwhile approaching the problem step by step, firstly by addressing the patient's understanding and active misconceptions about treatment regimens. If it is clear that the patient has not understood treatment requirements, this can be improved by reducing the complexity of the regimen and by providing written supporting material, either in the form of a handout or a booklet, for the patient to keep. Should the educational approach be insufficient, the second step is to assess motivation of the young person or family. With adolescents, where the attainment of autonomy and independence are uppermost, it is sometimes possible to manage the problem by increasing the patient's sense of control by negotiating which medications they need to take and when (Coupey and Cohen, 1984), coupled with increased medical supervision. In teenage girls non-compliance is commonly associated with concern about cosmetic side-effects such as excessive weight gain, cushingoid features, hirsutism. When possible, the team needs to help solve these difficulties within the context of adequate medical treatment – for example, by using an alternative immunosuppressive drug, providing dietary advice, depilatories and cosmetic measures when the problem is severe. Finally, psychological or family issues may play an important part, necessitating referral on to other specialists.

As transplantation programmes become increasingly successful, the assessment of quality of life is becoming more important (Henning *et al.*, 1988). For example, patients who have received liver transplants have been found to need fewer admissions to hospital and drugs than they did prior to the operation and to show an increase in growth and general development (Zitelli *et al.*, 1988). Other studies have highlighted that some children continued to have persistent delays and point out that positive outcomes in catch-up growth were usually determined by factors such as age, height and bone age pretransplant (Rizzoni *et al.*, 1986).

It is often assumed that children who have received transplants have serious mental health problems, but the evidence is inconclusive. Children who have received liver transplants have been described as having appreciable psychological problems (House *et al.*, 1983), whereas most children with renal transplants are said to be well-adjusted on formal psychiatric and psychological assessments (Bernstein, 1977; Klein *et al.*, 1984).

There is also a suggestion that children have emotional problems in accepting and integrating the new organ. On balance the evidence does not support this, although cases of children who experience difficulties do occur. They tend, however, to be children who had emotional problems before the transplant, and in these cases the transplant is likely to colour the way in which distress is manifested rather than be a causal factor in itself.

There is firmer evidence that children with transplants feel differently about themselves compared with other healthy children, particularly in terms of their self-esteem and body image. Many authors comment on the children's sensitivity about the physical changes caused by immunosuppressive therapies, their reactions to scars, their persisting short stature and deformities caused by bone disease (Bernstein, 1977). It is important to identify dissatisfaction with body image early on, as follow-up studies suggest that difficulties in this area are associated with emotional and social adjustment problems in later life (Brookes, 1983: Klein *et al.*, 1984).

Parents report difficulties in achieving an appropriate balance between protectiveness and independence at this stage. The main areas of concern are re-establishing old family patterns of interaction, coping with worries about the future and the side-effects of medication (Gold *et al.*, 1986). A particular stress is the death of another child, as this can reawaken their sense of vulnerability. In the case of renal transplantation, failure of the graft necessitating a return to dialysis is a similar factor. Evidence suggests that when good graft functioning is established, normal family routines re-establish themselves within a year (Korsch *et al.*, 1973). Studies of liver transplant families suggest that parental problems in adjustment are more entrenched (Gold *et al.*, 1986; Zitelli *et al.*, 1988). This is possibly because of the higher incidence of rejection and post-transplant complications, as well as the lack of alternative treatments should transplantation fail.

These arguments indicate a need for regular psychosocial reviews to be built into the medical outpatient assessment, so that problems can be identified early and appropriate help provided. There are critical transition points in the life-cycle of families that can prove to be a hurdle to successful adaptation. Consultations need not only to focus on medical aspects, but also to take into account more general issues, such as how the family are coping and whether the child's development is age appropriate, as it is only in integrating psychosocial and medical factors that optimal care can be provided.

The next issue to consider is that of family functioning and 'critical transition points' and their relationship to adjustment in more detail. How might families be more engaged into the process of identifying their needs and what would the care system have to do in order to facilitate this? If these changes were to take place, what might be the wider implications for child and family adjustment? These questions are addressed in the next chapter, where I describe a study aimed at altering patterns of interaction and communication between staff and families in an attempt to increase adaptation.

SUMMARY

- Organ transplantation is being viewed increasingly as the treatment of choice for several end-stage diseases. Following rapid advances in medical technology, psychosocial outcomes are taking on a new importance for both purchasers of services, transplant teams and recipients.
- The evidence in relation to paediatric liver transplantation indicates that prior to the operation children commonly have developmental delays and emotional and behavioural problems. Post-transplant, children and families often experience an exacerbation of pre-existing emotional problems, and at one-year follow-up, children typically show continuing developmental delays. Longer-term assessments of quality of life suggest that children may experience fewer hospital contacts and that over time psychological

difficulties reduce. However, many families continue to experience problems in adjusting to their child's condition.

- Helping families cope with transplantation, whichever organ is involved, involves teams recognising the differing coping styles of families and pacing communications to their needs, rather than to those of the transplant team. Communicating effectively with children requires an understanding of developmental psychology, and working with parents involves an appreciation of the literature on doctor–patient communication.
- Staff accuracy in gauging parental concerns can be highly variable. The situation in transplantation may be even more complicated owing to the specific pressures that families face. Psychological interventions involving the identification of families at risk as well as specific interventions to help coping are essential in promoting adjustment.
- Increasing survival rates following transplantation raise the issue of longer-term quality of life for children and their families. We lack good measures to assess this aspect and it is important that teams start to audit their effectiveness, taking into account medical, psychological and social outcomes. The evidence to date suggests that transplantation should not be viewed as a 'one off' procedure, rather it is a new illness with its own complications, requiring long-term medical intervention and psychological support.

Chapter 7

Family functioning

INTRODUCTION

There is a growing awareness of the need to treat whole families when paediatric problems present (John and Bradford, 1991; Sainsbury *et al.*, 1986). The development of this thinking can be traced back to the 1950s when theories of attachment were applied to parent–child separations following admissions to hospital (Bowlby, 1971; Robertson, 1958). These research findings, along with the Platt Report (1959), promoted changes in hospital policies concerning children and their parents. No longer were children expected to be isolated from their families during admissions: rather, the care-taker was encouraged to visit the ward and stay overnight if possible. The increasing attention paid to the psychological sequelae of childhood chronic illness has served also to highlight the importance of involving families in treatment (Bradford, 1990a; 1990b; Wallander *et al.*, 1989b) and it is now widely accepted that optimal care encourages parents to stay with their ill child in hospital and to take an active role in preparing and helping their child cope with the experience.

Modern paediatric medicine can be said to have three goals: to treat the disease, to prevent it interfering with the child's general development and to prevent it adversely affecting family functioning. As a consequence, paediatricians and others have had to develop an increasingly sophisticated understanding of the emotional needs of children and their families (Munson, 1986). Allied to these changes has been the growing awareness within psychology that more complex models of causation and intervention are required if the needs of children and their families are to be met. One avenue that appears to be particularly fruitful is to explore the role of family therapy in paediatrics. Whilst there has been a number of authors who have advocated such an approach (for example, Bingley *et al.*, 1980; Gustafsson and Svedin, 1988; Hodas and Liebman, 1978; Lask, 1982), there is surprisingly little information concerning how to put the ideas into practice in a medical setting.

BACKGROUND ISSUES TO WORKING WITH FAMILIES

Integrating family assessments and therapy into paediatrics is frequently problematic. One reason for this is that professionals use differing time-scales. For example, medical admissions are often short due to the rapid amelioration of symptoms. However, when admission is for psychological assessment and treatment, the rate of problem resolution is often considerably slower. This can lead to staff being put under pressure for beds, and psychological interventions having to occur against this background. As Honsing (1989) points out, new ways of working are unlikely to be accepted if they fail to make medical and nursing life less stressful!

A second problem is that for 'systemic thinking' to be integrated the unit needs to undergo a conceptual shift. The prevailing medical model has to change to incorporate psychological dimensions to explain the cause or maintenance of illness, as well as accommodating to an interactional, rather than linear, model of treatment (Bradford and Tomlinson, 1990). Inevitably, individuals will hold different philosophies about the origins and maintenance of illness and in doing so will place differing priorities on the child's mental and physical health. These decisions can have ramifications for the provision of space and time to see families as well as providing the potential for sabotage. Issues of power and territoriality can often be thrown into relief (Roberts and Wright, 1987).

Thirdly, not only will the team need to change its belief system, but the same has to occur in the patient and the family. Most commonly, when a child has entered hospital the family are organised into perceiving the problem as solely organic in origin. Investigations and treatments pursued during the admission continue to emphasise the organic nature of the problem. If medical personnel attempt subsequently to incorporate psychological dimensions, the family may well have difficulty in accepting the notion of a 'psychosomatic' illness.

WAYS FORWARD

A number of active steps can be taken to reduce these difficulties. Lask (1982) argues that the successful development of a working alliance with the medical team is dependent upon the development of mutually trusting relationships, in which the family therapist is considered an equally valued professional and therefore able to make specific contributions to the welfare of the child and the family. In facilitating this, Lask argues that regular case discussions need to be held in order to share views. This may also serve to help decrease issues of territoriality and conflicts over status (Rothenberg, 1977), as well as clarifying the family therapist's role and way of working.

The early involvement of the family therapist is also essential. This is important because it helps reduce the possibility of families and medical teams focusing exclusively on the physical element of illness. Munson (1986) also indicates the importance of the family meeting the family therapist with the paediatrician, as this enables clarification of the child's problem and the reason for the involvement of the mental health professional. Anders and Niehans (1982) argue that enlisting the collaboration of the senior paediatrician facilitates this process. Maintaining the paediatrician's involvement and utilising him/her as a co-therapist can have the duel benefit of helping families appreciate the interaction of organic and psychological factors in illness causation and maintenance, as well as reducing the possibility of team splits over 'ownership' of the problem.

At the time of admission, families have been catapulted into new experiences. This means that the family's equilibrium has been unbalanced. The homeostatic functions are often not operating as the family is having to adopt new roles temporarily to accommodate having a child in hospital (for example, a parent becomes a functional single parent as the spouse remains resident in hospital with one child). Lask (1982) indicates that this disturbance, if constructively used by the therapist, can bring energy and motivation for change, hopefully allowing a family to see the interaction between symptoms and family functioning.

I became interested with Mary John, a clinical psychology colleague, in exploring the role of family therapy in understanding child adjustment. As the studies in the preceding chapters have illustrated, it is clearly important to look at family patterns of interaction, but not to limit one's field of vision simply to these. It is also essential to consider what factors might be impinging on the observed patterns of interaction, such as characteristics of the child, for example temperament, and features of the environment, such as the functioning of hospital wards. This study seeks to integrate these ideas by analysing both family and ward functioning and how they interact together. We were particularly interested to explore what contribution 'structural family therapy' (Minuchin and Fishman, 1981) would have in helping us to understand and effect change in families and the ward system.

In the next section, I will use two case studies of families to illustrate our experience (names have been changed to protect anonymity). From this, a model emerges that we feel has implications in highlighting influences on adjustment as well as practical applications in how to intervene 'systemically' to help families cope better.

DESIGN

The study was carried out at a London teaching hospital with my colleague Mary John. The paediatric department consisted of a neonatal unit and four wards. The medical staff consisted of six consultants, a senior registrar, two registrars and four senior house officers. Each ward was run by a sister and a specific complement of nursing staff, all of whom were managed by a nursing officer. Weekly psychosocial meetings were held on the wards and attended by a psychologist, a social worker and members of the medical and nursing teams. All cases were discussed, with referrals being made if social or psychological factors were thought to be significant in the aetiology or maintenance of the problem.

FAMILY 1: THE LAWRENCE FAMILY

The family, consisting of Mr Lawrence (28), a builder, Mrs Lawrence (26), a housewife, Joseph (3) and Samantha (18 months), was referred to my colleague Mary John following a four-week admission for investigations into the two children's non-organic failure to thrive. The poor weight gain had been a feature for the past eighteen months.

The following actions were taken in promoting a systemic approach to working with the family.

Planning and convening the initial meeting

In order to develop a structural hypothesis about the Lawrence family and their relationship with the ward system, a meeting of hospital professionals was convened. Three problem areas were identified by the staff group: first, Mrs Lawrence's reluctance to care for the children whilst they were resident on the ward; second, her desire not to return home; and third, her increasing emotional attachment to one of the male medical staff. The hospital team was managing these problems, it seemed to us, by pursuing medical investigations, reinforcing Mrs Lawrence's under-involvement by taking responsibility for the children, and leaving unresolved the issue of her relationship to the ward doctor.

A structural hypothesis

The information obtained about the family from the meeting suggested to us that Mrs Lawrence's attempts to become emotionally involved with a junior doctor highlighted significant marital conflicts at home. Mr Lawrence's infrequent visits to the hospital pointed to a peripheral role, in relation to both his wife and his family. Furthermore, in light of the long-standing nature of the children's failure to thrive, we thought that Mr and Mrs Lawrence may not have successfully negotiated the changes in their family life-cycle (Carter and McGoldrick, 1981), in particular the transition from being a married couple to being parents with young children and the new roles this involves. Informal observations on the ward also suggested that the ward system had become triangulated into the marital and parenting conflicts between Mr and Mrs Lawrence and that the staff group was replacing the children in acting as a distance regulator in the marital and parental conflicts. The nurses' care of the children appeared to serve the function of further undermining Mrs Lawrence's ability to be an effective parent (Robinson, 1985).

Engaging the support of the ward

In order to re-establish an appropriate ward team/family boundary, a joint meeting was convened, involving the consultant paediatrician, ward psychologist and Mrs Lawrence. The aim of this was to gain support from Mrs Lawrence for a psychological assessment and to reduce the possibility of splits occurring over the treatment plan. The professionals presented a consistent, unified message concerning the role of psychological factors in the children's failure to thrive and the need for the family to engage in treatment. This resulted in Mrs Lawrence accepting the above ideas with her agreement to invite her husband to take part in treatment.

The family meeting

The family members' behaviour in the session confirmed several elements of the structural hypothesis. The parents were unable to negotiate an agreed strategy on child management issues. Mr Lawrence could be effective in his control of the children when his wife allowed him to take this role; Mrs Lawrence in contrast was frequently ineffective. The therapist's observations suggested that there were no boundaries between the parental and sibling sub-systems and that Mrs Lawrence would divert or avoid parental conflicts by shifting attention onto the children. We hypothesised that the function of the feeding difficulty in part was to serve as a 'distance regulator', in other words it served to help them avoid conflict and difficulties in their own relationship as parents.

Some support for the above ideas came from the parents' own explanation of what needed to change. Interestingly, Mr Lawrence saw the solution to the family problem lying in his wife becoming more distant from the children and joining more closely with him, and also in his reducing his working hours, thereby making himself more available to her. Mr Lawrence felt unneeded at home and as a consequence worked long hours and frequently visited his own parents. He was unhappy that he was so under-involved with his own family and that his wife seemed to be uninterested in him. Mrs Lawrence did not share his perception of his lack of involvement and did not see a particular need for him to spend more time with the family, as her view was that he would either be critical of her parenting or would interfere in the way she organised things.

When parental conflicts appear to be central in understanding the cause or maintenance of a childhood problem, it is very easy for a third party to become involved in such a way that they inadvertently compound the difficulty. Staff on paediatric wards can be vulnerable to this, as in their efforts to help the child it is always possible to lose sight of the wider context to the problem. We felt that certain staff had indeed become 'triangulated' into the parental and marital conflicts. For example, the ward sister's acceptance of mother and children continuing to stay in hospital over the weekends, even though it would have been appropriate for the family to have returned home, served to reinforce the physical distance between the parents in actually working together as a couple.

During the family meeting, a trans-generational family history was taken. This identified that Mrs Lawrence had had an extremely impoverished childhood, both physically and emotionally. Her mother had valued the sons of the family but not her daughters. She had left home at the age of 14 and had lived initially with a friend before moving in with her future husband's family. They were married when they were both 18.

As a result of this session, the parents acknowledged that as a couple they often failed to communicate their needs and that Mrs Lawrence had tried to bring up the children without the help of her husband in order to prove, in Mrs Lawrence's words, that she was 'an exemplary mother'. They agreed that they wanted to continue therapy to address these issues.

Reconvening the team

Following the assessment, a further meeting involving the paediatrician, ward sister, dietician and junior medical ward staff was convened. The children's feeding problems were put in the context of the parenting difficulties. The tensions between the parents were explained in terms of Mrs Lawrence's need to be a perfect mother and Mr Lawrence's perception that he had been displaced in his wife's affections by the children. All members of the team agreed that the children's problem was non-organic in origin and that psychological treatment was the most appropriate and should focus on gaining greater parental alliance and development of a less permeable boundary between the parental and sibling sub-systems. In addition it was suggested that Mrs Lawrence would benefit from some individual sessions to enable her to put her past into some perspective. With reference to timing, it was generally felt that the family work should take priority over the individual work at this stage owing to the seriousness of the children's condition.

Disengaging the family and ward system

Whilst an agreement had been reached as to the nature of the problem, it was clear to us that a number of meetings needed to be arranged with the nursing staff. As they had found themselves in a position of being *in loco parentis*, it was not surprising that several had become very attached to the children. To re-establish the professional/family boundary, nurses were placed in the new role of helping the parents take joint responsibility over the management of the children. This graded approach led to an effective discharge.

FAMILY 2: THE ROBERTS FAMILY

John Roberts (12 years of age) was the only son of Mr and Mrs Roberts (both aged 56). He had been admitted to a paediatric ward at the hospital with an initial diagnosis of Guillain-Barre syndrome (a rare disorder of the peripheral nervous system, resulting in paralysis; it typically commences at the feet and progressively moves up towards the head; the disorder can be fatal). Medical investigations had failed to confirm the provisional diagnosis and the paediatrician considered that there might be a psychological basis to John's problem.

The initial staff meeting

The focus of the meeting was to enable the therapist to understand how the doctors and nurses saw the problem and what information had been given to the family. The consultant had told the parents that a psychological opinion was necessary to enable him to develop an appropriate treatment plan; the parents had stated, however, that they felt that the problem was physical and not psychological. Nursing staff were split as to whether John's symptoms had an organic basis or not: whilst the nursing staff do not have the power to diagnose officially, this does not stop them from making observations, which we felt could be important in helping to understand the case.

John was described by the nursing staff as an amenable boy who enjoyed playing with children younger than himself on the ward and in the hospital school. His behaviour was noted to change when his parents visited him. On these occasions he would be quiet and passive, speaking only when spoken to. Staff indicated also that in discussions he did not appear interested in going home and was not concerned about his lack of mobility. A number of the nursing staff had encouraged John to stay on his bed playing a variety of board games, whilst other nurses were keen to encourage mobility in and around the ward.

A structural hypothesis

The marked change in John's mood following his parents' visits to the ward suggested to us that family conflicts could be significantly related to his symptoms. With reference to the ward team, we felt that splits were occurring over how John should be managed, owing to differing perceptions as to the cause of the problem. These splits appeared to be undermining any effective intervention and we hypothesised that this could be the result of the team reflecting dysfunctions within the family (Berkowitz and Leff, 1984). The involvement of the psychology service at this time could be seen as an attempt by the team to gain a consensus on the treatment plan.

Enlisting hierarchical support in the ward system

In order to give John clear guidance as to what was expected of him, it was decided to develop a plan to involve the hospital school and the physiotherapy department. The aim of this intervention was to keep some consistency over John's school attendance and to encourage him to become physically mobile again. We felt also that the plan would help to reduce the possibility of illness behaviours becoming reinforced (Fordyce, 1976). A meeting was convened involving the medical, nursing, teaching and physiotherapy staff; at that meeting the treatment plan was agreed and clear roles were negotiated for each relevant professional (Dubowitz and Hersov, 1976). A further meeting was then arranged with the paediatrician and the family to discuss these arrangements.

The family meeting

In the event the paediatrician was unable to attend this meeting. Initially the parents expressed anger at the fact that the paediatrician had asked them to see a psychologist, reiterating their view that the problem was organic in origin. Mrs Roberts took charge of providing the information on behalf of the family, whilst Mr Roberts appeared content to allow this pattern of communication to continue. When efforts were made to engage him into the session he would look to his wife to respond for him. John sat quietly during the session, until his parents began to argue about an aspect of his hospital care. At this point he took responsibility for defusing the argument by providing the solution to the dispute.

In an attempt to understand why the problem had arisen, time was spent exploring family change. An undisciplined 3-year-old American cousin and his mother had arrived to stay with them; this appeared to have provoked feelings of animosity as family life had become disrupted. The parents had not been able to confront their relative, with the result that John had experienced unusual feelings of tension and hate towards family members.

At the end of the session we felt that the alliance between the parents was extremely poor, resulting in little effective problem-solving and decision-making. The relationship between Mrs Roberts and John appeared enmeshed whilst Mr Roberts appeared disengaged and peripheral. A cross-generational alliance was evident and John's position in the hierarchy was such that he was either in charge of his parents or equal to them. He was very sensitive to his mother's needs, and when conflict started to occur between the parents, John's illness served to distract them from pursuing these issues. Mrs Roberts was very protective of John; he was not allowed to carry out activities that many boys of his age would enjoy. Instead he would spend the evenings with his mother completing physical fitness exercise regimes.

Reconvening the staff group

The professional team was reconvened after this assessment and an initial trial period of a ward and school-based rehabilitation programme was suggested. In this meeting it soon became evident that the staff continued to be divided in their view of treatment; the medical team viewed the problem as primarily psychogenic whilst some nursing staff saw the problem as primarily organic. When they attempted to resolve the differences, a symmetrical argument ensued which remained unresolved. Whilst the power relationship was such that the paediatrician could impose his view on the meeting, this did not occur. Instead, the paediatrician invited the psychologist to resolve the dilemma.

In thinking through the process that had occurred, we hypothesised that the paediatrician realised that if he had imposed a psychogenic diagnosis on the nurses and family, the result could have been the effective sabotage of the treatment plan, leading to a bed becoming blocked and the child's best interest not being served. It was clear we had become triangulated in these conflicts and that the dilemma could not be solved effectively. A new task for the group needed to be set. We decided to convene a further meeting to shift the focus away from who was right or wrong to a consensual task of helping the psychologist to find more effective ways of explaining the problem to the parents and finding a way to ensure the continuation of a treatment plan. An agreed formulation and treatment plan was reached that incorporated both psychosomatic and organic factors; this new formulation was discussed with the parents. The physiotherapy programme was developed further to include specific goals and a definition of the family's role in rehabilitation. Daily schooling would be compulsory and John's own school would be contacted for work to help bridge the gap between hospital and home. Family therapy would focus upon how the parents could help their son to develop age-appropriate strategies to cope with his worries.

Disengaging the family and ward system

The ward-based programme was successful in structuring staff interactions with John and his family, and resulted in John's partial recovery. But despite this, staff splits re-emerged when attempts were made
to discharge the family. These splits occurred when the parents expressed uncertainty as to whether progress would be maintained
when John returned home, and led to a number of nursing staff agree-
ing that he could remain on the ward longer and receive more
physiotherapy.

As discharge was proving problematic, the paediatrician and psychologist met the family to determine the next stage in the treatment
plan. It became clear that Mr and Mrs Roberts felt that John was not
ready to return home as he would not have sufficient space at home to
complete his recovery; his young cousin was still using his bedroom
and there would not be the time to devote to the physiotherapy programme. Time was spent discussing the gains John had made whilst
in hospital and how they could be maintained at home, as well as
helping his parents find solutions to John's lack of privacy at home.
The parents agreed to further family therapy sessions which involved
them monitoring progress, discussing this within the session and
thinking of ways of helping John cope with stress more effectively.
John would continue also to have a number of outpatient physiotherapy sessions. The family's agreement was communicated to the nursing team, who passively accepted the arrangement.

Following discharge the family was seen on five occasions. The focus was on increasing John's participation in extracurricular activities
with his peer group. The parents were encouraged to develop shared
activities. These two strategies led to Mrs Roberts spending less time
with John whilst giving Mr Roberts an opportunity to become more
involved with his son by helping him with age-appropriate activities
and sharing ideas on how to cope in a variety of situations. Efforts by
the therapist were also made to keep the staff group informed of progress through the psychosocial ward round. This was considered important to demonstrate that the discharge plan had been effective,
and is potentially a useful model of working with families in the future.

DISCUSSION

The two case reports illustrate the processes involved in integrating a
family therapy approach into a paediatric setting, as well as some of

the difficulties experienced in overcoming the 'organic' versus 'psychogenic' argument that is frequently played out in such settings. Six clear stages emerged as being important in working with families where illness presents as the main referral problem:

1 Convening an initial case conference
2 Developing a structural hypothesis
3 Gaining support from the ward system
4 Holding a family meeting
5 Reconvening the staff group
6 Disengaging the family and ward system.

The first stage, calling a case meeting, confirmed the importance of enlisting all staff who are central to the child's management, and in particular gaining the active involvement of the medical consultant (Lask, 1982; Munson, 1986). The aim of this meeting for the therapist is to help staff share their perceptions of the child and family. In doing so, the therapist gains an understanding of how the family is functioning as well as important information concerning how the hospital system relates to the family. Whilst the desirability of such meetings is clear, the difficulties in organising them should not be underestimated. In this context the initial meeting concerning the Lawrence family was made outside the ward psychologist's official work hours, perhaps suggesting that an extra commitment would be required. This demonstrated the need for initial flexibility on the therapist's part, awareness of the power and status hierarchies and consequently a need to be 'one down', in order not to overtly threaten the status quo.

Additional problems in setting up meetings were the competing demands that professionals found themselves under, as well as the problem of staff shortages. Whilst it is true that finding time to discuss cases can be difficult due to work pressures, we felt also that on occasions the difficulties were related to psychological issues being given less importance in relation to medical management. There is an issue of shifting some medical and nursing staff from holding an over-exclusive medical orientation.

The second stage, developing a structural hypthesis, involves integrating a number of ideas, including aspects of family functioning such as boundaries, hierarchies and alliances, the family's stage in the life-cycle, how the symptom relates to this and how the hospital system interacts with these elements. Thus with the Lawrence family it was important to enable the parents to become effective in their management of the two children whilst at the same time helping the staff to take on a more appropriate role. To achieve this, the therapist has to be 'joined' with both hospital and family systems (Minuchin, *et al.*, 1978).

Enlisting hierarchical support in the ward system is crucial in creating a structure that will allow psychological work to occur in a medical setting. Wynne *et al.* (1986) have described the importance of having those 'at the top' of the hierarchy in agreement with a treatment plan. The essential aim of the meeting is to reach a consensus on how the family will be helped, and the role of each professional.

At this third stage it may be necessary to incorporate elements of the wider hospital system in a tactical manner. For example, with the Roberts family it was important to include a physiotherapy plan (Dubowitz and Hersov, 1976) in conjunction with family therapy in order to avoid a symmetrical battle over which professional group had 'ownership' of the problem and to facilitate the parents' acknowledgement of psychological issues. As a result of this networking it should be possible to convene a meeting with the family, in conjunction with a senior medical colleague, where a clear formulation can be presented that incorporates both psychosomatic and organic factors. This serves to ensure that the parents perceive that the team is unified as well as maintaining the consultant in a central position and not challenging his authority and expertise in his or her own field.

We felt that the professional background of the therapist could be an important issue in gaining this hierarchical support. Paediatricians perceive psychologists generally as having clearly definable skills in helping children and families with emotional and behavioural problems. This established background provides sufficient status to convene meetings where psychological issues are involved. However, there is the potential problem of the system having rigid ideas about the psychologist's role within this setting; moving into the area of systemic thinking has not traditionally been considered the psychologist's area of expertise. This could be a problem, as other staff members may not welcome or consider the ideas worthy of attention as the professional was not employed as a family therapist, and as a consequence may attempt to focus the meeting on to more traditional territory.

Social workers in the paediatric setting also have expected roles that tend to focus on offering counselling and support to families as well as the practical element of advice on benefits. They could also convene a meeting on the basis of their background but again would have the potential problem of a rigid system if they wished to work in a 'new' way. Similar issues have been described in developing child psychiatric liaison/consultation services (Mrazek, 1985).

At the fourth stage, holding a family meeting, joining techniques proved to be very important as there were dilemmas for the families concerning the aetiology of the symptoms. It was essential to demonstrate respect for the parents' position within the family and to introduce change at a tolerable pace for them. Given that this could be a slow process, the need for enlisting hierarchical support was again confirmed, in order to avoid symmetrical positions being adopted in relation to whether or not treatment was effective.

Whilst we had the expectation that, ideally, all members of the family would be seen, we found that in practice greater flexibility was necessary in working with families in an inpatient paediatric setting. The reduction in the number of family members available did not detract from our main aim of placing physical health problems in a psychological systems context.

At stage five, reconvening the professional staff group, time is spent discussing the cases in a language that is meaningful to the professional group. It has been noted by a variety of authors that to ensure explanations are comprehensible and accessible the language should be as free from jargon as possible (Lask, 1982; Treacher, 1984). Nitzberg *et al.* (1985) have argued also that the therapists should think systemically but translate the ideas into an accessible and palatable language. We found that using linear explanations, which positively connoted the behaviour of individual family members, could be effective in achieving this. It also helped to facilitate the shifting of staff views away from the often-held belief that 'parentectomy' (Nitzberg *et al.*, 1985) was a desirable choice. The aim of reconvening the meeting, besides imparting information, is to ensure that the team continues to have a shared view of the problem and the way forward. As was found in the Roberts family, it is not unusual for splits to develop in teams, which can mirror the processes occurring in the family (Berkowitz and Leff, 1984). The meeting allows for tensions between professionals to surface, be recognised and worked through. The meeting also serves an educational and demystifying function in relation to the role of family therapy in paediatrics and the fruitlessness of organic versus psychogenic debates.

The final stage, disengaging the family and ward system, is essential if progress is to be maintained after discharge from hospital. This was illustrated by the Lawrence family where it was evident that the hospital system had taken over the care of the children, with

Mrs Lawrence's collusion. A number of structural manoeuvres were necessary to redress the professional–family boundary which involved promoting the parents to be effective whilst providing the ward staff with an alternative role away from parenting the children (Robinson, 1985). De Shazer (1982) has discussed in the 'Binocular Theory of Change' the way in which the family pattern of interaction can be altered by the team's way of interacting with them. Unless the team joins with the family to free them from their old pattern of interacting, the original symptomatology will continue. However, in the ward setting we felt that the nursing staff was replicating the patterns of interaction rather than joining with the family to promote change. An important task for the therapist is to help the medical and nursing team identify ways to co-operate productively with the family in the overall goal of creating change. The regular updating of staff, through the psychosocial meetings, as to the progress of therapy helps with the generalisation of these principles to other families.

The study highlights that family functioning can have a significant impact on the development and maintenance of illness symptoms and that hospital staff can play a key role in influencing whether these patterns of interaction become stuck or whether families are helped to change, thereby promoting patterns of adjustment.

In the next chapter, I will develop these ideas by considering how the organisation of support services in the community can impact on child and family coping.

SUMMARY

- Treating childhood problems requires the integration of medical, nursing and psychological care.
- Systemic approaches to understanding and intervening in chronic illness and disability appear highly appropriate as the emphasis is on exploring how the presenting problem impacts on the whole family and the role of the hospital in influencing subsequent adjustment.
- Structural family therapy can be a useful adjunct to understanding and working with paediatric cases. Problems in integrating the approach can be overcome by the therapist being flexible and working within the paediatric system at a pace that does not overtly threaten the status quo.
- Six stages appear to be important in the successful implementation of systemic thinking, which involve open communication,

joint planning, joining techniques, maintenance of hierarchies and establishing professional/family boundaries.

- In assessing the influence of family functioning on presenting problems the following actions help facilitate an action plan: convening an initial case conference; developing a structural hypothesis; gaining support from the ward system; holding a family meeting; reconvening the staff group and disengaging the family and ward system.

Chapter 8

Community services

INTRODUCTION

In this chapter I want to stand back from the issue of how the organisation of hospital services impacts on child and family adjustment and explore instead how people can be encouraged to work together to meet the needs of children and their families, once they have been discharged back to their local community. This is a very important area in the treatment of chronically-ill children because the majority of ongoing care is provided in the community, and therefore systems need to be in place to ensure that interventions started in hospitals dovetail into the local provision.

When I moved from working on a paediatric ward to a local community child psychology service, I received a number of referrals that were concerned with adjustment difficulties to chronic illness and disability. Most problems focused on how to reintegrate a child into mainstream schooling, or how best to maintain compliance with taking medications or how to re-balance family life so that the 'sick' child was not always the centre of attention, to the detriment of siblings. The striking feature of these problems was the failure of hospital services to think ahead as to what problems families might encounter. They also highlighted the lack of liaison with local services. Equally, as the problems referred had often been developing over a long period of time, it appeared that GPs and others had failed to pick up on the issues earlier. Often this delay meant that problems were now chronic and needed a multi-agency response to resolve the difficulty.

This chapter will explore these problems more fully and look at some ideas about how to ensure services do work more closely together. The examples used are taken from two community-based projects I was involved in (Bradford, 1993; 1994b). The children had a variety of chronic disabilities, for example learning disabilities and autism, and as such fall within Mattsson's (1972) definition of chronic disease outlined at the start of this book. Whilst the studies reported so far have concentrated more upon the physical illness aspect to chronic disease, I feel the projects do merit inclusion here, as they carry implications for working with children with a range of chronic diseases, whatever the underlying origin of the disorder might be.

MODELS OF SERVICE DEVELOPMENT

In thinking about the organisation of child health services, there are a number of useful documents to be aware of. Principal amongst these are the Department of Health's (1991) *Welfare of Children and Young People in Hospital* and *Child Health in the Community: A Guide to Good Practice* (1995). Both set out the principles that should guide the development and organisation of paediatric services to ensure that the needs of children and their families are met.

The Audit Commission, in their publication *Seen But Not Heard*, estimated that in 1991/92 approximately £2 billion was spent on community health and social services, of which £295 million was spent on paediatric services. In order for this money to be used as efficiently as possible, they advised that authorities needed to work more closely together to provide an integrated range of services.

In *Welfare of Children and Young People in Hospital* it is stated clearly that services should strive to 'provide for the child as a whole, for his or her complete physical and emotional well being and not simply for the condition for which treatment or care is required'. In doing so, services should be 'child and family centred with children, their siblings and their parents or carers experiencing a "seamless web" of care, treatment and support'.

Whilst the goal of more integrated services is one that we would all fully endorse, there is less certainty as to how it is to be achieved in practice. In my clinical practice, I often found that the transition from hospital-based care to community services was fraught with problems for families. Chief amongst these was the difficulty of accessing appropriate services and the apparent lack of communication between the hospital and local services and between the local services themselves in combining and coordinating their inputs. The simple fact is that effective collaboration between the various agencies is often very difficult to achieve. It is even more problematical when the child and family have complex therapeutic needs, as is the case in chronic disease.

Following the enactment of the Children Act (1989) in 1992, I became interested in how this piece of legislation might help the group of children I was working with. The Children Act was heralded widely as one of the most important provisions in child care legislation to be enacted, and amongst many of the principles it espouses is the idea that children's needs are paramount and that services should be organised in such a way that these needs are identified and catered for. The consequence ought to be that statutory services should stand back and evaluate collectively the extent to which they are achieving these goals. As such, the Act clearly addresses a key problem in the functioning of statutory services, in that it is not uncommon for agencies to be in ignorance as to the particular needs of their population, what other agencies offer and as a consequence where the gaps in service delivery exist. In practice this can often mean a lottery in service provision, with children and their carers passed between, missed or overwhelmed by services.

The desirability of closer collaboration between services and their 'consumers' at a philosophical level is not in doubt. However, the fact that services frequently have differing agendas means that, even with the best will in the world, disputes over the ownership of problems can result. Perhaps one litmus test of how well inter-agency working is set up in practice is to explore how children with complex needs are managed and how these needs are responded to. If services are functioning well at this level, this is a possible indicator of effective working at 'lower' levels in the continuum of care.

With this in mind, I was involved in two projects in Kent, which looked at the way in which Health, Education and Social Services worked together in assessing and providing services for children whom the Children Act (1989) would consider to be 'in need' as a consequence of their disabilities. The first study describes the setting up of a 'multi-agency consultation team' (MACT) the aim of which was to cut across inter-agency disagreements about whose responsibility it was to carry out certain actions. The second study details the setting up of a unit for children 'in need' which involved statutory agencies working together under one roof. These two studies may serve to stimulate ideas as to how more integrated services can be provided.

SETTING UP A MULTI-AGENCY CONSULTATION TEAM

Initial planning

The first task was to gain agreement from the Service Directors in Health, Education and Social Services that they would support the development of a project aimed at promoting joint working. Surprisingly, this was not as straightforward as might have been expected and several meetings were required before it was finally agreed that a small working party should be set up with representatives from Health, Education, Social Services and the Family Health Services Authority, with the task of putting forward a proposal for inter-agency working, to be considered by the Joint Child Planning Team (JCPT). This latter body was the key group consisting of representatives from statutory and voluntary agencies who met monthly to look at ways of promoting joint working.

Problems identified

The working party identified that children with complex therapeutic needs, who often required input from several different agencies in a coordinated fashion, would be a particularly appropriate group to target for a multi-agency approach. At that time, there was no system set up where children and families could access at one point a multi-agency perspective of their needs. Where joint planning had taken place over particular cases, it was apparent that this had not always been sufficient to resolve difficulties, as perceived by the agencies themselves or the service users. It was also clear that there were several cases where agencies had been unable to agree an intervention plan and that, typically, these concerned children where progress depended on financial considerations (for example, out-of-county placement, or additional staff being made available within schools) and no conclusion had been reached between the agencies as to whose responsibility it was to meet the cost. This had led to a 'therapeutic limbo' for a number of children and their families.

Proposed solution

The suggestion put forward to the JCPT was that a small multi-agency consultation team (MACT) should be set up, consisting of senior representatives from each of the statutory services. The aim of the team would be three-fold: to offer a forum where any agency could access a multi-agency perspective on cases of complex need; to make recommendations to Service Directors in Health, Education and Social Services as to the most appropriate way forward in cases where planning had become stuck; and to provide information to managers as to where gaps in service delivery existed, so that a more rational approach to resource allocation could be developed.

With these objectives in mind, an operational policy was suggested for the team's functioning.

Operational policy

A key aim was not to build additional levels of bureaucracy into an already complex system. It was decided, therefore, that all agencies should be encouraged to identify potentially suitable children and families in need by using their existing planning and review procedures, for example case conferences, children's panel and case supervision.

To ensure that the team did not become overwhelmed by referrals, two sets of 'eligibility' criteria were specified:

Agency criteria

Either   All three agencies recognised a need for joint planning over a particular case.

or   Two agencies agreed that for effective therapeutic intervention to occur, the third agency needed to become involved in a joint planning process.

And

Process criteria

Either   No other forum was available to carry out the joint planning process.

or   A forum did exist, had been utilised, but had not resulted in a satisfactory resolution, as defined by one of the agencies involved.

Once these were satisfied, referrers were requested to ensure that their senior manager as well as the family gave consent to referral and that all other agencies involved in the case were informed of referral to the team. To aid the process, a flow diagram was developed (see Figure 8.1).

With reference to the team itself, it was suggested that a 'core' group would consist of one representative from each of Health, Education and Social Services. In addition, other professionals, for example, community paediatrician, child psychiatrist, would be invited to join the group to advise on particular cases. It was estimated that for each

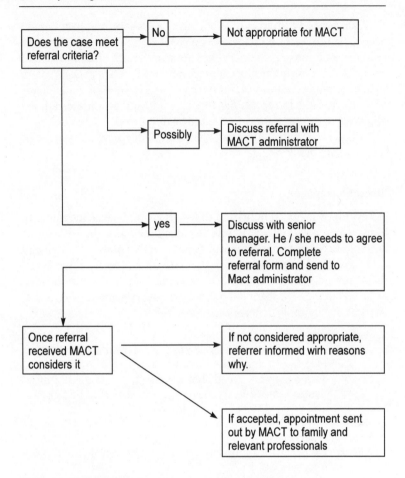

Figure 8.1   Referral to Multi-Agency Consultation Team
Source: Bradford, 1993: 358

case referred approximately four hours of administrative support would be necessary.

As to functioning, it was proposed that the team should run for a year, at which point its impact would be evaluated. The team would meet monthly, with a day set aside for each case. The morning would be devoted to a pre-assessment consultation with the network of professionals involved in the case to clarify issues and responsibilities. The afternoon would involve a family assessment and drawing up of the teams' recommendations and suggested intervention plan. These

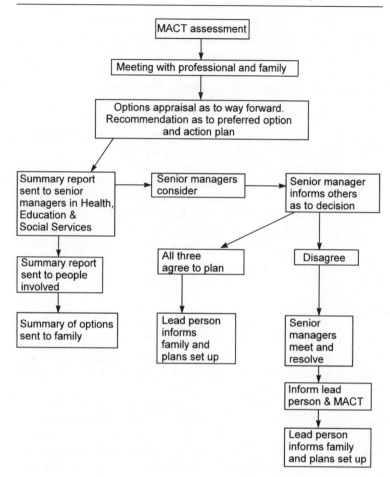

Figure 8.2 Process to decision making following MACT referral
Source: Bradford, 1993: 359

plans were to be circulated subsequently to all those involved in the day, as well as to senior managers (see Figure 8.2).

Operation

The above proposal was presented to the JCPT and agreement was reached that the project would go ahead, with a Special Needs Manager nominated as the Education Department's representative on the team, with Social Services putting forward a senior practitioner, and the Health Service the Head of Clinical Child Psychology. As part of the discussion, it was emphasised that the success of the proposal rested, in large part, upon the service directors' willingness to accept the recommendations made by MACT. If these were not sanctioned, at least to a significant level, then clearly MACT would not have contributed anything to resolving the presenting difficulty and in effect would be superfluous.

Not surprisingly this placed service directors in a rather difficult position: they did not want to be bound by decisions that could have financial implications, but at the same time they recognised that cases did exist that required an inter-agency package and that the Children Act (1989) did place a duty on services to work jointly to meet these needs. To establish whether service directors would be able to back MACT it was agreed that an initial pilot would be carried out involving three cases, one to be referred from each of the agencies involved in the team. Name have been changed to protect anonymity.

Case 1: 'Mark'

A social worker referred a 10-year-old boy who was the third of three brothers, all of whom had severe learning difficulties and severe, challenging behaviour. The two brothers had already been placed in two separate out-of-county, fifty-two-week boarding schools, and the parents were requesting the same for this boy as they were unable to cope with him at home. A package of care had been set up by Social Services, involving respite, link family and family aid in an attempt to contain the situation, but increasingly it was being seen as untenable owing to the deterioration in Mark's behaviour and the family's difficulties in containing him. Many conferences had been held to discuss the situation, but apparently with no satisfactory resolution.

The network consultation involving seven professionals from Health, Education and Social Services revealed that plans had become stuck owing to the agencies failing to agree whether Mark should be placed in residential school, whether the family could cope if additional support was provided and whether appropriate services were available locally or whether an out-of-county placement was required. The central theme was that inadequate resources were allocated to the case, with the dispute revolving around what resources were required and who should fund them.

Consultation focused on clarifying what Mark's needs were which led to agreement between all involved that he required constant one-to-one supervision both in and out of school. The school agreed that Mark would be able to remain with them, provided additional support was forthcoming. It was also recognised that the family required more support than was currently provided and that developing a package of care locally was more desirable than referral out of county, as it would meet Mark's needs more effectively (for example, maintain contact with family and community) and in the longer term would be considerably cheaper than the year-on-year costs of an out-of-county specialist placement, assuming one could be found.

The family meeting explored these conclusions and led to MACT's recommendation that Mark should remain at his current school, with an additional classroom assistant as well as psychological help being provided by Education and Health respectively. Furthermore, it was felt that Education should explore what provision could be found locally to provide Mark with a weekly boarding placement during term time. For weekends and school holidays it was recommended that Social Services should provide intensive support involving additionally funded family aid time, over and above the existing package of respite care. Education were nominated as the lead agency to co-ordinate and monitor these plans.

Recommendations were also made by MACT to senior managers of the need to explore setting up a dedicated residential unit for children with learning difficulties and severe challenging behaviour, as the current practice was to finance out-of-county placements, rather than developing services locally.

Follow-up four months after these recommendations had been made revealed that Mark continued to attend his local school. A classroom assistant had been provided, although there had been no liaison with Health over the provision of psychology input. Additional support had been forthcoming for the family via increased family aid time. As to accommodation for Mark, he was still living at home. Potentially suitable local accommodation had been identified, although discussions were still ongoing within the Education Department as to the feasibility of this option. The longer-term recommendation of the need to develop a small residential unit had been highlighted to service managers and Social Services had initiated a costing exercise to determine the cost benefits of out-of-county provision versus developing a local resource. The outcome of this exercise was not available at follow-up.

Overall it was felt that the situation at home was barely being contained and that unless both immediate accommodation and longer-term provision were provided, then the prognosis for Mark and his family remained very bleak.

Case 2: 'Nicole'

Nicole, a 7-year-old girl with severe behaviour problems, who required one-to-one help and supervision to prevent her harming herself or other children, was the second case in the study. She had been diagnosed as having a pervasive developmental disorder, associated with brain damage, with the possibility of sexual and physical abuse having also occurred. The parents were unable to cope with her behaviour and Social Services were currently involved under child protection procedures. Her specialist school placement was making no headway either educationally or behaviourally, and the referral was made by the Special Needs Manager in Education as it was clear that the situation, at both home and school, was becoming increasingly untenable.

In the consultation all professionals were unanimous in their view that Nicole's needs were for a consistent regime to modify her behaviour, and that to achieve this, a high degree of structure with minimal changes in her life needed to be provided. In addition, she required speech and language therapy, tuition in small groups and long-term psychotherapy. Options discussed to meet these needs were:

1   Maintaining the current placement, which was felt overall to be undesirable.
2   A residential placement which, again, was felt not to meet Nicole's needs as she would return home at weekends and holidays.
3   A fifty-two-week boarding placement which was considered the desired option and which the parents were in agreement with.

The consultation team recommended that, in the short term, additional support should be provided at school by the allocation of an additional classroom assistant; at home, a package of family aid, link family and sessional work for Nicole needed to be set up. In the longer term, a fifty-two-week residential placement needed to be identified, with costs for this spread equally between the three agencies. Social Services were nominated as the lead agency for short-term plans and Education for the residential placement.

At follow-up, four months later, it transpired that the long-term plan for an out-of-county placement, with costs split equally between the agencies, had not been supported by the Health Department, and Social Services had not as yet reached a decision. The recommendations for the immediate future had been implemented, in that a classroom assistant had been allocated and increased family aid time had been provided. Overall it was felt that the situation continued to be unsatisfactory.

Case 3: 'Adrian'

Adrian was a 13-year-old boy who had long-standing problems of anger control, violence, poor self-esteem, peer difficulties and academic under-achievement. He was an only child who lived with his mother, the father having left the family. He was attending a special school for children with emotional and behavioural difficulties, but was reported to be making no real progress. He had previously attended child guidance over a number of years, for a combination of family therapy and individual counselling, and had been interviewed under child protection procedures following concerns that he had been sexually abused, although no evidence was subsequently found. He had been the subject of numerous inter-agency case conferences. The referral was made by a consultant paediatrician, who was concerned that, despite the efforts of the agencies, his behaviour was continuing to deteriorate and in the near future his family placement would break down.

The morning consultation, involving paediatrician, social worker and headmaster, highlighted that there was some confusion as to what the various agencies were attempting to achieve with Adrian and why. It became clear that the agencies had differing treatment aims and expectations as to what was possible, which ranged from therapeutic optimism to the feeling that services were attempting to contain an untenable situation. A particular area of disagreement between the agencies in the past had been whether Adrian should be offered a boarding school placement, with Education and Social Services taking diametrically opposite views. The afternoon session with the family confirmed that the identified problems were indeed occurring and that the family were in some confusion as to what solution people were attempting to reach. Adrian's mother felt that the best solution would be for a boarding school to be found.

MACT's formulation was that the agencies were not working together owing to a lack of agreement as to what was the overall goal of intervention and that planning had become stuck owing to the lack of resolution as to whether boarding school was appropriate. Whilst this issue remained unresolved, the agencies and the family lacked a common therapeutic aim, with the agencies pulling in different directions. It was not clear whether work was focused on helping Adrian to remain at home, or on helping him to move on to a boarding school.

MACT identified three available options: that Adrian remain at home and continue to attend his current school; that Adrian be placed in a fifty-two-week boarding school placement, which would probably be out of county; or that Adrian attended a local residential school, with home visits at weekends and holidays. The preferred option for all concerned was the latter, and it was recommended that this should be pursued by the Education Department, with ongoing therapeutic services provided by the Health Department. It was also recommended that Social Services should continue to offer support to the family during Adrian's weekends and holidays at home. Finally, MACT suggested that Adrian's therapeutic needs required prioritising: social skills training and help with anger control seemed to be more appropriate than the in-depth psychotherapy that was currently offered. These ideas were discussed with the family and professionals, who agreed to take up the recommendations, with Social Services identified as the lead agency for both coordinating and monitoring these plans as well as organising a liaison meeting between the various therapists involved in the case in order to clarify roles/responsibilities.

The case was followed up four months later. Adrian had been placed at a residential school and had settled in well, following preparation and support by Social Services. The professionals had met to clarify roles, and overall the case had been monitored and coordinated by the lead agency. It was felt that tensions at home had reduced as a result of Adrian living away from home and that this had had a beneficial effect on the relationship between Adrian and his mother when he returned at weekends and holidays. Therapeutic plans had not been set up at the school and it was agreed that this was a gap that still needed to be addressed.

DISCUSSION

What were the key features in developing the MACT proposal and putting it into operation? It was essential to have the backing of service directors. The fact that they, along with the JCPT, were willing to sanction the protocol gave it sufficient status for it to be taken seriously by potential referrers and for it not to be viewed by families as 'just another talking shop' where nothing actually was resolved. Equally, the service directors' assurance that they would back up decisions made by MACT represented a very important step in coming to grips with the difficulties presented by the cases.

The use of referral criteria in the setting up of MACT was important as, in effect, they operated as a control mechanism, a threshold that needed to be crossed before a case could be referred. The significance of this was that it ensured that only those cases that were complex were seen, thereby ensuring that the team did not become overwhelmed. Also, by setting stringent eligibility criteria, we felt that it might highlight to potential referrers the need to attempt joint planning between agencies, which, in itself, might produce a resolution to some of the difficulties.

In terms of operation, the network consultation proved essential in generating hypotheses (John and Bradford, 1991) as to how best to intervene. A common theme to all the team's recommendations was the nominating of a lead agency, that is, identifying one service as responsible for monitoring the overall intervention. This was felt to be important in ensuring that MACT did not place itself in a case management role, with the responsibility for monitoring and following up recommendations. It had been envisaged that a key function of the team was to offer consultation and that to achieve this it was essential that referrers realised that the management of the case remained with them, rather than with the team. In addition, the nominating by MACT of a lead agency, which was empowered to take more responsibility than the others, served the function of cutting across some of the organisational confusion as to who was doing what by promoting a hierarchical difference between three apparently equal agencies.

Evaluating the effectiveness of MACT is difficult and depends to a large extent on the yardstick used. Contrary to some expectations, it was possible for the three agencies constituting MACT to reach agreement on the way forward for each of the cases. Thus real interagency working that involves negotiation and agreement is possible. Furthermore, the recommendations made did result in additional resources being targeted to each case, in a coordinated fashion, and the overall process did identify the shortfall in therapeutic services available to meet the needs of children and families, which was potentially helpful to managers in their planning of service developments.

However, the follow-up at four months did reveal that MACT's recommendations were not fully sanctioned, particularly when significant financial issues came to the fore, thereby underlining the difficulty for managers in supporting decisions without additional finance being forthcoming from, for example, the commissioners of services. In the cases of Mark and Nicole the longer-term plans had not been resolved by managers, and, as a result, it could be argued that little had changed for the children and families involved. Understandably, several of the professionals involved in these cases expressed frustration at the outcome and argued that MACT could never truly deliver if it did not have its own budget to meet its own recommendations.

The issue of a dedicated budget had, in fact, been considered at length in the early planning stages of setting up MACT, as a way of ensuring that MACT had influence. The notion had been rejected, however, on the grounds that, as senior managers had agreed to back MACT's decisions, there was no need for a budget. In any event, as some of the cases referred to the team were likely to need on-going financial support, possibly over a number of years, a finite budget could not deal with this year-on-year expenditure.

A further issue to take into account in evaluating the outcome of the three cases is the amount of staff time taken in reaching the recommendations. For each referral to the team an entire day was set aside, requiring the input of three senior professionals. In addition, administrative support was required for half a day for each case, and for the morning consultations a total of seventeen staff attended. Thus, some 109 hours of staff time was spent over three cases.

This cost needs to be balanced against the fact that each case was creating significant difficulties for the families themselves and the professionals involved. In addition, all of the cases had been subject to lengthy multi-professional discussions previously, although clearly no resolution to the problems had been forthcoming. It is perhaps of note that MACT, in reviewing the options available, concluded in two of the cases that a local solution to presenting difficulties was viable, as opposed to pursuing the alternative of expensive out-of-district placement. Arguably this resulted in significant financial saving, as well as ensuring that disruption to the children and their families was minimised.

Clearly the evaluation of multi-agency working needs to take into account the costs not only in terms of inputs (staff time etc), but also in terms of outputs (for example, the extent to which the decisions made are cost effective, and are acceptable to families). The choice of a period of four months to follow up the cases was inevitably arbitrary. Since the follow-up, further meetings have taken place between the professionals and managers who referred both Nicole and Mark, with the outcome that significant progress has been made. The commissioners in Health, Social Services and Education have become involved and agreed jointly to fund the necessary placement for Nicole. Equally progress has been made in resolving the issue of Mark's placement, and the costing exercise on developing a local resource for children with challenging behaviours has been completed.

One outcome that was unexpected, but with the benefit of hindsight is possibly predictable, was a steady reduction in the number of referrals made to MACT. Whilst this might appear a depressing outcome indicating a breakdown in joint working arrangements, in fact the opposite is the case. One spin-off from the exercise was the decision made by the commissioners from the agencies to set up regular meetings between themselves to explore joint commissioning ventures. This, in effect, made MACT redundant, as the commissioners were able to resolve issues of joint finance without MACT's input being required.

THE DEVELOPMENT OF BEAUMONT HOUSE CHILDREN CENTRE

MACT had been set up to overcome difficulties in planning and resourcing where services had become stuck. As such, it had the strength of being able to target children and families with known difficulties, but also had the weakness of not providing any input to those families whose difficulties were not identified or were less serious. In the light of the above experiences, I became aware that MACT was addressing only part of the problem in meeting the needs of children.

It is possible to think of three levels of intervention. Firstly, there are actions aimed at preventing difficulties occurring in the first place (primary prevention). Examples could include immunisation programmes, parent training workshops, Aids awareness campaigns and sex education to prevent teenage pregnancy. Secondly, there are interventions that aim to identify and reduce difficulties as early as possible, in order to stop them becoming more marked (secondary prevention). Child health screening programmes, 'drop in' facilities and well man/woman clinics are typical examples of this approach. Finally, there are efforts that seek to contain or ameliorate a known problem, with the overall aim being to promote quality of life, whilst recognising that the underlying problem cannot be 'cured' or eradicated (tertiary prevention). MACT represented an example of this last level of intervention, as it was concerned only with children where services had come to an impasse, where a number of interventions had already been attempted and had been unsuccessful, in the context of chronic problems and disabilities. As such, MACT was targeting children at a tertiary level and did not look at issues of primary and secondary prevention.

The Children Act (1989) has recognised the importance of meeting needs at all three levels when it talks about helping children 'at risk' and 'in need'. Clearly children at risk are those who have suffered or might suffer significant harm (sexual, physical, emotional abuse or neglect). Children in need (who, in the context of this book, are our major interest) fall into two broad categories: those whose health and/or development is likely to be impaired without the provision of services, and those who are disabled. 'Disabled children' are those who might have, for example, a sensory impairment, suffer from a mental health disorder or are permanently handicapped by illness, injury, or congenital deformity.

Children with chronic illnesses or disabilities clearly fall under the heading of 'children in need'. This raised the following question for me: how can services be set up in the community to help these children and their families which are not simply reactive or problem solving in the way MACT was? How could one start to identify children in need earlier on and intervene in such a way as to achieve the goal articulated by the Department of Health (1991), namely 'to promote and preserve good health and where illness does occur, to ensure that children are given the best care and attention in a way that mitigates physical and emotional distress'.

The present organisation of services tends to result in children's needs being looked at in isolation by each agency. The Children Act (1989) encourages services to work together in carrying out assessments of need, so that children are seen 'in the round', rather than being subjected to disjointed and poorly coordinated assessments. Following on from the success of MACT, a further proposal was developed for the setting up of an inter-agency assessment and treatment centre to provide services to children 'in need'. A bid for joint finance monies was made to the JCPT, who agreed the resourcing for the development of the Beaumont House Children Centre and its staffing. A disused, centrally based children's home was identified as a suitable location, and monies were allocated for its refurbishment, the recruitment of staff and a recurring budget to 'buy in' services if they were not available locally.

Operation

In order to facilitate the development of the centre, two groups were formed: a management group, which consisted of senior representatives from the three statutory agencies, and an operational policy group, comprising local practitioners from the agencies, teachers and voluntary organisations.

The management group's task was to resolve issues relating to the philosophy of the centre, and to develop a model of service delivery. This group reported to the JCPT. The operational policy group was concerned with the day-to-day running of the centre, including developing systems for monitoring referrals, informing service users about the centre, and keeping the management group informed about 'management' issues that needed to be resolved. In order to ensure that consumers' views were fed into this process, a users group was also established. This involved setting up a system whereby those people who used the centre, either to run groups or as actual participants, had an opportunity to express their views. Figure 8.3 details these arrangements.

Management issues

The first issue was to gain agreement between the three agencies as to the purpose and philosophy of the centre and how the agencies were

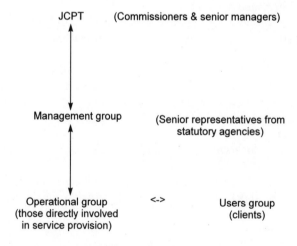

Figure 8.3   Organisational arrangements for the development of the project
Source: Bradford, 1994b: 33

to work together. Inevitably, the different agencies had agendas and priorities that were not always congruent with each other, and there was a tendency initially for each service to see the new centre as a solution to their own particular problem, whether it be long waiting lists, dissatisfaction with services currently on offer or the need to provide interventions to particular client groups for 'political' reasons.

Following a series of meetings it was recognised and agreed that the centre was a new opportunity to develop services based on common ground between the agencies and that it would not function if one agency agenda became the predominant one. Consequently, the philosophy agreed upon emphasised that the centre should aim to provide a centre of excellence, where complex cases needing input from at least two of the agencies could be referred for assessment. This multi-professional assessment would then result in a treatment plan that the centre would either carry out itself or refer on to other agencies; if the necessary therapeutic expertise was not available locally, then the centre would buy in treatment resources. In addition to this assessment/treatment/coordination role, it was felt that the centre should offer outreach services, such as offering consultation and training to ensure that preventive interventions were set up locally in communities.

In order to meet some of the pressures that all agencies were under to provide certain services, it was agreed that eligibility criteria would be developed. These were as follows:

- Children aged 0–8 years
- Children whose development may be significantly impaired by a complex of education/health/social/emotional and intellectual difficulties
- Children with emotional and behavioural difficulties requiring therapeutic input and whose needs cannot be met elsewhere
- Children 'at risk' of needing future provision to meet special educational needs and whose needs could be met by pre-school intervention
- 5–8-year-olds having the potential to be or having been excluded from school
- Children 'at risk' of being placed on Child Protection Register
- Children 'at risk' of being accommodated by the local authority.

Referral process

The process of referral to the centre is illustrated in Figure 8.4. The ideal solution to ensuring appropriate referral to the centre was to

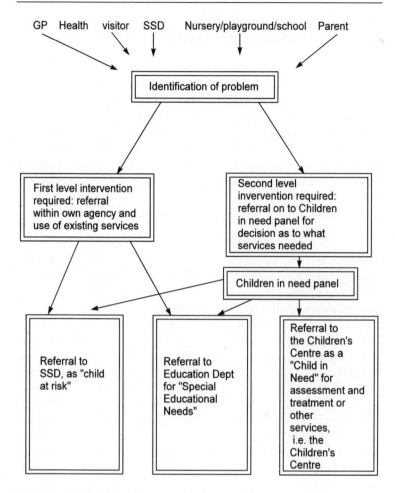

Figure 8.4   Referral process to the Children's Centre
Source: Bradford, 1994b: 34

have a process that identified children in need, and that was not bureaucratic or slow.

Following negotiations with the Child Health Department, it was agreed that their coordinating meeting, where the community paediatrician met with health visitors, social workers and others to identify children in need of specific help, would be reorganised. The meetings were renamed 'Children in Need Panel', with the age range of children discussed at the panel widened from 0–5 years to 0–8 years. In addition, an increased profile of educational personnel on the panel was agreed, as was the attendance of the manager of the centre.

Staffing

Joint finance money was made available for the appointment of a child clinical psychologist, social worker, speech and language therapist and clerical support. In addition, a significant budget was allocated for 'buying in' services. Those services already available, for example child psychiatry, portage, family aids, etc., would be offered a base at the unit to facilitate access and coordinated intervention plans.

CONCLUSION

Developing services across the traditional barriers set up by statutory services is both an exciting and frustrating experience. It is possible to develop a shared vision of services that attempts to see children 'in the round', but, as the two projects illustrate, the process is both time consuming and complex. Without compromises and a degree of trust between agencies, such projects are very difficult to get off the ground.

It is a great pity that there has been very little written about community interventions that aim to identify and meet the needs of children with chronic disorders, because these are the services that carers will need to access most of the time. The two studies in this chapter highlight ways in which community services could ensure that the needs of children are better met. This is an issue to which I will return in the final chapter of the book when I explore ways in which hospital and community interventions could become more integrated and coordinated.

SUMMARY

- Research on community-based interventions and models of how to meet the needs of children once they move from hospital care to community services is surprisingly lacking.
- Effective collaboration between agencies is often difficult to achieve. The interface between statutory services can be tense as a result of differing duties placed on each service and the way in which they are funded. Children and their families/carers who have complex therapeutic needs present particular challenges in

that agencies need to work together if they are to produce a coordinated and integrated package of care.

- A multi-agency consultation team (MACT) and a Children's Centre were set up in an attempt to overcome some of these problems of inter-agency cooperation. Experience from these two projects suggests that meeting the needs of children can be achieved if a number of essential steps are taken including:
  1 gaining the backing of senior managers and all 'key players'
  2 setting clear eligibility criteria, referral routes and decision-making processes
  3 nominating one agency to take lead responsibility for monitoring the care plan
  4 evaluation to highlight what works and what areas need further refinement.

Part III

Implications for theory and practice

Chapter 9

Theories of adjustment

INTRODUCTION

A reasonable criticism that can be levelled at much of the psychological research in chronic childhood disease is that it lacks a clear theoretical basis. If one looks at the key journals that publish research in this area (for example, the *Journal of Pediatric Psychology*), it is evident that there is a wealth of studies, all employing a variety of assessment tools, with different populations, with different aims in mind. An overriding issue, therefore, is to integrate this diverse literature theoretically and to be able to utilise this applied research in the clinical setting.

Through experiments and reflections on clinical practice I have explored several factors that I believe influence adjustment to chronic disease. The approach I have taken, however, could be open to the criticism that the studies have simply added to the 'shopping list' of psychological variables that impact on child and family adjustment. Whilst such a criticism over-simplifies the case, it does deserve, nevertheless, to be taken seriously. After all, if we are to make progress in helping families to cope effectively, we need to start to draw together into a coherent model what can appear, at times, to be disparate and contradictory findings.

In this chapter my aim is to provide an overview on theories that have attempted to explain the mechanisms underlying adjustment. This will then provide a backdrop from which to consider the results from my studies. In the next chapter I will explore which models underpin these results and what the implications are for the development of a more unified theory of adjustment.

THEORETICAL APPROACHES

One consistent theme in the literature has been to explore whether specific psychosocial 'risk' and 'resilience' factors influence child and family adjustment. A number of common threads have started to emerge from this literature, as highlighted by Lavigne and Faier-Routman's (1992) meta analysis and recent reviews by Garrison and McQuiston (1989), Eiser (1990) and Pless and Nolan (1991). Davis (1993) has summarised the state of the art in relation to the influence of psychosocial risk factors as follows:

- Disease category does not clearly predict adjustment, although children with brain dysfunction, disability or sensory impairment have a greater incidence of psychosocial problems.
- Severity of disease as assessed by parents (not professionals) is associated with poorer adjustment.
- The gender of the child is not associated with adjustment.
- Psychological problems in children appear to increase as children get older, with adolescence being a particularly troublesome time.
- As the degree of debilitation and pain increase, there is an associated increase in psychological difficulty.
- Diseases with a higher probability of fatality are associated with greater levels of psychological disorder, both in children and their parents.
- The visibility of disease appears to predict good child adjustment.
- Socio-economic status is not consistently related to the level of adjustment in either the child or the parents.
- Family variables such as open, honest communication, lack of conflict, family cohesion, emotional expressiveness and family stability are predictive of the ability of the child and parents to cope with the disease and disease control.
- Family size, marital status and ethnicity do not appear to predict child and parent adjustment.
- Parental depression and ill health increase the risk of problems with the child.
- Concurrent stresses, both within and outside the family, are predictive of outcome in maternal and child adjustment.
- Previous severe psychological problems in the parents are associated with difficulties in adapting to disease.
- There is some evidence that increasing parental age is related to greater adjustment.
- Social or emotional support, including marital satisfaction, is related to level of parent and child adjustment.

(Davis, 1993: 13–14)

With the accumulation of evidence that psychosocial factors do influence child and family adjustment, a number of models have been proposed that attempt to explain how these risk and resistance factors might operate. Broadly, there are three theories that merit attention: Lipowski's (1970) model of adjustment, Pless and Pinkerton's (1975) reformulation of Lipowski's model and Wallander *et al.*'s (1989b) attempt to integrate a number of theories into a single conceptual model.

MODELS OF ADJUSTMENT

In describing the theories, it may be helpful to think of a case study. This may assist in both clarifying how the theories work and how they differ from each other.

David: a case study
David is a 10-year-old who has cystic fibrosis. Over the last year he has complained of severe stomach pains and as a consequence has frequently missed school. He has been investigated extensively, although no organic cause for the pains could be identified.

Lipowski's (1970) model

Lipowski (1970) suggests that disability and illness are both forms of psychological stress, as they both share in common the threat of suffering loss. The model proposes that, under these conditions, an individual will seek to reduce the perceived threat by using coping strategies to preserve 'bodily and psychic integrity'.

In Lipowski's model, it is hypothesised that the individual has at their disposal two broad categories of 'coping styles' – cognitive and behavioural. Furthermore, it is hypothesised that the determinants of coping include interpersonal, disease-related and environmental factors. *Interpersonal factors* include the child's age, personality, intelligence and social background. *Disease-related factors* refer to the type of disease, its location, rate of onset, prognosis, severity and visibility, whilst *environmental factors* relate to attitudes of the parents and significant others to the disease and their perceptions of its implications (see Figure 9.1).

Thus, according to Lipowski's (1970) model, there are a number of *predisposing conditions* such as poor housing or low intelligence that place the child at increased risk of adjustment difficulties. These conditions combine with *precipitating factors*, such as the reactions of others and features of the disease itself, to create a crisis. Whether or

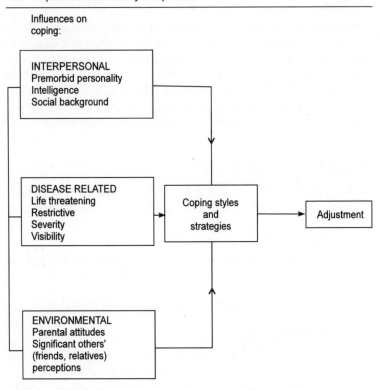

Figure 9.1   Lipowski's (1970) model of child adjustment to chronic disease

not this leads to adjustment problems is largely the result of *perpetuating factors*, namely the coping styles and strategies used by the child and their family.

If we relate Lipowski's ideas to the case study of David, the model places particular emphasis on coping styles and strategies as mediating adjustment. Thus, David's stomach aches might be seen as a function of inappropriate or insufficient coping resources to deal with stress. Underlying this might be a predisposition to feelings of anxiety ('premorbid personality') or the negative reactions from 'significant others'.

Whilst these hypotheses are eminently sensible, the model as a whole has been the subject of some criticism. For example, Lipowski fails to define what he means by 'adjustment', and as a result it is difficult to test his model. For example, if 'adjustment' refers to the extent to which a child functions 'normally' in everyday life, this is quite a different concept from 'adjustment' being used to refer to the extent to which a child and the family arrive at a realistic acceptance of the condition and the limitations it imposes. Depending on which definition is used, the model would use very different measures to determine adjustment.

The model also fails to specify how the various risk factors might interact and, indeed, whether all variables are equally important in influencing adjustment. Lipowski's (1970) two hypothesised coping styles (cognitive and behavioural) can also be questioned, as the evidence suggests that this typology does not adequately represent the range of responses that an individual might make. Carver *et al.* (1989), for example, have identified thirteen different strategies that might be involved in coping with a chronic illness.

Pless and Pinkerton's (1975) model

In the light of some of these issues, Pless and Pinkerton (1975) developed Lipowski's (1971) basic model by suggesting that adjustment is a dynamic process that continues from childhood through adult life and that is shaped and influenced by feedback loops (see Figure 9.2).

In this expanded model, Pless and Pinkerton (1975) hypothesise that genetic, social and family factors determine in large part a child's attributes (for example, temperament, personality or intelligence). These attributes then interact with characteristics of the disease (severity, location, etc.), and the reactions and attitudes of family, peers, teachers and 'significant others'. So far this is very much in line with Lipowski's model. Where Pless and Pinkerton have developed the model is to suggest that the net result of these interactions determines the child's self-concept and coping style and, as a result, the child's adaptation. Over time, they hypothesise that 'feedback loops' are set up, whereby the child's adjustment is influenced by the dynamic interplay of all these factors, which reflect the child's current life situation as well as their past experiences and expectations.

In relation to the case study of David, Pless and Pinkerton's model places particular emphasis on his current self-concept and self-esteem, and on exploring how past as well as present interactions serve to exert a negative influence on his coping resources.

Underlying Pless and Pinkerton's (1975) model are two clear assumptions. Firstly, there is the notion that functioning in early childhood sets a template for later adjustment in both adolescence and adulthood. According to the model, psychological disturbance associated with physical illness in childhood persists essentially

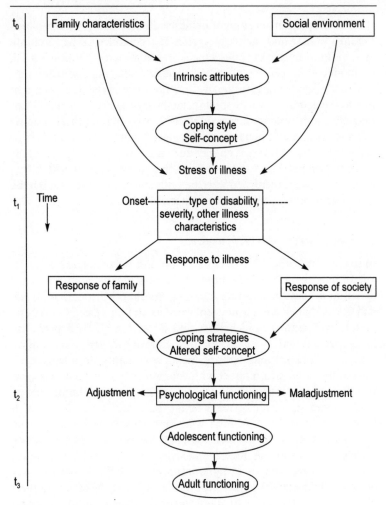

Figure 9.2 Pless and Pinkerton's (1975) model of child adjustment to chronic disease
Source: Pless and Pinkerton, 1975

unchanged into adulthood. The second assumption is that adjustment can be defined as freedom from abnormality. Underlying this is the notion that adjustment is synonymous with the individual child functioning within a 'normal' range. As a consequence, Pless and Pinkerton (1975) suggest that adjustment can be assessed using what is termed 'norm referenced tests', such as intelligence tests, personality measures, school attainments tests and the like. They are 'norm referenced' in that an average score can be stated to which the child's individual score can be compared.

The strength of Pless and Pinkerton's (1975) model is that it is explicit about the assumptions it makes, which helps when it comes to testing how robust the model actually is. The evidence so far indicates that its underlying assumptions have not been supported substantially. For example, the notion that pathways from childhood to adult adjustment are set early can be questioned. A review by Rutter (1985), for example, highlights that a number of transition points in the child's life can impinge on later outcomes, both in a protective way, to promote adjustment (such as developing friendships and social supports) as well as in a negative way, to reinforce cycles of disadvantage (such as failures at school and family discord). Equally, the idea that adjustment is an unalterable state is at odds with various outcome studies that have examined the influence of psychological treatments on specific difficulties associated with chronic disease, such as noncompliance (La Greca, 1988) and distress during medical procedures (Jay, 1988).

Pless and Pinkerton's (1975) model can also be criticised for lacking predictive power. It is not contentious to suggest that adjustment is influenced by an individual's self-concept and coping responses. What is more problematic is establishing which aspects in particular impact on adjustment. Moos and Shaefer (1984) make the point, for example, that the coping strategies people use are not inherently adaptive or maladaptive in themselves, but rather are skills that are effective in one situation but may not be so in another.

From a clinical point of view, the challenge is to understand and predict which children, under what circumstances, with what outcome are affected by chronic disease, and which strategies are most effective in promoting adjustment. It is not apparent that Pless and Pinkerton's (1975) model provides the answers to these questions, as the research studies that have been conducted in relation to the model have yielded several inconsistent and inconclusive results (see Eiser, 1990).

Wallander *et al.*'s (1989) integrated model

The most recent model to emerge in the research tradition of exploring the variability in child and family adjustment as a function of risk and resilience factors is that advanced by Wallander and colleagues

(1989b). They have proposed a model of child and maternal adaptation that integrates the conceptual models put forward by Pless and Pinkerton (1975), Moos and Shaefer (1984) and Lazarus and Folkman (1984). As I have already outlined Pless and Pinkerton's ideas, I will briefly review the other two models.

Moos and Shaefer's (1984) crisis theory

This theory is concerned with how people respond to and cope with major life crises and transitions. Moos and Shaefer (1984) hypothesise that the diagnosis of an illness represents a crisis, as a diagnosis threatens one's own personal and social identity. As a consequence, the individual will seek to re-establish an equilibrium by employing problem-solving strategies. When these strategies prove insufficient, either because the individual's coping response is inadequate, or because the event was particularly novel or major, Moos and Shaefer (1984) hypothesise that the individual will be thrown into turmoil. They hypothesise further that this crisis represents a 'turning point': either the individual comes to cope successfully with the crisis, resulting in 'personal growth and maturation', or maladaptive responses

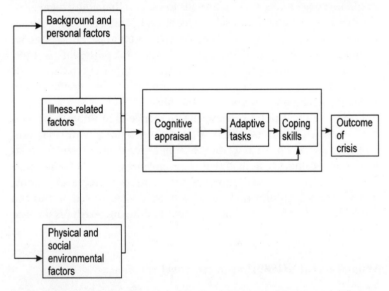

Figure 9.3   Moos and Shaefer's (1984) conceptual model for understanding the crisis of physical illness
Source: Moos and Shaefer, 1984

become established, resulting in 'psychological deterioration and decline'.

Moos and Shaefer (1984) suggest that a number of risk factors come into play in influencing an individual's appraisal of a situation and their subsequent use of coping strategies. These fall into four categories: demographic variables (for example, age, gender); personal variables (for example, maturity, ego strength), illness variables (for example, visibility, pain) and environmental variables (for example, social support, personal space). Moos and Shaefer's model is summarised in Figure 9.3.

Lazarus and Folkman's (1984) model of stress and coping

Lazarus and Folkman's (1984) model (illustrated in Figure 9.4) hypothesises that stress and coping involve continuous interactions and adjustments between the person and their environment (Rutter *et al.*, 1993). Stress is said to occur when the demands on a person tax or exceed that person's resources or ability to cope. Coping is hypothesised to be the problem-solving process by which people attempted to manage the discrepancy between the demands made and resources available.

The model identifies two key concepts in understanding stress responses: cognitive appraisal and coping.

Cognitive appraisal

Cognitive appraisal involves the individual assessing whether a demand threatens their well-being and whether they have the resources available to meet this. This judgement itself entails two components which Lazarus and Folkman (1984) define as primary and secondary appraisal. In the first, the individual is said to assess whether a particular event (for example, the diagnosis of a chronic disease) is irrelevant, benign or stressful. If it is the latter, the event is appraised further as to whether it involves harm–loss, threat or a challenge. Harm–loss refers to the amount of damage that has occurred already, threat is the expectation of future harm and challenge is the opportunity to achieve growth and mastery.

Following this judgement process, secondary appraisal starts, although the two processes may occur almost simultaneously and feedback into each other. The task of secondary appraisal is for the individual to determine what resources are available for coping and, if enacted, what the consequences are likely to be.

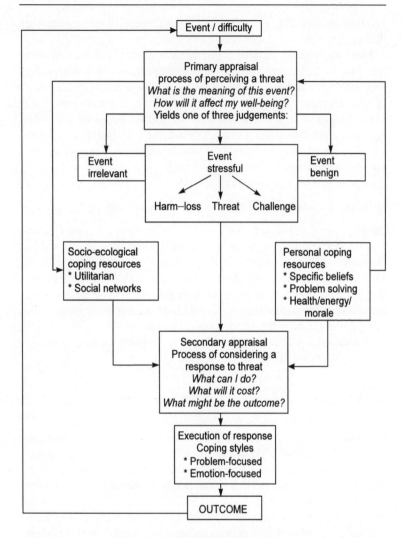

Figure 9.4 Lazarus and Folkman's (1984) model of stress and coping
Source: Rutter *et al.*, 1993

Coping

Having appraised the problem and determined the resources available, an individual will seek to master the situation by selecting a coping strategy or mechanism. Lazarus and Folkman (1984) distinguish two major functions of coping: firstly, to change the situation for the better, that is, to solve the problem if possible; and secondly to manage the somatic and subjective components of stress-related emotions. The two functions can be opposite to each other but can also support each other.

The model hypothesises five categories of coping resources: *utilitarian*, including socio-economic status, money, available services; *health, energy or morale*, including pre-existing physical or psychiatric illness; *social networks*, including close interpersonal relationships; *general and specific beliefs*, including self-efficacy, mastery and self-esteem; and *problem-solving skills*, including intellectual abilities, cognitive flexibility and analytic skills.

Review of the models

Taking the models proposed by Pless and Pinkerton (1975), Moos and Shaefer (1984) and Lazarus and Folkman (1984), Wallander *et al.* (1989b) attempt to integrate the above ideas into a unified conceptual theory of adaptation to chronic illness and handicap. This is illustrated in Figure 9.5.

Within the model, it is not assumed that the presence of a chronically sick or handicapped child necessarily represents an adverse event for the family. A view is taken that, as a consequence of having a child with a disorder, families are confronted by an increased number of potentially stressful situations, which can lead to difficulties, if not managed successfully.

In seeking to explain the variability in child and family adjustment to chronic illness, Wallander *et al.*'s (1989b) model places particular emphasis on the role of stressors and the individual's competence. Stressors are defined as 'the occurrence of problematic situations requiring a solution or some decision-making process for appropriate action' (Varni and Wallander, 1988: 215). Varni and Wallander hypothesised that coping with these stressors is the result of the person's competence, where competence is viewed as 'the effectiveness of the coping responses emitted when an individual is confronted with problematic situations' (Varni and Wallander, 1988: 215).

The implication of Wallander *et al.*'s (1989b) model is that adjustment can be understood as being a function of the level of strain experienced, which is influenced by the nature of problems encountered and the person's ability to cope successfully with these. The model postulates that adjustment is further influenced by risk

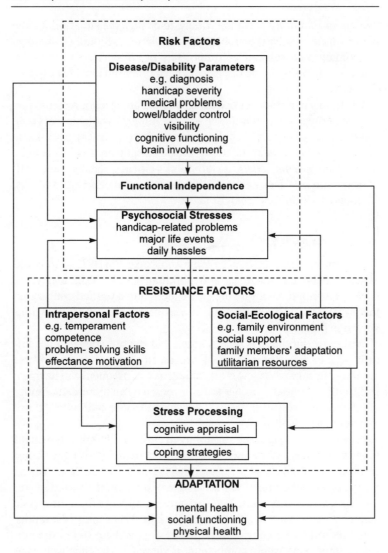

Figure 9.5   Wallander *et al.*'s (1989b) model of child and maternal adaptation to chronic conditions
Source: Wallander *et al.*, 1989b

and resilience factors. Variables that are thought to increase the risk of poor adaptation fall into three domains: factors relating to the child's *disease and disability* (for example, severity and visibility); the child's level of *functional independence* and *psychosocial stressors*, including stresses relating to the disease itself, as well as other co-existing life events and 'daily hassles'.

The impact of these risk factors on adaptation is moderated by three sets of resistance factors, namely: *intrapersonal* (including the child's temperament and problem-solving ability), *social-ecological* (including the family environment and social supports) and *coping resources* (such as cognitive appraisal and coping strategies). Wallander *et al.* (1989b) hypothesise that these factors influence adaptation in both direct and indirect ways. For example, diseases that are more life threatening may impinge on maternal adjustment in a direct way, through the anxiety associated with the disease, or impact in an indirect way as a result of the disease involving the mother in increased amounts of care giving. Alternatively, good adaptation might result, where the disease imposes few restrictions or where the family has a high degree of effective social supports that can act as a 'buffer' to moderate levels of stress.

If we return to the case study of David, we can see that Wallander *et al.*'s model offers a much more complex and detailed explanation of the parenting difficulties, in comparison to that advanced by Lipowski and Pless and Pinkerton. They borrow several of the concepts from these models, but in doing so, clarify to a much greater extent the interdependence of risk and resistance factors and how they operate. Wallander *et al.*'s model is much more *multi-factorial* in that it includes many elements omitted in the earlier models and as such does not suggest that adaptation, or adjustment, is solely a function of coping skills or a child's self-concept.

Wallander *et al.* (1989b) argue that their model is applicable to any paediatric disorder and as a consequence they propose that a non-categorical approach to studying the effects of chronic disease should be adopted. As discussed in Chapter 1, under this paradigm it is hypothesised that the commonalities between diseases are greater than their differences, as children and their families are thought to face common challenges to successful adaptation. In practice, this has meant that Wallander and colleagues have tended to group together children with differing diagnoses and to analyse the effect of risk and resilience factors on the group as a whole, rather than studying single diagnostic categories. In testing the model, Wallander *et al.* (1990) have argued that it is not possible to validate their model as a whole, rather it is only feasible to analyse single or small groups of variables to see if they do operate in the hypothesised direction.

Wallander *et al.*'s (1989b) model represents the most up-to-date, and some would say the most sophisticated and coherent, theoretical framework to emerge so far. As such it is worthy of more detailed inspection to see whether the evidence supports their theory. In the next section, I will review the studies carried out by Wallander *et al.* to test their model.

EVIDENCE FOR WALLANDER *ET AL.*'S MODEL

Wallander *et al.* (1989b) hypothesise that disease and disability factors have both a direct and indirect effect on child and maternal adjustment. They identify seven variables as being important: the child's diagnosis; severity of the handicap; occurrence of medical problems; visibility of the disorder; lack of bladder and bowel control; whether cognitive functioning is impaired; and whether the condition is associated with neuropathology. The relationship between these factors, as well as the child's functional independence on adjustment, has been explored by Wallander and colleagues in a series of six studies.

Impact of specific diagnosis

Wallander *et al.* (1988) tested the hypothesis that child maladjustment would vary as a function of their diagnostic condition. Mothers of 270 chronically ill and handicapped children aged 4–16 completed a standardised screening tool for psychiatric disorder, the Child Behaviour Check List (CBCL) (Achenbach and Edelbrock, 1983). Children included in this study had a diagnosis of either juvenile diabetes, spina bifida, juvenile rheumatoid arthritis, haemophilia, chronic obesity or cerebral palsy.

Analysis of parental responses to the CBCL indicated that, taken as a whole, the children did indeed have higher behavioural and social competence problems in comparison to a normative sample of healthy children (10 per cent versus 2 per cent). However, analyses of the adjustment problems experienced by the ill children failed to reveal any significant differences as a function of diagnostic group. In other words, whether the child had, say, spina bifida or juvenile rheumatoid arthritis did not result in differing scores on the CBCL.

Wallander *et al.*'s (1988) results indicated that whilst there was a five-fold increase in psychological problems in children who have a chronic disease in comparison to healthy peers, it is important not to lose sight of the fact that the vast majority of the children did not experience difficulties. Indeed, many of the children were found to have no significant adjustment problems at all. The conclusion appears to be, therefore, that children with a chronic disorder are a population at risk of psychological difficulties, but that these difficulties are not inevitable and are not determined by the child's diagnosis.

The fact that children's overall scores on the CBCL did not vary as a function of which diagnostic group they were in is interesting, particularly in the light of Wallander *et al.*'s assertion that a non-categorical approach should be adopted in research programmes. The evidence from their study would tend to support such a view, as maladaptation was not predicted by the child's diagnosis.

Impact of disease severity, functional independence and chronic strain

In the light of a lack of any apparent direct relationship between a specific diagnosis and child maladjustment, Wallander *et al.* (1989c) investigated the role of disability parameters and chronic disability-related strain on adaptation. Their idea was to test the notion that diseases that involved the child's mother in substantially increased amounts of care giving might be associated with increased rates of stress and strain on the mother, which in turn might contribute to poorer child and maternal adjustment. They hypothesised further that factors that might underpin the need to give more care could include certain disease factors (for example, seriousness and painfulness) as well as the child's 'functional status'. This latter aspect refers to 'how capable the child is in meeting the demands of activities of daily living, functioning in the community and communicating to others relative to expectations for his or her age' (Wallander *et al.*, 1989c: 25).

Fifty mothers of 6–11-year-old children with a congenital physical handicap (cerebral palsy or spina bifida) completed a series of questionnaires to determine adaptation. Again the CBCL was used to define child adaptation, whilst maternal adjustment was assessed by two measures: the Malaise Inventory (Rutter *et al.*, 1970) and by a questionnaire designed for the study which assessed social-recreational activities and contacts.

The child's functional status was determined in two ways. Firstly, a researcher rated the severity of the child's condition using a five-point scale (Rutter *et al.*, 1970). In addition, the child's intellectual functioning was tested using a battery of standardised cognitive assessments.

Results from these various measures indicated that the children were rated as having significantly more emotional and social functioning problems in comparison to a normative sample. However, the total level of difficulty reported did not vary as a function of the child's diagnostic group, which replicates the finding reported by Wallander *et al.* (1988). Mothers of the children studied reported more mental and health complaints in comparison to a normative sample of mothers of healthy children, although again these rates of distress did not vary in relation to the child's diagnosis.

In testing their hypothesis for a mediating effect between the risk factors (disability parameters and chronic strain) and maternal and child emotional adjustment problems, Wallander *et al.* (1989c) have failed to establish any significant associations. In other words, neither the severity of the child's condition, the presence of a learning difficulty, nor the child's functional independence predicted the occurrence of behavioural problems, as rated by the mother; nor were the mothers' own ratings on the Malaise Inventory related to these same variables. What the results did confirm was that children and their mothers report more adaptation problems in comparison to a healthy sample.

Impact of disease severity, medical problems, bowel and bladder control and functional independence

Wallander *et al.* (1989a) investigated further the relationship between the child's physical health status and his or her psychosocial adjustment. They hypothesised that their earlier study (Wallander *et al.*, 1989c) had failed to produce significant results, as they had not assessed the child's health status using objective parameters, rather they had relied upon a 5-point rating completed by a researcher. By attending to this problem, in conjunction with studying a single handicapping condition, Wallander and colleagues hypothesised that children with spina bifida would show an increased rate of maladjustment in comparison to a normative sample, and that maladjustment would be related, firstly, to the child's scores on individual physical health measures and, secondly, to their overall disability score.

In this study, Wallander *et al.* (1989a) determined the child's physical health status on the basis of medical records and parental reports regarding the child's spinal cord lesion level, number of operations to replace shunts, number of operations on skin ulcers below the waist, total number of operations the child had undergone, ambulatory status (for example, whether the child required a wheelchair) and bladder function. Child maladjustment was determined by the child's score on the CBCL, which was completed by the mother.

Sixty-one children aged 4–16 with spina bifida were included in the study. Results revealed that this group of children did have a higher incidence of adjustment problems in comparison to a normative sample, but that none of the above disease and disability parameters, nor the child's overall disability score, predicted the emotional/behavioural adjustment difficulties reported.

These results failed, therefore, to support Wallander's hypothesis concerning the mediating role that specific disease parameters might play (such as the degree of physical or intellectual disability) in influencing child adjustment.

Impact of functional independence and psychosocial stress

In the light of the above, Wallander *et al.* (1990) moved on to explore the hypothesis that the child's level of functional independence might significantly influence maternal adaptation, through the mediating effects of maternal psychosocial stress. Specifically, they proposed that a child with poor independence skills would cause more major life events for the mother (for example, major financial expenditure associated with altering the home environment), daily hassles (for example, complications in daily transport) and handicap related problems (for example, child being isolated from peers), compared to a child with relatively better skills, and that these problems would play a significant mediating role in predicting maternal adjustment.

A total of 119 mothers of children aged 2–18 years, with a physical or sensory disability, were mailed a questionnaire that evaluated the nature of the child's disability via parental responses to a twenty-nine-item disability checklist. In addition, parents were asked to comment upon the child's functional independence, by completing the Vineland Adaptive Behaviour Scales (Sparrow *et al.*, 1984). Maternal adaptation was assessed by their self-reports on a Physical Health Measure (Belloc *et al.*, 1971), a Mental Health Inventory (Veit and Ware, 1983) and a Social Contacts and Resources Questionnaire (Donald and Ware, 1982). Maternal psychosocial stress was measured by the Life Experiences Survey (Sarason *et al.*, 1978); Daily Hassles and Uplifts Scale (Kanner *et al.*, 1981) and a scale developed for the study that assessed the problems that the child's condition caused for the parent.

Analyses using multiple regressions failed to support Wallander *et al.*'s (1990) hypothesis of an indirect relationship between a child's level of functional impairment and maternal adaptation. No statistically significant association was found between the child's level of functional independence and maternal stress. Nor was an association found for the child's level of functional independence and maternal adjustment problems. The only association that was established was between mothers' level of stress and their mental health, although maternal stress did not mediate any indirect association between child functional independence and maternal adaptation.

These results indicate that factors related to the child's disease or disability do not impact on maternal adjustment. The fact that mothers reported mental health problems therefore needs to be explained by other factors. Wallander *et al.* (1990) suggest that relevant dimensions might include maternal temperament, social support and coping resources.

So far we have seen that Wallander and colleagues have largely failed in their attempts to show that certain risk factors explain and predict child adaptation. What about the role of resistance factors which the model suggests may also play a part in influencing adaptation? Wallander *et al.* (1989b) identified three relevant factors: social and ecological factors, intrapersonal factors and stress-processing abilities. They have reported two studies in relation to social-ecological factors (social environment and family resources), although they have yet to explore the effects of intrapersonal factors or stress-processing abilities in buffering the effects of the hypothesised risk factors. What do the results so far tell us?

Impact of the social environment

Wallander *et al.* (1989d) investigated the relationship between the 'social environment' and adaptation in mothers of physically handicapped children. Wallander *et al.* (1989d) hypothesised that four dimensions of the social environment would influence maternal adaptation: utilitarian resources, the handicapped child's adjustment, psychosocial family resources and the availability and use of services.

In order to test the above hypothesis, mothers of fifty children aged 6–11, with central nervous system lesions (spina bifida and cerebral palsy), completed a series of questionnaires. 'Utilitarian resources' were defined as:

> the structural characteristics of the family which may aid it in dealing with the acute and chronic problems related to the child's han-

dicap [namely] family income, mother's education, family size, presence of a child older than the handicapped child, duration of the marriage and mother's age.

(Wallander *et al.*, 1989d: 376)

'Psychosocial family resources' referred to 'the family's characteristic mode of receiving and interacting with the social world, including within and external to the family' (Wallander *et al.*, 1989d: 377). They operationalised this rather vague definition by asking mothers to complete the Family Environment Scale (Moos and Moos, 1981), to determine the degree of family support; the Dyadic Adjustment Scale (Spanier, 1976) to assess marital satisfaction; and the Social Support Questionnaire (Sarason *et al.*, 1983), to assess the number of people available to provide support.

Service utilisation was determined by providing mothers with a checklist of twenty services and asking them to indicate which, if any, had been used in the child's life. The child's handicap severity was determined by information provided by the mother in association with one of the researcher's observations of the child over an hour, when a series of cognitive assessments were completed. Maternal adaptation was defined on the basis of the Malaise Inventory and Social and Activities Questionnaire, with child adjustment determined by the mother's rating on the CBCL.

Multiple regression analyses indicated that 34 per cent of the variance in maternal adaptation was explained by a combination of family and utilitarian resources and the use of services. Variables found to be of particular relevance were: extent of family and social support, marital satisfaction and duration of marriage. Neither the child's disability status (severity, extent of cognitive impairment nor level of functional independence), nor child adjustment (occurrence of emotional/behaviour problems), nor family social economic status were significantly associated with maternal maladjustment.

Impact of family resources

Wallander *et al.* (1989b) further tested the hypothesis that utilitarian family resources and the family environment would help to protect the child from maladaptation. They studied 153 children aged between 4–16 years, with one of five chronic conditions: juvenile diabetes, juvenile rheumatoid arthritis, chronic obesity, spina bifida or cerebral palsy. Child adjustment was defined by mother's ratings on the CBCL. 'Family resources' were defined in two ways: 'psychological resources', which were determined on the basis of mother's ratings on the Family Environment Scale (analysed using the five sub-scales of: cohesion; expressiveness; organisation; control; conflict), and 'utilitarian [i.e. practical] resources', which were determined by the family's income and maternal education level.

Children's scores on the CBCL were subjected to a multiple regression analysis. Results indicated that child maladjustment was related to one dimension on the Family Environment Scale (occurrence of family conflict), but not to any of the other dimensions assessed. Low scores on the social competence sub-scale of the CBCL (involvement in organised clubs, hobbies, etc.) were found to be correlated with family conflict, as well as parental control and a lack of family cohesion. With reference to the role of 'utilitarian resources', maternal educational level and family income accounted for only a small amount of the variance in behaviour problems (7 per cent), and a slightly higher amount in social competence (24 per cent).

These results indicate that child maladjustment correlates with family conflict, poor family cohesion and poor parental control and, to a lesser extent, with financial hardship and maternal education level. The fact that Wallander et al.'s analysis relies on correlations does not answer the question of cause and effect. For example, are children's behaviour problems the cause or the result of family conflict?

Overall, the results from Wallander and colleagues' five studies suggest that their model, as originally conceived, has not proved to be as robust as might have been hoped. Drawing on a range of theoretical ideas, Wallander and colleagues' hypothesis, that risk and resistance factors interact in a particular way to influence adjustment, has not received substantial support. The review of Wallander and colleagues' research indicates that several of the predictions made by their conceptual model have not been substantiated, whilst others have received only tentative support.

In the next chapter, I will revisit the results from my studies and explore what implications they have for Wallander's model of adjustment and whether the results obtained can throw any light on the reasons why Wallander et al.'s research has largely failed to support their theoretical model.

SUMMARY

- The early models of adjustment (for example, Lipowski, 1970; Pless and Pinkerton, 1975) have tended to emphasise the role of coping strategies and the child's self-concept in attempting to explain the variability in child adjustment to chronic disease. A number of criticisms can be made of these models, not least that that they commonly fail to be supported by research studies.

- Wallander *et al.*'s (1989b) conceptual model arises from the tradition of exploring how individual risk and resilience factors interact to influence child and family adaptation to chronic diseases. Wallander *et al.*'s (1989b) formulation represents the most coherent theory to date, and by specifying the relationship between factors, the model is unique in making specific predictions as to which children and families are most at risk of poor coping, as well as the reasons why.

- The review of Wallander and colleagues' research indicates that several of the predictions made by their conceptual model have not been substantiated, whilst others have received only tentative support. There is a need to reformulate Wallander *et al.*'s (1989b) model so that its predictive validity can be strengthened.

Chapter 10

Reappraisal of theories of adjustment

INTRODUCTION

In the preceding chapter, I presented three theories that have attempted to explain the psychological mechanisms underlying adjustment to chronic disease and disability. In discussing the strengths and weaknesses of these, it became apparent that none has stood the test of time, in that research has often failed to support the ideas underpinning the theories. In this chapter I want to explore what might be some of the reasons why these models have proved inadequate, by revisiting my own studies.

I believe that, in considering the studies together, four key factors emerge that can be considered to influence adjustment. These are: family patterns of interaction; 'doctor–patient' communication; the health care environment; and health beliefs. The important issue for me is how might these factors operate? Equally, what are their wider theoretical implications and how might Wallander *et al.*'s (1989b) model be developed to take these factors into account?

FAMILY INTERACTION

A common theme that ran through the studies was the effect that family interaction had upon adjustment. For example, in the X-ray study we saw that child distress was associated with parental discipline style, which appeared to be part of a wider picture of how the parents related to their child. Similarly, in the family therapy study it became clear that certain patterns of family interaction were associated with children's illness behaviours and an exacerbation of symptoms. In these studies and others I argued that family interactions did not occur in a vacuum, but were influenced by characteristics of both the child, such as stranger sociability, and the environment, such as the behaviour of staff. Thus, it seems important to take a 'systems' perspective – that is, an orientation that explores the inter-connections between people and events – if we are to unravel the pathways underlying adjustment.

What are the implications of this for Wallander *et al.*'s (1989b) theory? In their model, Wallander *et al.* acknowledge the role of the 'family environment' in adaptation and in two studies they have explored the impact of 'family resources' on outcomes. However, in doing so, Wallander and colleagues have relied exclusively upon pen and paper measures (for example, the Family Environment Scale, Moos and Moos, 1981), which were completed by the child's mother. This methodology can be criticised on the grounds that such scales assess only one person's perception of family functioning. Furthermore, reliance upon such questionnaires is inevitably limited as it is questionable whether the intricacies of family life and the patterns of interactions that surround this can be adequately captured by a forty-five-item questionnaire. A related point is that adaptation is defined by the child's scores on the Child Behaviour Check List. As we have already seen in Chapter 1, use of this measure with chronic illness populations has been heavily criticised (Perrin *et al.*, 1991).

From a theoretical standpoint, Wallander *et al.*'s (1989b) formulation also has a number of weaknesses. For example, in their model, 'family environment' is conceptualised as a 'resistance' factor, which operates in such a way as to promote adjustment and acts as a buffer against 'risk' factors. It is not clear from their own research, however, whether this is correct, as their studies (Wallander *et al.*, 1989b; Wallander *et al.*, 1989d) highlighted that certain family environments, namely those characterised by conflict, low cohesion and poor parental control, were associated with childhood behaviour problems and delays in social competence. As such, this would appear to be more indicative of risk than resilience.

One reason for the confusion as to whether family environment is a risk or resistance factor lies in the fact that Wallander and colleagues do not precisely define what is meant by 'risk' and 'resistance'. Rutter (1985: 600) has referred to resistance or 'protective' factors as 'influences that modify, ameliorate, or alter a person's response to some environmental hazard that predisposes to a maladaptive outcome'. He goes on to argue that resilience factors are not simply the opposite of risk factors. To treat them as if they are is, in fact, to deal with aspects of the same variable. Rutter also makes the point that resistance to stress is relative, not absolute, and that the degree of resistance is not a fixed quality – rather it varies over time and according to circumstances. Rutter's (1985) analysis draws attention to the importance of conceptual clarity when discussing risk and resilience factors. It is theoretically necessary to distinguish between the two, in order to understand their relative effects, which Wallander's model, and many others, fail to do.

On the basis of my research, I believe it would make more sense for Wallander *et al.* (1989b) and other similar models to place the family environment as a risk factor. I also think we need to be clearer as to what is being referred to, by, for example, re-labelling 'family environment' as 'family interaction', and specifying what dimensions of family interaction are thought to be important.

Whilst there are many different approaches to analysing family interaction and many different views as to what dimensions of behaviour should be assessed, it seems to me that my results concerning the influence of family functioning on child adjustment are consistent with the model proposed by Minuchin *et al.* (1975) and that, as such, Minuchin *et al.*'s model represents an important theory which could be incorporated into Wallander's model.

Minuchin *et al.*'s (1975) model of psychosomatic illness

Minuchin *et al.* (1975) have attempted to explain the development of illness behaviours and symptoms in children by analysing family patterns of interaction. Their model contains two key hypotheses: firstly, that certain types of family organisation are closely related to the development and maintenance of psychosomatic symptoms in the child, and secondly, that the child's psychosomatic symptoms play a major role in maintaining the family homeostasis. They suggest that in order for a psychosomatic illness to develop, three factors in conjunction are necessary:

    (i) the child is physiologically vulnerable, that is a specific organic dysfunction is present;

   (ii) the child's family shows the transactional characteristics of: enmeshment, over-protectiveness, rigidity and lack of conflict resolution; and

  (iii) the sick child plays an important role in the family's patterns of conflict avoidance and this role represents an important source of reinforcement for the symptoms.

(Minuchin *et al.*, 1975: 1032)

Within this model, Minuchin *et al.* (1975) hypothesise that the transactional patterns of enmeshment, over-protectiveness, rigidity and lack of conflict resolution provide the context for children and their families using illness as a mode of communication.

The four constructs that Minuchin *et al.* propose warrant some clarification. 'Enmeshment' refers to 'a high degree of responsiveness and involvement... and can be seen in the interdependence of relationships, intrusions on personal boundaries, poorly differentiated perception of self and other family members and weak family subsystem boundaries' (Minuchin *et al.*, 1975: 1033). The clinical presentation includes an excessive 'togetherness' and sharing, with family members frequently intruding into each other's thoughts, feelings and communications. For example, family members may finish each other's sentences; equally, children may feel able to join with one parent in criticising the other, and to an observer it may be unclear whether the parents are in control or whether the child is.

'Over-protectiveness' occurs when family members become overly concerned for each other's welfare. Minuchin *et al.* (1975) give the example of how a sneeze can set off a flurry of handkerchief offers, and how conversations can be punctuated frequently by complaints and queries about illness symptoms such as tiredness or discomfort. Where over-protectiveness is a dominant feature, signs of distress act as cues to family members as to the approach of dangerous levels of tensions or conflict, which can then lead on to distracting behaviour to avert this.

'Rigidity' is said to occur when the family are so committed to maintaining the status quo that opportunities for change are perceived as significant threats and therefore to be avoided. For example, when a child in an 'effectively' functioning family reaches adolescence, the family is likely to be able to negotiate successfully a change to its rules and transactional patterns, to allow for age-appropriate increased autonomy, whilst still preserving family continuity. Rigid families may well be less able to negotiate such changes and indeed may deny that there is any need for a change in the balance of relationships.

As a result of rigidity, over-protectiveness and enmeshed transactional patterns, Minuchin *et al.* (1975) argue that the family's threshold for conflicts is reduced. In order to avoid conflict (which is seen as a key motivation in Minuchin's *et al.*'s (1975) formulation as a lack of arguments ensures the survival of the family unit), problems are left unresolved or avoided where possible. Families may present, for example, with a problem or difficulty, only to fall into patterns of communication, such as avoidance and 'detouring', which ensure that no resolution is possible.

When the above conditions are satisfied, Minuchin *et al.* (1975) hypothesise that two phases occur: 'turn on' and 'turn off'. In the former, a family conflict would trigger the occurrence of illness symptoms in the child; the latter comes in to play when the conflict had been avoided, thereby allowing the symptoms to recede. Minuchin *et al.* (1975) propose that certain family interactions are associated with a failure to progress from the turn on to turn off phases. They refer to these interactions as: triangulation, parent–child coalition and detouring.

In 'triangulation', the child is said to be put in the position whereby he/she is unable to express him/herself without siding with one parent against the other. Thus, patterns of communication where one parent overtly or covertly asks the child to make a choice between the parents places that child in a bind and results in continued conflict and stress. Where a 'parent–child coalition' is evident, the child is likely to side with one parent against another and may become the conduit for the unexpressed conflict between the parents. In the third type of pattern, 'detouring', parents are hypothesised to submerge their own difficulties into the child. The child becomes the focus of their attention, thereby ensuring that underlying conflicts are denied.

Whilst Minuchin *et al.*'s (1975) model identifies 'pathological' patterns of interaction, it does not suggest that these are necessarily abnormal. Families who function well are also likely to show similar patterns of interaction at times of stress and conflict. What distinguishes these families from 'psychosomatic' ones is the inability of the latter to move on from maladaptive sequences and their use of illness as a habitual way of avoiding conflict.

Minuchin and colleagues have reported a number of studies that appear to confirm that the hypothesised risk factors of enmeshment, over-protectiveness, poor conflict resolution and rigidity are indeed associated with the following conditions: poor diabetic control (Minuchin *et al.*, 1975; Anderson *et al.*, 1981; Bobrow *et al.*, 1985;), asthma (Minuchin *et al.*, 1975; Gustafson *et al.*, 1987), anorexia (Minuchin *et al.*, 1978) and other 'psychosomatic' conditions, such as headaches and gastrointestinal disorders (Minuchin *et al.*, 1975).

Whilst the model is not without its limitations (Coyne and Anderson, 1989; Woods, 1994), it does appear to offer a way forward in thinking about how family interactions mediate adjustment and what dimensions might be important to explore.

'DOCTOR–PARENT' COMMUNICATION AND INTERACTION

A second theme to emerge from my studies was that adjustment was influenced by the nature and quality of communication between families and health care staff. By referring to 'doctor–parent' communication, I do not wish to imply that the focus should be limited to medical personnel and individual parent interaction. Rather, the notion of 'doctor–parent' communication serves as shorthand notation for interaction between all health care staff and all relevant family members. For example, in investigating the stresses imposed on parents as a consequence of their child's chronic disease, I drew attention to the way in which the medical system's management of the emotional aspects of the child and family's care was a significant source of dissatisfaction. It seemed that the organisation of services often meant that parents failed to have their emotional needs met, thereby adding further barriers to successful coping. Underlying this was a failure in communication, whereby parents frequently failed to ask the questions they wanted, and clinicians and others failed to meet their needs for information, discussion and emotional support. It seems that parents commonly complained that they were not told enough and that the way in which they were given information was unsatisfactory too. This failure to meet parents' needs is implicated as an important mediating mechanism to subsequent adjustment.

In Wallander et al.'s (1989b) model it is assumed that outcomes (mental health, physical health and social functioning) are the net result of the interplay between risk and resistance factors, which are largely conceived in terms of 'stable person factors', for example temperament and stress-processing abilities. This formulation places particular emphasis on adaptation being the consequence of individual attributes. The results from my studies challenge this assumption as it seemed that the way in which staff responded to families was of equal, if not greater, importance.

It is apparent that, in coming to terms with a chronic condition, the child and his or her family do not attempt to do so in isolation. The very fact that the child has an illness means that they are very likely to become involved with the medical care system. In the research programme it was hypothesised that both the way in which that system operates, and the nature of the staff interactions with the child patients and their families, would have a significant effect on the adjustment of the child and their family. The results, in supporting this notion, highlight that Wallander *et al.*'s (1989b) model fails to pay adequate attention to this aspect.

What theoretical models might help to elucidate the link between hospital services and psychological outcomes for children and their parents? In the following section two models that have been developed within the framework of doctor–patient communication are considered.

Korch's (1968) affective model

Early studies that explored the determinants of patient satisfaction emphasised affective aspects of the interaction (for example, Korsch *et al.*, 1968; Korsch and Negrete, 1972). Korsch *et al.* (1968), for example, found through analysing 800 interviews between mothers and paediatrician that maternal satisfaction correlated with two main features.

Firstly, satisfaction correlated with the way in which the doctor was perceived by the mothers: those doctors who behaved in a 'friendly' way, as opposed to 'businesslike', and understood the mother's concern, as well as showing 'positive' communication skills, produced significantly greater satisfaction than those who did not. Secondly, an important part was played by the mothers' expectations. Mothers who expected that the doctor would prescribe a course of treatment, for example, or offer a diagnosis were much more satisfied when those expectations were met than when they were not. Satisfaction is thus in part a product of what the parent brings to the encounter and not just what happened during the interaction (Rutter *et al.*, 1993).

Ley's (1977) cognitive model

A second theoretical approach has emphasised the role of cognition in patient satisfaction. Ley and colleagues (1988) have conducted a series of studies in relation to their theory that satisfaction is the product of how much the patient understands of what the doctor says and how much is remembered. Satisfaction, in turn, is hypothesised to lead to compliance with the doctor's advice and treatment regimen (see Figure 10.1).

The research evidence supports Ley's model, as dissatisfaction has been found to be correlated with poor recall and comprehension. Equally, helping patients to understand and recollect the information imparted results in increased satisfaction, which in turn impacts

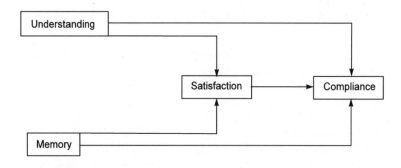

Figure 10.1   A model of satisfaction and compliance: Ley (1988)
Source: Ley, 1988

on compliance. Where dissatisfaction with a consultation occurs – and according to a recent review of the literature this is a very common feature (Ley, 1988) – mothers have often been found to be non-compliant with the advice they had received (Korsch and Negrete, 1972). Conversely, improving clinicians' communications correlates with both patient satisfaction and compliance, as well as a quicker recovery from surgery and shorter lengths of stay in hospital (Ley, 1988).

As to why patients might fail to understand and recall what they are told, a number of important factors have emerged. Korsch *et al.* (1968) found that much of the language used by doctors was too difficult for patients to follow, as it was frequently interspersed with medical terminology and jargon. Equally, Roth *et al.* (1962) highlight that patients have their own theories concerning illness and its treatment, which may be at variance with received medical wisdom. These findings illustrate that not only do most people have very little precise medical knowledge, but that unless active misconceptions are identified and corrected, there is a possibility of communication breakdown. A related issue is that patients are often found to be reluctant to ask clarifying questions, or to raise particular worries. Again in the Korsch study, it was found that 24 per cent of parents did not ask the doctor questions, even though they wanted more information, and 76 per cent of parents' main worries and 63 per cent of their expectations about treatment were not communicated. It is salutary to note that the results of my research programme found a similar magnitude of problem, this despite the fact that the two studies are separated by twenty-five years.

THE WARD, HOSPITAL AND WIDER HEALTH CARE ENVIRONMENT

So far, I have suggested that adaptation is influenced by family inter-action and by the nature and quality of communication between families and health care staff. If we widen the focus, it becomes clear that these elements are influenced, in turn, by aspects of the environment, for example the ward, the hospital and the 'community' once the family is discharged back home.

The studies concerned with staff accuracy and the role of family therapy, as well as the review of organ transplantation, highlight the importance of the environment in which children and families find themselves in influencing adjustment. The studies suggested that the way in which a ward operates, its structure, culture, mode of function-ing and the atmosphere it conveys, is likely to have a significant effect on patient–staff interactions and parents' perceptions of the adequacy of emotional support.

The impact of the ward environment on adjustment is an issue that has been generally neglected in the research to date. This is surprising given the established finding that, for example, child behaviour is in-fluenced by both home and school environments. In the study that ex-plored the integration of 'systems' approaches into a paediatric ward it was found that the hospital context was a major determinant of how children and families adjusted. When the ward was helped to change its interaction with the families, this resulted in a change in the families' own behaviour.

This raises the intriguing question of what factors impinge on staff in their interactions with children and families? One interesting model that has been advanced suggests that 'anxiety' may be a key in-fluence.

Menzies Lyth's (1988) theory of social systems as a defence against anxiety

Menzies Lyth (1988) has described from a psychoanalytic perspective how anxiety, tension and distress in nursing staff result in particular relationships developing with patients. According to Menzies Lyth (1988) these interactions are sanctioned, and indeed required, by the hospital system as a way of containing this anxiety. She suggests that 'socially structured defence mechanisms' (Menzies Lyth, 1988: 50) develop over time, the aim of which is to protect nurses from the emotional burden of their work.

Some of the common defence mechanisms that Menzies Lyth has identified include:

Splitting up the nurse–patient relationship, whereby contact is regulated by ensuring that the nurse has several patients to look after, and that emotional contact is limited by organising the interaction around tasks.

Depersonalisation, categorisation and denial of the significance of the individual. Uniforms, wards all having the same layout, the use of routines (all patients having to wash at the same time), referring to bed numbers and particular illnesses and to 'patients' (for example, 'the patient in bed twelve', or 'the liver transplant in intensive care') rather than to people as individuals, are all ways in which the patient–staff relationship is kept at an emotional distance.

Detachment and denial of feelings. By reducing the individual distinctiveness of people and avoiding strong emotions, the possibility of attachments developing is decreased. The physical relocation of nurses from one ward to another and the implicit culture of 'stiff upper lip' in the face of adversity both contribute to the ongoing process of depersonalisation.

The attempt to eliminate decisions by ritual task-performance. Ensuring that task lists are presented, with precise instructions about the way each task must be performed, the order of tasks and the time for their performance, is identified as one way in which personal involvement is reduced by interactions becoming ritualised.

Purposeful obscurity in the formal distribution of responsibility whereby the boundaries to roles are left vague so that the individual can evade responsibility and the relationship between different layers of the organisation are left unclear so that responsibility becomes defuse.

The reduction of the impact of responsibility by delegation to superiors. By avoiding decision-making by passing the issue up a management chain, the individual can limit their sense of personal responsibility.

Whilst alternative interpretations can be offered to the dynamics Menzies Lyth (1988) has described, her work is important in drawing attention to the importance of the hospital and ward as environments which, by necessity, regulate patient and carer relationships in the context of illness. In support of this notion, it was found in the study exploring parents' experiences of medical care that some families felt that nursing staff deliberately avoided them when they were upset and that, generally, the emotional aspects of their child's care were a source of dissatisfaction.

Whether a psychodynamic explanation for staff's behaviour accounts completely for the finding is questioned by the study on staff accuracy. That study found that one reason for the gap between what parents say they need and what they report they received appeared to lie in the fact that staff often failed to identify accurately the difficulties that parents faced. The important issue from a theoretical point of view is that attention needs to be paid to the characteristics of the environment where research is carried out. This is important, not only in interpreting the results, but also in highlighting that the ward environment might be a risk factor in its own right in understanding the variability in adaptation to chronic childhood illnesses.

HEALTH BELIEFS AND THEORIES OF ILLNESS

In many ways, I see this final influence on adjustment, health beliefs and theories of illness as having completed a circle. I have argued that family interaction and the way staff respond, which are both shaped by the environment, have a major influence on adjustment. Underlying much of this are people's – the child's, parents' and staff's – beliefs about illness, its causation and its treatment. Thus thoughts and feelings drive behaviour and behaviour informs and shapes people's beliefs.

This issue has been touched upon in all the studies, ranging from mothers' beliefs about the impact that previous miscarriages had on their relationship with their child, through staffs' beliefs about the psychological effects of chronic disease and their role in providing support, to parents' feelings about seeking help for psychological problems.

The influence of health beliefs was also explored in the study, which examined the determinants of child adjustment, where I found that, contrary to Wallander *et al.*'s (1989b) original hypothesis, a child's 'objective' health status was not the key variable in predicting adjustment. Rather, maternal perceptions and beliefs about the impact of the disease on the child appeared to be of far greater significance. This study also served to highlight that many of the mothers included felt that the occurrence of emotional and behavioural difficulties in their children was directly related to their disease, despite the fact that most mothers also rated their children as being in good health.

These initially puzzling results on reflection point to a dynamic interplay between mothers' perceptions of the child's condition, occurrence of behaviour problems, poor maternal mental health and beliefs about their own coping, which suggest that the processes underlying adaptation are more complicated than proposed by Wallander *et al.* (1989b). The results raise the possibility, for example, that health beliefs and theories of illness may both be important elements to incorporate into any model that attempts to explain the pathways involved in adjustment to chronic disease. I will detail two theories to illustrate this point.

Rosenstock's (1974) Health Belief Model

The Health Belief Model was developed initially in an attempt to explain people's failure to take up preventive and screening programmes. It has been applied subsequently to the more general issue of how people respond when they become ill and factors that influence compliance. The model is illustrated in Figure 10.2.

The model hypothesises that behaviour is dependent on two main variables: the value an individual places on a particular goal; and the individual's estimation of the likelihood that a given action will achieve that goal. Applied to health, the variables become the desire to avoid illness (or to recover if one is already ill) and the belief that particular conditions can be prevented (or overcome) by specific behaviours (Rutter *et al.*, 1993). Three dimensions are identified that un-

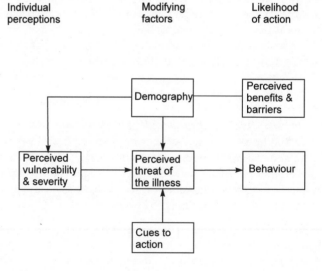

Figure 10.2   The Health Belief Model
Source: Rutter *et al.*, 1993

derlie action: perceived susceptibility or vulnerability; perceived severity; and perceived benefits and barriers. Thus, 'health behaviours' are dependent upon the individual's beliefs about their own risk of, say, acquiring a particular illness, what the implications would be if they did succumb to the illness, and an analysis of what costs versus benefits would accrue, if some action was taken now. 'Cues to action' are also hypothesised to play a key role in alerting the individual to the possible need for some health-related behaviour. For example, the development of illness symptoms or mass media campaigns or significant others identifying a potential problem could all act as cues for the person to consider action, based on their health beliefs.

The importance of the Health Belief Model in the context of the current research programme and Wallander et al.'s (1989b) conceptual model is that it draws attention to the role of beliefs in mediating health-related behaviours, and therefore adaptation. The Health Belief Model highlights the fact that parents are not passive recipients in the process of adjustment, but rather that health outcomes are influenced by their own perceptions of, for example, the cause of disease, what influence they can exert over it and what barriers to effective action are in place.

With reference to the study on the long- term effects of liver disease, it was hypothesised that mothers are unlikely to seek mental health services if they perceive the underlying cause of their child's behavioural problems as being liver disease, as they might feel little benefit would result. This raises the wider issue of the potential relationship between parents'and children's theories of illness and their adaptation.

Leventhal *et al.*'s (1982) self-regulation processing system

Leventhal *et al.* (1982) have proposed a theory that attempts to explain the information-processing mechanisms involved in the way patients perceive and respond to bodily complaints. Underlying this model is the notion that patients develop theories as to the nature of their illness, and acquire representations or 'scripts'as to disease symptomatology and treatment. According to Leventhal *et al.*:

> When individuals notice a bodily sensation or a change in mood or behaviour, they may believe it represents some malfunction or illness. These events are observed and interpreted by comparing them with one's own personal history and other people's past experience. From a series of such events an individual constructs a

representation of the illness episode or problem and then creates a coping plan which may or may not include formal medical treatment. This illness representation reflects the operation of an underlying information-processing mechanism, designed to regulate the individuals' relationship to environmental events.

(Leventhal *et al.*, 1982: 56)

Within this model, coping behaviours are seen as the culmination of interpretation, planning and appraisal, all of which are influenced by the patient's theory of illness and its associated behaviours. According to Leventhal *et al.* (1982), theories are developed over time and are the result of feedback loops which successively provide templates to which experiences can be compared. Under this paradigm, the individual searches for physical symptoms to make sense of illness labels and labels symptoms on the basis of expectations.

There is evidence from both the adult and child literature concerning the notion of illness scripts. For example, Fordyce (1976) has highlighted how dysfunctional cognitions concerning pain can become reinforced over time by the hospital and family, to the detriment of the patient's adjustment. Work by Nelson (1986) has demonstrated also that even young children develop scripts concerning illness, its treatment and how to respond. Furthermore, attending to the cognitive and affective aspects of communications, and linking these to the individual's health beliefs, has been found to have a significant impact on patient's subsequent health-related behaviour (Ley, 1988; Janz and Becker, 1984).

The importance of the above model for Wallander *et al.*'s (1989b) theory of adaptation and the current research programme is that it highlights the crucial role of practitioner communications in influencing coping. Firstly, adjustment can be hampered if inappropriate or insufficient information is made available, as patients will be reliant on their own formulations as to what is going on, which might be different from the reality. Secondly, patients with 'inappropriate' scripts concerning the illness episode, its treatment and how to cope with it could have such scripts reinforced if communications fail to challenge the underlying beliefs and expectations. For example, a patient in chronic pain might believe that their condition was incurable, and that their life-style should therefore reflect this, when in fact the illness need not be so devastating and may have only a limited impact on the person's quality of life.

Thus, adjustment does not appear to be solely the function of an individual's stress-processing abilities, as proposed by Wallander *et al.*

(1989b), but rather the result of how these abilities combine with the scripts already held, in conjunction with the hospital system and the way in which illness symptoms are responded to by staff.

SUMMARY, INTEGRATION AND IMPLICATIONS

I have suggested some ways in which current theories of adjustment could be developed to take into account the wider literature from health psychology and systemic therapy. The results from my research highlight four influences on adjustment (see Figure 10.3): family interaction, patterns of communication, the ward and general health care environment and health beliefs.

I believe there are a number of theories that underpin these influences, namely: Minuchin *et al.*'s (1975) model of family functioning, Korsch *et al.* (1968) and Ley's (1988) models of doctor–patient communication, Menzies Lyth's (1988) notions of systems developing defences and Rosenstock (1974) and Leventhal *et al.*'s (1982) theories of how health beliefs develop and impact on adjustment.

By focusing on these aspects, I do not wish to imply that other factors might not be of equal or even greater importance (such as social supports, the child's self-concept, self-efficacy and cognitive development); it is simply that they have not been directly addressed in this research programme. In the model detailed in Figure 10.3, the variables identified all have the potential to interact with each other, rather than operating in isolation. For example, poor child adjustment could be the result of poor family functioning, where patterns of interaction become reinforced by a hospital system which fails to respond to the emotional needs of the family. This could be the result of communication problems between the family and the health care system, which in turn might be related to illness scripts and beliefs. Underlying this could be influences exerted by significant others in the family's social support network or by coping resources available.

In the context of Wallander *et al.*'s (1989b) theory of adaptation it seems that if we are to develop an adequate conceptual model then we need to broaden our horizon from simply identifying risk and resilience factors (the 'shopping list' approach I referred to earlier) to developing a multi-level approach that understands the child, the family and the wider care system and how they inter-relate and impact upon each other. We also need to move away from defining adjustment purely in terms of the absence of pathology. There are several ways that adjustment could be operationalised. As Pless and Pinkerton (1975)

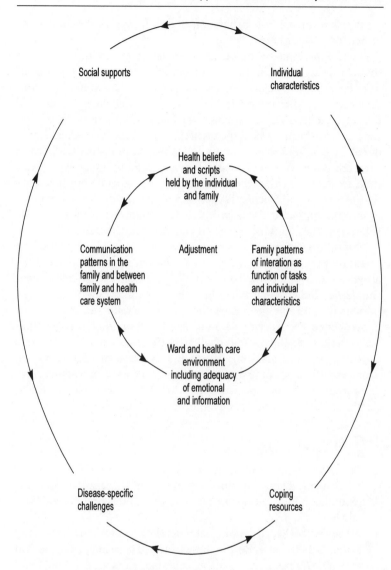

Figure 10.3   A model of risk factors involved in adjustment to chronic childhood disease

have discussed, adjustment is a difficult concept to define and within the literature it has been used variously in the research to indicate: a lack of pathology, the child achieving developmentally appropriate tasks, a lack of sick role behaviour, or acceptance of the limitations imposed by the disease.

I believe there may be some merit in defining adjustment in relation to the behaviours that a child and his or her family show in coping with illness. If we do this, the focus of attention shifts to the way in which children and others behave in relation to the specific challenges presented by their condition. These challenges might include dealing with pain, incapacitation (both physical and mental), distress during medical procedures, developing and maintaining adequate relationships with health care staff, compliance with medical advice, maintaining a 'positive' attitude, reintegrating into school and maintaining adequate family functioning (Moos and Shaefer, 1984). As such, the meaning and demands of chronic childhood disease will change as a function of the child's development, the family life-cycle and, possibly, the disease itself.

This approach moves away from the current emphasis within the literature which tends to suggest that 'adaptation' is equivalent to the absence of psychopathology. Equally, it implies that adjustment should be studied longitudinally, rather than at a one-off, arbitrary point in the child's illness. Research activities should be directed, as a consequence, at gathering data on how children and families do behave in relation to the various challenges they face, so that a context is provided for understanding behaviours that become dysfunctional. This would also go some way to answering the issue of whether non-categorical or disease-specific approaches need to be taken in studying the effects and influences of chronic childhood disease.

SUMMARY

- The research programme identifies four key factors that influence adjustment. These are family patterns of interaction, 'doctor–parent' communication, the ward and health care environment and health beliefs.
- A number of theories from health psychology and systems therapy are identified that underpin these factors. These include Minuchin *et al.*'s (1975) model of family functioning, Korsch *et al.* (1968) and Ley's (1988) models of doctor–patient communication, Menzies Lyth's (1988) notions of systems developing defences and Rosenstock (1974) and Leventhal *et al.*'s (1982) theories of how health beliefs develop and impact on adjustment.
- In explaining why Wallander *et al.*'s (1989b) model has not been largely supported, it appears that it fails to pay sufficient attention to

these dimensions and often lacks conceptual and theoretical precision when it discusses the relationship between the risk and resilience factors and their impact on adjustment. Furthermore, Wallander *et al.* have relied extensively upon descriptive pen and paper measures that may not be adequately sensitive to test their model or to tap the issues involved in chronic disease.

- Studies need to adopt approaches that define adjustment in ways other than the absence of pathology. Equally they need to take a more longitudinal perspective and rely more upon observational methodologies.

Chapter 11

An overview

INTRODUCTION

In this final chapter, I want to pull together what I see as being the key themes that have run through the book. I will start with the studies and then move on to explore how the themes identified relate to clinical practice by highlighting key issues in the development of paediatric services. Returning full circle, in the final section of the book I will consider areas for future research.

THEMES IN THE STUDIES

One of the key themes has been the need to rethink how we understand and investigate the psychological effects of chronic disease. As I highlighted in the introduction (pp. 7–10), there has been increasing dissatisfaction with the 'pathology' and 'deficit' models that have been applied to chronic childhood disease, because it has become clear that they do not adequately characterise the way in which most families react to and cope with this challenge. These models have also failed to elucidate the reasons why some children and their families adjust to the challenges presented by chronic illness, whilst others fare less well.

As a consequence, I believe a shift in emphasis is starting to take place, with the pessimistic assumptions of inevitable psychopathology being gradually replaced by a recognition that many families adjust well. This new approach is perhaps best expressed by Perrin and MacLean's (1988) contention that families coping with a chronic childhood disease should not be considered 'deviant', but as ordinary people coping with abnormal circumstances.

A related theme has been the need to develop new models to explain child adjustment to chronic disease. In exploring the theories that have been suggested so far, it became clear that we still have a long way to go. Despite this, models such as Wallander's are to be welcomed as they do represent coherent attempts to explain the available data. The fact that, to date, they have not proved to be as robust as might have been hoped does not mean they have no value. Rather we need to explore ways of making them more reliable and valid by exploring other influences on adjustment and suggesting new ways in which they might work.

A third theme has been to plead for more 'ecologically valid' assessment tools. By this, I mean that we need to recognise that chronic disease does create specific challenges and, as a consequence, we need to develop measures that can address these issues more effectively. Unfortunately, the development of such measures remains a largely neglected area, with the literature still dominated by assessment tools from the broader mental health field. Perhaps this indicates that we still perceive adjustment as being synonymous with the absence of mental health difficulties and, as such, we may need to develop new ways of understanding and defining adjustment before we can start to replace or supplement our current measures.

Allied to the need for more sensitive measures is the desirability of widening the focus from studying the reactions of *either* the child or family, to include the complex inter-relationships between family members. There are many models that could guide such an endeavour and I believe integrating ideas from health psychology and systemic theory holds particular promise in starting to unravel the pathways underlying adjustment. If such an approach was taken up, I believe we might start to develop a more sophisticated, multi-level understanding of the child, their family and the wider care system and how they inter-relate to influence adjustment and health-related behaviours.

In the studies presented a range of childhood conditions were included, from liver disease to congenital heart disease and learning difficulties. In studying such a range of chronic disorders, I have come down on the side of adopting a non-categorical approach to studying the effects of chronic disease. Whilst there is growing support for this approach, it would be wrong to lose sight of some of the unique challenges that can face some children in coping with their disease (for example, transplantation). At a practical level, given that individual illness conditions often occur relatively infrequently, perhaps we need to look at ways of combining disorders in relation to the challenges they present, so that larger samples can be generated.

A final theme has been my desire to challenge the traditional division between academic and applied approaches. For too long, theory and practice have existed as if they were separate entities. It is almost as if there is a gap between the activities of researchers and clinicians, with research programmes frequently not addressing the practical concerns of clinicians, and equally, important research findings failing to be utilised by clinicians to improve their practice. With the conceptual shift in emphasis to investigate the factors that influence outcomes, I believe that researchers and clinicians will need to work more collaboratively, as each becomes more reliant upon the other.

THEORY INTO PRACTICE

Taken as a whole, my studies point to aspects of family interaction, 'doctor–patient' communication, the health care environment and health beliefs as being important influences on adjustment. What are the implications of this for clinical practice?

The need for effective communication

One of the first implications is the need to ensure adequate communication between healthcare staff and child patients and their families. It goes without saying that children and their families benefit from sensitively provided information, coupled with the opportunity to clarify concerns and acquire the necessary skills to manage their treatment as independently as possible. However, this is not always achieved, which raises the question of what are the problems or barriers to effective communication?

Stein and Jessop (1985) suggest that chronic illness creates a need for skill in providing on-going 'care' rather than 'cure'. They argue that this presents specific challenges because the training that medical personnel receive emphasises the biomedical needs of child patients in relation to specific diagnoses, as opposed to their emotional needs and the commonality of these needs across diagnostic conditions. A related point is made by Stabler (1988) who argues that medical training focuses upon what she terms 'divergent problem solving skills' which seek to reduce the patients' presenting problem to its constituent elements. Such training can result in consultations becoming a fact-finding activity (Winefield, 1992), which may have the unfortunate effect of inhibiting families from raising emotional concerns or problems. According to Waitzkin (1989), doctors and others regulate interactions with patients by using questions, interruptions and topic changes, in order to shift the patient away from psychosocial sources of distress. Pantell *et al.* (1982) have similarly illustrated that paediatricians rarely conversed directly with their child patients, preferring instead to rely on parental accounts.

Difficulties in doctor–patient communication are not uncommon, therefore. As I discussed in Chapters 4, 5 and 6, parents often felt that they were unable to raise certain issues and that these concerns often persisted for considerable lengths of time. The implication appears to be that we need to set up training to improve communication skills and provide more generally based education to reinforce the type of challenges that children and families face, and the problems that can result.

Whilst the above is undoubtedly necessary, it is unlikely to be all that is required. For example, Maguire *et al.* (1986a; 1986b) investigated the effect of a 'communication skills training programme' on junior doctors' interviewing skills. They found that doctors schooled in interviewing were indeed better than their untutored peers and that these doctors maintained their superiority over conventionally trained doctors at five years follow-up. Despite this, the 'trained' doctors still performed poorly in using open questions, asking about the psychosocial impact of health problems, providing adequate information, and often failed to discover the patient's own views, expectations and responses to the treatment plan or to mention prognosis. This example highlights the danger of introducing changes that do not take into account the environment or context where the training is to be used. If work practices militate against, or neutralise, the use of newly acquired skills, clearly the solution is not simply to offer more training.

It is of note that the majority of communication programmes are designed for junior medical staff and are viewed as a supplement to their medical training. The challenge, therefore, is how best to transfer these programmes on to a ward and how to develop an atmosphere whereby all staff, not solely the most junior, see effective communication with families as being a key task and responsibility, which all share jointly. Consultants as well as nursing and other staff should ideally be involved in developing skills to provide what has been called 'the patient centred consultation' (Winefield, 1992). At a pragmatic level, it may be necessary to see the solution as one that evolves over a period of time. Georgiades and Phillimore (1975) have warned of the danger to the 'hero innovator', in believing that cultural changes can be introduced quickly. It is more realistic to see improvements in doctor–patient communication occurring in a piecemeal fashion, with doctors and others being encouraged to become more involved in the issues on a case-by-case basis. The setting up of 'psychosocial' ward rounds, so called 'heartsink' meetings, case conferences, seminars, teaching events and joint cases are all ways in which communication can be put on to the agenda. In a similar vein, the auditing of parents' perceptions of the adequacy of information and emotional support can provide important feedback to all involved as to their effectiveness, and elucidating the links between psychological and medical outcomes can encourage a more unified approach. These issues were explored in some depth in Chapters 4, 5 and 7.

Counselling and support

A second major clinical theme to arise from the studies is the need for counselling and support. Counselling can be defined as:

> any situation in which there is mutual agreement that one person should interact with another in an attempt to help... by listening to and communicating with the person, it also has the more general intention of attempting to make people feel good about themselves.
>
> (Davis, 1993: 3)

Providing the right emotional atmosphere for children and their families to raise worries, emotional problems and the like is clearly an essential ingredient in promoting patterns of adjustment. The fact that it is a prerequisite for effective care (Pot-Mees, 1989) raises the important issues of who should provide it, to whom, how and when. Where a lack of clarity does exist this can set the scene for inter-professional rivalries and fragmented services, as was explored in Chapters 6 and 8.

With reference to counselling families, there is often a lack of agreement as to whether this should be provided by the doctor, nurse or other member of the team. For example, some writers have advocated that the physician should be the primary resource for emotional support for the family (Pless and Pinkerton, 1975). Mattsson and Gross (1966) call for the 'continuous reassuring support of the paediatrician' (quoted in Pless and Pinkerton, 1975: 203) as being essential for the emotional and social adaptation of their child patients. In a similar vein, Spencer and Behar (1969) see the paediatrician as someone who provides 'a strong authoritative, but accepting figure' (quoted in Pless and Pinkerton, 1975: 203), whilst Battle (1972) advocates the paediatrician's role as being similar to that of an 'ombudsman', who advises, counsels and organises services, whilst at the same time helps the family to understand and accept a treatment plan. Holdaway (1972), in recognising that chronic illness commonly presents a complex picture of physical, social and educational problems, asks rhetorically: 'who other than the doctor is better placed to grasp their full implications?' (quoted in Pless and Pinkerton, 1975: 203).

Budetti (1981), on the other hand, suggests that doctors have little specific training in counselling and the coordination of care and queries whether it should be their role. Nuckolls (1981) considers that nurses are ideally placed to take on the task, whilst Bergman *et al.* (1979) and Lowit (1973) vote for the social worker as being the most appropriate professional. Psychologists have similarly seen themselves as taking a key role. Brantley *et al.* (1981: 232) believe that psychologists play a useful intermediary role between physician and family, as 'families do not expect their physician to offer suggestions and advice around problems of living with disease'.

The above highlights, on the one hand, that there is potential for professional rivalry, and on the other, that there is no one professional group who can lay claim to a unique role in counselling families. Indeed, this latter state of affairs is highly desirable as it is the role of all professionals to respond sensitively and skilfully to the emotional needs of children and their families. In many ways it is less important who provides the support, as long as there is a recognised system set up for identifying those children and families 'in need', so that the appropriate help can be mobilised. Issues around screening for psychological problems were explored in Chapters 3, 4 and 5.

Mental health services and chronic illness

Whilst support can be provided by any member in the team, interventions in respect of specific psychological difficulties should be provided by the appropriately trained professional. Given that children with a chronic disease experience between one-and-a-half to three times the rate of emotional and behavioural problems in comparison to their healthy peers (Pless, 1984), it might be expected that mental health services for these children and their carers would be flourishing and in great demand. This does not appear to be the case, however. For example, Cadman *et al.* (1987) found that most children with emotional difficulties who also had a chronic disease failed to receive the help they needed. Three-quarters of the children who had a psychiatric disorder failed to access appropriate mental health services, despite the fact that a large majority were under the care of their physician.

These findings raise a number of questions. Do children fail to receive appropriate help due to the paediatrician failing to identify the problem, or is it the result of families not raising the concern in the first place? Alternatively, are the problems identified but families fail to take up the referral to mental health services, possibly due to the stigma attached, or is it all the result of those services not being available in any case?

Garrison and McQuiston (1989) argue that most parents do want help and that the blame for non-referral lies squarely at the door of the medical profession who act as gatekeepers to other services, and who may judge referral on as unnecessary. Others have suggested that families of children with physical disorders may not place nearly so much value on good mental health of their children as professionals do. Cadman *et al.* (1984) argue that there is commonly a conflict of values between the family and physician that results in families failing to take up services offered. Families may resent the idea that they are 'not coping' and see the possibility of being referred on to a mental health professional as a sign of criticism, blame or failure. Certainly it is important to explore parental attributions and health beliefs as part of the process of developing a working alliance with the family.

Stein and Jessop (1985) have discussed the problems that can occur in engaging families:

> Chronic illness lowers self-esteem and isolates a family, as parents' guilt and self-blame over producing a child who is not 'perfect' interact with the negative reactions of others. There may be social isolation because of practical difficulties in handling the child's condition or because a family's need to protect itself and the child from the outside world. These experiences can lead to defensiveness, hostility and anger, or alternatively, to great passivity on the part of the family. In either case, the consequences can make it extremely difficult for the health care provider to engage in a meaningful reciprocal relationship with the family.
>
> (Stein and Jessop, 1985: 390)

As to whether psychological and psychiatric services are available, Drotar and Bush (1985) make the point that accessing mental health services is complicated by the fact that most children live in communities distant from where their physical care is based. This can create difficulties because families may not be able to get to services at the hospital because of the distances involved, and equally may not feel that local provision is adequate, because support workers may not have sufficient experience or knowledge to deal with the particular issues created by their child's disease. Thus they fall down the gap in service provision.

I feel that there is no single reason why families commonly fail to receive the level of help that might be of benefit to them. Engaging families entails skill and time on the part of the primary care team or the specialist involved in the child's care. Paediatricians and others need to be aware of the common issues faced by families in coping with a chronically sick child. Equally, they need to be competent in identifying and eliciting the families' worries, and to know when to refer on. In doing so, families need to be engaged in the process so that they feel actively involved, rather than passive recipients. Admissions to hospital often entail a loss of personal control, because the hospital takes over and life starts to revolve increasingly around the routines and expectations of the system. For some families, being referred to see another health care worker can feel like yet another violation of personal autonomy. If this is to be avoided, or at least minimised, referrals need to be handled sensitively, and to involve the families' active agreement so that a partnership develops between the child/family and the hospital system. Ways in which this might be achieved were explored in Chapters 4, 5, 7 and 8.

Of course, the opposite problem can occur when staff over-zealously identify cases, when in fact an effective intervention might be to provide the child with additional stability through the reliable presence of family or hospital staff. Alternatively, the professionals' own work-related stress can lead to counterproductive labelling of a highly stressed, but mentally healthy child as emotionally disturbed. Helping staff to recognise their own reactions, and how these might colour their appraisal of the child and family, could well be more productive than taking the referral on. Issues relating to the need to develop effective working alliances with both medical and nursing teams, as well as the child and family, are clearly central.

Effective paediatric liaison

One way in which the emotional needs of children and families can be identified and met is through paediatric liaison activities. Collaborative working between medical, nursing, paramedical and mental health professionals requires that a forum is available for the discussion of children and families 'in the round'. The way in which this is approached is commonly through psychosocial ward rounds, case discussions, so called 'heartsink meetings', seminars, journal clubs, grand rounds and research programmes.

I believe that mental health services should not be geared singularly to mental health issues. As most children do not have mental health problems, as defined by formal classification systems (for example the *Diagnostic and Statistical Manual of Mental Disorders*, 4th ed.) it is clearly inappropriate to limit the focus to these issues. This raises the important point as to whether evaluations of children's adjustment should be approached with mental health and psychiatric nosologies in mind. There is an argument for suggesting that equating adjustment to mental health outcomes is unnecessarily restricting.

The implication of this is that it is essential that the traditional approach to treating the 'mind' and 'body' as two separate entities is replaced by a recognition that in all physical complaints there is a psychological consequence. The task is to identify those children and families where psychological aspects represent either a major contributory cause in the genesis of bodily complaints, or where psychological reactions significantly influence the course of the disease process. Equally, in seeking to blur the distinction between mind and body, psychosocial outcomes should be integrated with medical outcomes so that the evaluation of services addresses both aspects – an issue that was emphasised in all the studies.

Medical, nursing and other professionals need to be aware of the potential impact of individual differences, as well as family and ward dynamics on disease processes. It is important that the recognition of risk factors, however, does not lead to labelling of families. For example, the constellation of family patterns identified by Minuchin *et al.* (1975) are not in themselves 'pathological'; there is evidence to suggest that these styles of interaction are common when families are confronted by a crisis, and to that extent are 'normal' (Kazac, 1989; Minuchin *et al.*, 1975; Valesco De Parra *et al.*, 1973). Indeed, the point was made in Chapters 5, 6 and 7 that under certain conditions, for example the need to keep a child emotionally stable and free from infection, the patterns of family interaction described by Minuchin *et al.* (1975) might well be highly adaptive.

It is important, therefore, for the clinician or researcher not to jump to premature diagnostic conclusions as to the impact and role of family dynamics in the child's adjustment to chronic disease. What can be said at this stage is that, at a conceptual level, a clear distinction needs to be made between aspects of family life that constitute a risk and those that represent protection. Minuchin *et al.*'s (1975) model provides an important starting point from which a typology of family interaction can be developed.

Achieving effective paediatric liaison in meeting the needs of children and families can be a long-term process owing to a number of barriers (Roberts, 1986; Stabler, 1988). Firstly, there is the issue of hierarchical and status differences between the professionals involved. This may militate against the medical profession seeking help from others, owing to a belief that they do not have an important contribution to make. Drotar (1983) has referred to this phenomenon as 'the illusion of certainty', that is, the medical profession's belief that as everyone is a 'psychologist', there is no benefit to be gained by referring on. This situation can become reinforced where only the most 'difficult' or extreme cases are referred on for help, as it may be that intervention will not produce dramatic gains. This then confirms to the referrer their original view that other services have a limited role, and thus families with more ameliorable problems may not be referred on.

A second barrier concerns the way in which problems are thought about by differing personnel. As a result of their training, physicians use a process of 'differential diagnosis', which may well differ from the way others approach a presenting problem. A related point is that the prevailing 'medical model' tends to value 'hard' data and convergent problem-solving skills, whereas services concerned with emotional health frequently operate on the basis of 'soft' data and utilise divergent solutions to problems. This lack of an agreed model can result in problems in identifying and working collaboratively with families.

Thirdly, there are problems over what Roberts (1986) has called 'turf' disputes. These refer to the tensions that can develop when one professional group starts to 'move in' to another's territory. Where resentment or suspicion at the arrival of new disciplines becomes a dominant feature, joint working becomes more difficult and can result in tensions over which profession 'owns' a particular problem and who is best equipped to help the family with their problem.

Finally, collaboration can be made difficult by doctors' prior experiences. Where they have failed to intervene successfully in the emotional problems of their patients, this can serve as a negative reinforcement to working jointly with mental health professionals.

For example, Duff *et al.* (1972) found that junior doctors often picked up on underlying psychological reasons for families seeking medical help, but when they tried to intervene, their advice was largely ineffective. Duff *et al.* (1972) suggest that these frustrations encourage doctors to take on an increasingly medical role, and to pass the case on to others in relation to other concerns. A similar point is made by Stein and Jessop (1988) when they suggested that as chronic conditions are not amenable to short-term solutions, and indeed the problems presented are commonly multi-factorial and complex, this can result in frustration and a sense of impotence, if health care personnel seek rapid and simple solutions. Chapter 8 explored how such difficulties might be overcome.

Psychology services in chronic illness

As a clinical psychologist, I make no apologies for addressing this issue. Whilst you may not be a clinical psychologist, the following may link with concerns that your own discipline is facing. If not, at least it may explain some of the reasons why psychologists act the way they do on the ward or in paediatric teams.

Clinical child psychology is a growing discipline. Where the medical professions' perceptions of paediatric psychologists have been explored, the results tend to suggest that they are seen as offering a rather circumscribed role (for example, Mrazek, 1985), with the emphasis on cognitive assessments and behaviour modification. Equally, psychologists are seen as operating from within a child psychiatry paediatric liaison team, with their activities coordinated by the team leader.

Psychologists themselves have called for a more independent role, with a wider remit (for example, Kazak, 1989; Roberts and Wright, 1982; Roberts, 1986; Stabler, 1988). Stabler and Mesibov (1984), in reviewing the requests they had received from paediatricians, found that the most frequently requested service was diagnostic psychological testing, followed by treatment. Requests for consultations, that is offering advice or an opinion to the doctor without the case being referred (Steinberg, 1988), were rare, and even fewer referrals asked for the psychologist to be involved in community follow-ups, subsequent to the child's discharge from hospital. Charlop *et al.* (1987), in describing their out-patient paediatric psychology service, report that most requests received were for treatment of non-compliance, tantrums and aggression.

The picture that emerges from these surveys is that, in developing new locations for their work, psychologists have nonetheless continued to carry out remarkably similar activities to their traditional roles in child and adolescent mental health clinics. Whilst there is no doubt that the roles of assessment and treatment are important ones to be involved in, it does raise a wider problem of how to improve the wellbeing of children in general, in both the hospital and community, if the focus of psychological activity is limited to those few cases who are referred.

There is an argument to say that the model of service delivery that is developing is inherently flawed. It is recognised that not all children with psychological problems are identified and referred on, and therefore the cases that are seen can represent only an arbitrary tip of the iceberg. It is also established that many children access paediatric hospital services – by 5 years of age, a quarter of British children have been admitted to hospital at least once (Butler, 1980) – and that forms of psychological distress as a result of the illness and its treatment are common reactions (Quinton and Rutter, 1976). In contrast, there are only some 292 full-time equivalent clinical child psychologists employed in the NHS in the United Kingdom (Manpower Planning Advisory Group, 1990), with just over a third (36 per cent) of child psychology departments offering sessions to acute paediatrics (*Child and Adolescent Mental Health Services*, 1995). Clearly, the gap between the level of need and the service available is such that defining child psychology services solely in terms of direct patient assessment and treatment has significant drawbacks.

The tensions between what psychologists are asked to do and what they feel they ought to do is illustrated by the Management Advisory Service Report (1989), which recommended a reconceptualisation of the psychologist's role, away from direct patient work to a more consultative model based on prevention. The challenge is to produce a mix of activity that allows psychology to have as wide an impact as possible, within a context that commonly perceives psychologists as offering circumscribed areas of expertise.

Models are generally lacking as to how this might be achieved, although Chapters 7 and 8 do provide some ideas on how to develop joint working arrangements and consultancy. Stabler (1988) has also considered this problem and outlines three possible ways for widening the scope of psychological presence within paediatrics. She refers to these as: 'resource consultation', 'shared care giving consultation' and 'process-educative consultancy'.

The process in the resource consultant model is akin to a medical consultation, where the doctor in charge of a case requests specific input from a colleague concerning a specific question. For example, referring on for an intelligence test in the context of a child presenting with Down's syndrome is essentially the same as requesting an X-ray to exclude cancer. They share in common a problem-solving activity, where the professional is given an 'expert' role to play. The limitation of this model, however, lies in the fact that the professional is asked to comment only upon the question posed by the referrer, and as a consequence their input is similar to that of a technician: skilled but limited in focus. Stabler (1988) contrasts this with the 'shared care giving consultation' model.

In this model, a dialogue is set up between the family, psychologist and referrer. The psychologist and paediatrician would communicate prior to referral on for a psychological evaluation, thereby allowing proper preparation of the family and clarification of the exact nature of the presenting problem. Thus the psychologist is not 'prescribed' by the doctor, rather the family is involved in decision-making and might be offered a joint appointment with the paediatrician.

The third model Stabler describes, which is more truly consultative, is the process-educative consultation. In this model the paediatrician remains in overall charge of the case, but seeks advice from the psychologist as to how best to tackle a specific issue, without the psychologist necessarily seeing the case.

This kind of liaison is likely to emerge only after close collaboration has already occurred between paediatrician and psychologist. It also demands a level of skill on the paediatrician's part as they have to evolve sufficient psychological knowledge to incorporate suggestions and advice concerning what are likely to be complex psychosocial issues. It also calls for a good deal of trust between the parties involved. The way in which such working arrangements can be enhanced was considered in Chapter 7.

Combined and integrated services

If paediatric liaison and the roles that different professionals play can be sources of tension, developing liaison and shared care between hospitals and the child's local services is even more complex. In order for families to receive the practical help they need, services need to be combined and integrated in such a way that a comprehensive range of support is available and accessible. For this to occur there needs to be good communication between the differing parts of Social, Health and Education Services.

Unfortunately such communication is often lacking, with the result that any one service may be in ignorance as to what the others offer; there is often a difference in perception between hospital and community services as to who should be doing what. For example, Pless *et al.* (1976) found that GPs and hospital specialists had differing views as to who should exercise lead or shared responsibility in the care of children with a variety of chronic conditions. It is interesting to note, however, that the medical profession, whether hospital or community based, was united in its view that mental health services did not have a role to play.

From a consumer's point of view these poor organisational arrangements often result in what appears to be fragmented services. Kanthor (1974), for example, reports that 68 per cent of families with a child with spina bifida felt that neither the specialists nor the primary care team picked up their concerns. This has prompted some clinicians to call for 'community chronic illness support workers' (Perrin, 1985) to bridge the gap between hospital and home-based care.

The issue of how to improve joint working is clearly complex and surprisingly little research is available to guide activities. In the studies reported in Chapter 8, the key dimensions appeared to be: clarifying responsibilities to reduce territorial disputes; seeing children and their families 'in the round', so that single features, such as the child's disease, do not predominate over everything else; encouraging joint ownership of presenting problems so that the tendency to 'pass the buck' is interrupted; and setting up clear lines of communication that are sanctioned and supported by organisations.

These results demonstrate the importance of developing services that respond to need, rather than attempting to fit problems into existing service structures. Children need to have access to services that assess complex problems and develop individual packages of care. An important element within this is acting proactively, rather than waiting for problems to reach such a level that services have to intervene. Such crisis interventions are often less effective than carefully planned and resourced pieces of work. As hospital services continue to devolve to community-based centres, with the primary health care team being given wider responsibilities and powers as a result of the Community Care Act (1990) and Children Act (1989), locally based solutions to presenting difficulties are likely to become more prevalent, with the role of hospital-based services being correspondingly reduced (Kings Fund Centre, 1991).

FUTURE RESEARCH

I have argued already that future research needs to develop measures that are sensitive to the issues faced by children and their families. The tendency to use assessment tools derived from the broader mental health field has severe limitations as they are likely to miss important aspects of the child and family's experience, whilst at the same time potentially over-estimating the difficulties that can occur (Walker et al., 1990).

Disease-specific measures have started to emerge, such as the Functional Disability Inventory (Walker and Greene, 1991), and the Observational Scale of Behavioural Distress (Jay et al., 1983), but it is concerning that their emphasis is on measuring problems, or negative reactions. Surely, we should be developing measures that tap competencies and strengths and not just difficulties? A related point is that measures that are developed need to be compatible with and easily integrated into clinical practice. At the current time we have some interesting measures that are simply too complex and cumbersome to be utilised in busy paediatric wards. As Drotar (1989) and Pless and Nolan (1991) have observed, a balance needs to be struck between scientific rigour and the realities of clinical practice.

I believe that future research should become less concerned with measuring difficulties and more interested in exploring what factors contribute to resilience and successful coping, how children and families do adjust to the challenges they face and the processes that underlie this. In making this shift, conceptual clarity will need to be brought to bear as to what factors constitute a risk and those that are protective. On the basis of the studies reported earlier, the issue of parental and child perceptions of disease and its prognosis needs to be further explored, because beliefs, expectations and appraisals are implicated as important mediating mechanisms in child and family adjustment. Understanding children's health beliefs and scripts are important goals in their own right and it is surprising that this remains a relatively neglected area.

Equally, we need to explore what factors influence a family's ability to solve problems successfully and adjust to the challenges of chronic disease. Ideally, longitudinal approaches should be employed rather than snapshot assessments. Coping should be studied from a developmental perspective, in which the child and family are studied over time, on measures that link behaviours to adaptive life outcomes (Drotar and Bush, 1985). Within this, more attention needs to be directed at the wider care system and how this impacts on child and family adjustment.

The focus of research also needs to be more balanced, with increased attention being paid to children with chronic disease presenting in community and primary care settings. To date there has been an over-emphasis upon hospital care, when in fact most chronically ill children, for most of the time, live at home and access community services. Studies that rely exclusively on hospital-based samples may produce findings that are not applicable to the remainder of ill children, if for no other reason than the mere fact that one group is in hospital whilst the other is not. Applied research in community settings is likely to become more important as the balance of services available shifts more to community settings. This in turn will highlight the need to develop models of service delivery for these children and their families to ensure that optimal care is provided.

What might be the important dimensions of family functioning to explore? A number of models have emerged in the literature that suggest some intriguing avenues (Doherty *et al.*, 1994). Firstly, as already discussed, there is Minuchin *et al.*'s (1975; 1978) formulation, with the important dimensions identified as enmeshment, over-protection, rigidity and poor conflict resolution.

A second area derives from the work of Reiss *et al.* (1986), who argue that family 'coordination' mediates the family's ability to handle serious illness and the resulting relationships with the health care system. Coordination refers to 'the family's level of readiness to experience itself as a single unit, especially in times of stress' (Doherty *et al.*, 1994). This paradigm suggests, therefore, that the extent of family coordination can influence the way in which the challenges created by illness are responded to and, in particular, whether the family becomes organised around health problems.

A third area concerns the dimension of 'expressed emotion'. Evidence from studies of schizophrenia highlights that continuing negative criticism and intrusiveness by a parent towards a mentally ill family member is a strong predictor of relapse and re-hospitalisation after treatment for the illness (Leff and Vaughn, 1985; Vaughn, 1988). Whilst this dimension has been poorly studied in relation to children and families, there is some tentative support for the notion that expressed emotion could be an important factor in understanding the variability in child adjustment to chronic disease.

A fourth avenue concerns the growing number of 'family assessment' measures that have their roots in systems theory. Whilst the majority of these originate from America and Canada, which possibly raises issues of cultural specificity, they are of importance in postulating dimensions of 'healthy' and 'unhealthy' interaction in families. Of particular note are Olson's (1986) Circumplex Model, with its parameters of cohesion, adaptability and marital satisfaction, and The McMaster Model (Epstein *et al.*, 1978), which is based on the assumption that family functioning is related to the accomplishment of essential functions and tasks. It describes seven dimensions that distinguish between healthy and unhealthy families: problem-solving, communication, roles, affective responsiveness, affective involvement and behavioural control, plus general functioning.

The integration of ideas from health psychology and systems theory, in conjunction with these more sophisticated ways of assessing family functioning, will enable future research to extend the existing models of adjustment. I believe the challenge will be to use these ideas to develop a sophisticated multi-level approach that understands the child, the family and the wider care system and how they inter-relate and influence each other.

In conclusion, it is only in integrating psychosocial and medical care and ensuring that hospital and community services are coordinated that children and families can be helped to meet the challenges they face. Collaboration between clinicians and researchers in developing sensitive measures to explore the effectiveness of the interventions offered, and to draw up guidelines for good practice and optimal service delivery, represent major goals for those working in this field. I hope that this book has contributed to the developing debate as to how children and families at risk of adjustment problems might be identified, possible pathways underlying successful adaptation and how services could be organised to promote patterns of adjustment.

SUMMARY

The main points in this chapter can be summarised as follows:
- Paediatric services need to be based on effective communication between health care staff and the family. There are a number of barriers to achieving this and interventions need to ensure that the entire care system develops a model of 'patient-centred care'.

- Counselling and support for children and families is necessary to promote adaptation. Who provides such support is probably less important than making sure a system is in place to ensure that children and families 'in need' are identified.
- Accessing specialist psychological care is often difficult. This results from gatekeepers to referral not identifying concerns, or not acting on what they are told; families' resistance to involvement with mental health professionals and the lack of appropriate services.
- Problems in joint working and engaging families can be reduced if effective paediatric liaison is set up. The differing working styles and orientations of professions need to be acknowledged and skills used to optimum effect. Particular attention needs to be directed at reducing the gap between hospital and community services if families are to avoid fragmented care.
- Future research needs to develop measures sensitive to the issues faced by children and their families and needs to be more focused upon factors that contribute to resilience and successful coping. We need to be developing models that provide a sophisticated multi-level approach to understanding the child, the family and the wider care system and how they inter-relate and influence each other.

References

Achenbach, T. and Edelbrock, C. (1983) *Manual for the Child Behavior Checklist and Revised Behavior Profile*. Burlington, VT: University Associates in Psychiatry.

Ainsworth, M., Blehar, R., Water, E. and Wall, S. (1978) *Patterns of Attachment. A Psychological Study of the Stranger Situation*. Hillsgate, NJ: Lawrence Erlbaum.

Alagille, D., Odievre, M., Gautier, M. and Dommergues, J. (1975) Hepatic ductular dypoplasia associated with characteristic facies, vertebral malformations, retarded physical, mental and sexual development and cardiac murmur. *Journal of Pediatrics.* 86, 63–71.

Anders, T. and Niehans, M. (1982) Promoting the alliance between pediatric and child psychiatry. *Psychiatric Clinics of North America.* 5, 241–258.

Anderson, B., Miller, J., Auslander, W. and Zantiargo, J. (1981) Family characteristics of diabetic adolescents: relationship to metabolic control. *Diabetes Care.* 4, 586–594.

Andrews, W. (1987) Pediatric liver transplantation: the Dallas experience. *Transplant Proceedings.* XIX, 3267–3276.

Audit Commission (1994) *Seen But Not Heard.* London: HMSO.

Azarnoff, P. and Woody, P. (1981) Preparation for children for hospitalisation in acute hospitals in the United States. *Pediatrics.* 68(3) 361–368.

Barbarin, O., Hughes, D. and Chesler, M. (1985) Stress, coping and marital functioning among parents of children with cancer. *Journal of Marriage and the Family.* 47, 473–480.

Battle, C. (1972) The role of the pediatrician as ombudsman in the health care of the young handicapped child. *Pediatrics.* 50, 916–922.

Becker, M., Maiman, L., Kirscht, J. and Haefner, D. (1979) Patient perceptions and compliance: recent studies of the Health Beliefs Model. In R. Haynes, D. Taylor and D. Sackett (eds) *Compliance in Health Care*. London: Johns Hopkins University Press.

Bedell, J., Giordani, D., Amour, J., Tavormina, J. and Boll, T. (1977) Life stress and the psychological and medical adjustments of chronically ill children. *Journal of Psychosomatic Research.* 21, 237–242.

Belloc, N., Breslow, N. and Hochstim, J. (1971) Measurement of physical health in a general population survey. *American Journal of Epidemiology.* 93, 328–336.

Bennett, A. (ed.) (1976) *Communication Between Doctors and Patients*. London: Oxford University Press.

Bentovim, A., Barnes, G. and Cooklin, A. (eds) *Family Therapy, Vol. 2: Complementary Frameworks of Theory and Practice*. London: Grune and Stratton.

Bergman, A., Lewiston, N. and West, A. (1979) Social work practice and chronic pediatric illness. *Social Work in Health Care*. 4, 265–274.

Berkowitz, R. and Leff, J. (1984) Clinical team reflect family dysfunction. *Journal of Family Therapy*. 6, 68–79.

Bernstein, D. (1977) Psychiatric assessment of the adjustment of transplanted children. In R. Simmons, S. Klein and R. Simmons (eds) *Gift of Life: The Social and Psychological Impact of Organ Transplantation*. New York: John Wiley.

Bibace, R. and Walsh, H. (1980) Development of children's concept of illness. *Pediatrics*. 66, 912–917.

Bingley, I., Leonard, J., Hensman, S., Lask, B. and Wolff, O. (1980) Comprehensive management of children on a paediatric ward: a family approach. *Archives of Disease in Childhood*. 55, 555–561.

Blun, R. (ed.) (1984) *Chronic Illness and Disabilities in Childhood and Adolescence*. New York: Grune and Stratton.

Bobrow, E., Adeuskin, T. and Siller, J. (1985) Mother–daughter interaction and adherence to diabetes regimes. *Diabetes Care*. 8, 145–156.

Boutsen, A. and Gilbert, A. (1987) Costs of liver transplantation: financing and social aspects. *Transplant Proceedings*. XIX, 3363–3366.

Bowlby, J. (1971) *Attachment and Loss. Vol. 1*. London: Penguin.

Boyle, C. (1970) Differences between patient's and doctor's interpretations of common medical terms. *British Medical Journal*. 286–289.

Bradford, R. (1986) *The Identification, Description and Prediction of Child Distress During a Non-invasive Medical Procedure*. Unpublished thesis submitted in partial fulfilment of the British Psychological Society's Diploma in Clinical Psychology. Leicester.

—— (1990a) The importance of psychosocial factors in understanding child distress during routine X-ray procedures. *Journal of Child Psychology and Psychiatry*. 31(6) 973–982.

—— (1990b) Parents' experiences of the care provided by medical services whilst looking after chronically ill children. *Early Child Development and Care*. 59, 43–51.

—— (1991a) Staff accuracy in predicting the concerns of parents of chronically ill children. *Child: Care, Health and Development*. 17, 39–47.

—— (1991b) Children's psychological health status – the impact of liver transplantation: a review. *Journal of the Royal Society of Medicine*. 84, 550–553.

—— (1993) Promoting inter-agency collaboration in child services. *Child: Care, Health and Development*. 19, 355–367.

—— (1994a) Children with liver disease: maternal reports of their adjustment and the influence of disease severity on outcomes. *Child: Care, Health and Development*. 20, 393–407.

—— (1994b) Setting up an inter-agency assessment and treatment centre for children 'in need'. *Clinical Psychology Forum*. 63, 32–35.

Bradford, R. and Singer, J. (1991) Support and information for parents. *Paediatric Nursing*. May, 18–20.

Bradford, R. and Spinks, P. (1992) Child distress during hospitalisation: implications for practice. *Journal of Clinical Otolaryngology.* 17, 130–135.

Bradford, R. and Tomlinson, L. (1990) Psychological guidelines in the management of paediatric organ transplantation. *Archives of Disease in Childhood.* 65, 1000–1003.

Brantley, H., Stabler, B. and Whitt, J. (1981) Programme considerations in comprehensive care of chronically ill children. *Journal of Pediatric Psychology.* 6, 229–238.

Breslau, N., Salkever, D. and Staruch, K. (1982) Woman's labour force activity and responsibility for disabled dependants. *Journal of Health and Social Behaviour.* 67, 344–353.

Breslau, N., Weitzman, M. and Messenger, K. (1981) Psychological functioning of siblings of disabled children. *Pediatrics.* 67, 344–353.

Bridges, K. and Goldberg, D. (1984) Psychiatric illness in in-patients with neurological disorders: patients' views on discussion of emotional problems with neurologists. *British Medical Journal.* 289, 656–658.

Brookes, A. (1983) A survey of children treated for 5 years or more by dialysis or transplantation to determine the quality of life in long-term survivors of chronic renal failure. *Journal of Child Psychology and Psychiatry Newsletter.* 7–12.

Budetti, P. (1981) Child health professionals: supply, training and practice. In Select Panel for the Promotion of Child Health, *Better Health for our Children: A National Strategy. Vol. 4.* Department of Health and Human Services. Publication no. 79–55071. Washington DC: US Government Printing Office.

Burgess, D., Martin, H. and Lilly, J. (1982) The developmental status of children undergoing the Kasai procedure for biliary atresia. *Pediatrics.* 70, 624–629.

Burnstein, A. and Meichenbaum, D. (1979) The work of worrying in children undergoing surgery. *Journal of Abnormal Child Psychology.* 7, 121–132.

Bush, J., Melamed, B., Sheras, P. and Greenbaum, P. (1986) Mother–child patterns of coping with anticipatory medical stress. *Health Psychology.* 5(2) 137–157.

Butler, N. (1980) Child health and education in the seventies: some results on the 5-year follow-up of the 1970 British birth cohort. *Health Visitor.* 35, 81–82.

Byng-Hall, J. (1995) *Rewriting Family Scripts.* New York and London: Guilford Press.

Cadman, D., Boyle, N. and Offord, D. (1988) The Ontario Child Health Study: social adjustment and mental health of siblings of children with chronic health problems. *Journal of Developmental and Behavioral Pediatrics.* 9, 117–121.

Cadman, D., Goldsmith, C. and Bashim, P. (1984) Values, preferences and decisions in the care of children with developmental disabilities. *Journal of Developmental and Behavioral Pediatrics.* 5, 60–64.

Cadman, D., Boyle, N., Szatmari, P. and Offord, D. (1987) Chronic illness, disability, and mental and social wellbeing: findings of the Ontario Child Health Study. *Pediatrics* 79, 705–712.

Cadman, D., Rosenbaum, P., Boyle, N. and Offord, D. (1991) Children with chronic illness: family and parent demographic characteristics and psychosocial adjustment. *Pediatrics.* 87, 884–889.

Campbell, D. and Draper, R. (eds) (1985) *Applications of Systemic Family Therapy. The Milan Approach.* New York and London: Grune and Stratton.

Carr, A. and McDonnell, J. (1986) Wilson's disease in an adolescent displaying an adjustment reaction to a series of life stressors: a case study. *Journal of Child Psychology and Psychiatry.* 27, 697–700.

Carter, B. and McGoldrick, M. (1981) *The Family Life Cycle.* New York: Gardner.

Carver, C., Scheier, M. and Weintraub, J. (1989) Assessing coping strategies: a theoretically based approach. *Journal of Personality and Social Psychology.* 56, 267–283.

Cassel, S. and Paul, M. (1967) The role of puppet therapy on the emotional responses to children hospitalised for cardiac catheterisation. *Journal of Pediatrics.* 73, 233–239.

Charlop, M., Parrish, J., Fenton, L. and Cataldo, M. (1987) Evaluation of a hospital-based outpatients pediatric psychology service. *Journal of Pediatric Psychology.* 12(4) 485–503.

Child and Adolescent Mental Health Services: Together We Stand (1995) Health Advisory Service. London: HMSO.

Clarke, G. and Cook, D. (1992) *A Basic Course in Statistics* (3rd edition). London: Edward Arnold.

Colonna, J., Brems, J., Hiatt, J., Millis, J., Amet, M., Quinones, W., Berquist, W., Besbris, D., Britt, J., Goldstein, B., Nuesse, K., Ramming, K., Saleh, S., Vargas, J. and Busuttil, A. (1988) The quality of survival after liver transplantation. *Transplant Proceedings.* XX, 594–597.

Coupey, S. and Cohen, M. (1984) Special consideration for the health care of adolescents with chronic illness. *Pediatric Clinics of North America.* 31(1) 211–219.

Coyne, J. and Anderson, B. (1989) The 'psychosomatic family' reconsidered II: Recalling a defective model and looking ahead. *Journal of Marital and Family Therapy.* 15, 139–148.

Craft, M. (ed.) (1979) *Tredgold's Mental Retardation* (12th edition). London: Balliere Tindall.

Cunningham, C. (1979) Parent counselling. In M. Craft (ed.) *Tredgold's Mental Retardation* (12th edition). London: Balliere Tindall.

Dahlquist, L., Gil, K., Armstrong, D., Delawyer, D., Greene, P. and Wuori, D. (1986) Preparing children for medical examinations: the importance of previous medical experience. *Health Psychology.* 5(3) 249–259.

Dare, J. and Hemsley, R. (1986) Design and evaluation of a questionnaire to identify emotional distress and its causes in parents of children with liver disease. Paper presented at the 58th British Paediatric Association Meeting. York.

David, L. and Goldstein, N. (1974) Psychological investigation of Wilson's disease. *Mayo Clinic Proceedings.* 49, 409–11.

Davis, H. (1993) *Counselling Parents of Children with Chronic Illness or Disability.* Leicester: British Psychological Society Books.

Deisher, R., Engel, W. and Spielholz, R. (1965) Mothers' opinions of their pediatric care. *Pediatrics.* 42, 82–88.

DeMaso, D., Campis, L., Wypij, D., Bertram, S., Lipshitz, M. and Freed, M. (1991) The impact of maternal perceptions and medical severity on the adjustment of children with congenital heart disease. *Journal of Pediatric Psychology.* 16(2) 137–150.

Department of Health (1991) *Welfare of Children and Young People in Hospital.* London: HMSO.

—— (1995) *Child Health in the Community: A Guide to Good Practice.* London: HMSO.

Department of Health and Social Services (1989a) *Working for Patients: The Health Care Service: Caring for the 1990s.* London: HMSO.

—— (1989b) *Caring for People: Community Care in the Next Decade and Beyond.* London: HMSO.

Department of Social Services (1989) *Children Act.* London: HMSO.

De Shazer, S. (1982) *Patterns of Brief Family Therapy. An Ecosystemic Approach.* New York and London: Guilford Press.

Diagnostic and Statistical Manual of Mental Disorders (1994) (4th edition, revised) Washington DC: American Psychiatric Association.

Doherty, W. and Baird, M. (eds) (1987) *Family Therapy and Family Medicine: Towards the Primary Care of Families.* New York and London: Guilford Press.

Doherty, W., McDaniel, S. and Hepworth, J. (1994) Medical Family Therapy: an emerging arena for family therapy. *Journal of Family Therapy.* 16, 31–45.

Donald, C. and Ware, J. (1982) *The Quantification of Social Contacts and Resources.* Rand Health Insurance Experiment Series, R-2937-HHS. Santa Monica CA: Rand Corporation.

Drotar, D. (1983) Transacting with physicians: fact and fiction. *Journal of Pediatric Psychology.* 8, 117–127.

—— (1989) Psychological research in pediatric settings: lessons from the field. *Journal of Pediatric Psychology.* 14, 63–74.

Drotar, D. and Bush, M. (1985) Mental health issues and services. In N. Hobbs and J. Perrin (eds) *Issues in the Care of Children with Chronic Illness.* London: Jossey-Bass.

Drotar, D. and Crawford, P. (1985) Psychological adaptation of siblings of chronically ill children: research and practice implications. *Journal of Developmental and Behavioural Pediatrics.* 6, 355–362.

Drotar, D. and Strum, L. (1988) Parent–practitioner communication in the management of non-organic failure to thrive. *Family Systems Medicine.* 6(3) 304–316.

Drotar, D., Bastiewicz, A., Irvin, N., Kendell, J. and Klaus, M. (1975) The adaptation of parents to the birth of an infant with a congenital malformation: a hypothetical model. *Pediatrics.* 56, 710–717.

Drotar, D., Doershuk, C., Stern, R., Boat, C., Boyer, W. and Matthews, L. (1981) Psychosocial functioning of children with cystic fibrosis. *Pediatrics.* 67, 338–343.

Dubowitz, R. and Hersov, C. (1976) Management of children with non-organic (hysterical) disorders of motor function. Development Medicine and Child Neurology. 18, 358–368.

Duff, R., Rowe, D. and Anderson, F. (1972) Patient care and student learning in a pediatric clinic. *Pediatrics.* 50, 839–846.

Eiser, C. (1990) *Chronic Childhood Disease: An Introduction to Psychological Theory and Research.* Cambridge: Cambridge University Press.

Emede, R. and Brown, C. (1976) Adaptation to the birth of a Down's syndrome infant: grieving and maternal attachment. *Journal of the American Academy of Child Psychiatry.* 17, 299–323.

Epstein, N., Bishop, D. and Levin, S. (1978) The McMaster Model of Family Functioning. *Journal of Marriage and Family Counselling.* 4, 19–31.

Evans, B., Kiellerup, R., Stanley, R., Burrows, G. and Sweet, B. (1987) A communication programme for increasing patients' satisfaction with general practice consultations. *British Journal of Medical Psychology.* 60, 373–378.

Fielding, D. (1985) Chronic illness in children. In F. Watts (ed.) *New Perspectives in Clinical Psychology. Vol. 1.* Leicester: British Psychological Society Books.

Fine, R. (1989) Non-compliance in paediatric patients with chronic renal failure. Paper presented at the 20th Annual Conference of the European Working Group on Psychosocial Aspects of Children with Chronic Renal Failure, Hanover.

Fordyce, W. (1976) *Behavioral Methods for Chronic Pain and Illness.* St Louis: Mosby.

Forrest, G. and Standish, E. (1985) The outcome of supportive psychotherapy for parents after perinatal bereavement. Paper presented at the Royal Society of Medicine Meeting in Edinburgh, April.

Garrison, W. and McQuiston, S. (1989) *Chronic Illness During Childhood and Adolescence: Psychological Aspects.* London: Sage.

Gayton, W., Friedman, S., Tavormina, J. and Tucker, F. (1977) Children with cystic fibrosis. 1. Psychological test findings of patients, siblings and parents. *Pediatrics.* 59, 888–894.

Georgiades, N. and Phillimore, L. (1975) The myth of the hero innovator and alternative strategies for organisational change. In C. Kiernan and F. Woodford (eds) *Behaviour Modification with the Severely Retarded.* London: Associated Scientific Publishers.

Gold, L., Kirkpatrick, B., Fricker, F. and Zitelli, B. (1986) Psychosocial issues in pediatric organ transplantation: the parents' perspective. *Pediatrics.* 77, 738–744.

Goldberg, D. (1972) *The Detection of Psychiatric Illness by Questionnaire.* London: Oxford University Press.

Gortmaker, S. and Zappenfield, W. (1984) Chronic childhood disorders: prevalence and impact. *Pediatric Clinics of North America.* 31(1) 3–18.

Graham, P. (ed.) (1987) *Epidemiological Approaches in Child Psychiatry.* London: Academic Press.

Greenbaum, P., Cook, E., Melamed, B., Abeles, L. and Bush, J. (1988) Sequential patterns of medical stress: maternal agitation and child distress. *Child and Behaviour Therapy.* 10(1) 9–18.

Greenberg, M. and Marvin, R. (1982) Reactions of pre-school children to an adult stranger: a behavioural systems approach. *Child Development.* 53, 481–490.

Gross, A., Stein, R., Levin, R., Dale, J. and Wojnilower, D. (1983) The effect of mother–child separation on the behaviour of children experiencing a diagnostic medical procedure. *Journal of Consulting and Clinical Psychology.* 51, 783–785.

Gustafson, P. and Svedin, C. (1988) Cost effectiveness: family therapy in a pediatric setting. *Family Systems Medicine.* 6, 162–75.

Gustafson, P., Kellman, N., Ludvigsson, J. and Cererbald, M. (1987) Asthma and family interaction. *Archives of Disease in Childhood.* 62, 258–263.

Gyll, C. (1977) *Children and X-rays.* National Association for the Welfare of Children in Hospital Newsletter.

Hall, D. (1992) Child health promotion, screening and surveillance. *Journal of Child Psychology and Psychiatry.* 33(4) 649–658.

Hardman, A., Maguire, G. and Crowther, D. (1989) The recognition of psychiatric morbidity on a medical oncology ward. *Journal of Psychosomatic Research.* 32, 235–240.

Hauser, S., Jacobson, A., Wertlieb, D., Weiss-Perry, B., Follansbee, D., Wolfsdorf, J., Herskowitz, R., Houlihan, J. and Rajapark, D. (1986) Children with recently diagnosed diabetes: interactions within their families. *Health Psychology.* 5, 273–296.

Haynes, R., Taylor, D. and Sackett, D. (eds) (1979) *Compliance in Health Care.* London: Johns Hopkins University Press.

Henning, P., Tomlinson, L., Rigden, S., Haycock, G. and Chatler, C. (1988) Long term outcome of treatment of end-stage renal failure in childhood. *Archives of Disease in Childhood.* 63(1) 35–40.

Hilgard, J. and LeBarron, S. (1984) *Hypnotherapy of Pain in Children with Cancer.* California: William Kaufmann.

Hobbs, N. and Perrin, J. (1985) *Issues in the Care of Children with Chronic Illness.* London: Jossey-Bass.

Hodas, G. and Liebman, R. (1978) Psychosomatic disorders in children: structural family therapy. *Psychosomatics.* 19, 11–21.

Hoffman, L. (1981) *Foundations of Family Therapy: A Conceptual Framework for Systems Change.* New York: Basic Books.

Holdaway, D. (1972) Educating the handicapped child and his parents. *Clinical Pediatrics.* 11, 63.

Honsing, T. (1989) Stories, reflections and miracles: introducing family therapy to in-patient settings. *Family Systems Medicine.* 7, 443–453.

Horowitz, W. and Kazak, A. (1990) Family adaptation to childhood cancer: siblings and family system variables. *Journal of Clinical Child Psychology.* 19, 221–228.

House, R., Dubovsky, S. and Penn, I. (1983) Psychiatric aspects of hepatic transplantation. *Transplantation.* 36, 146–150.

Hyson, M. (1981) Going to the doctor. A developmental study of stress and coping. *Journal of Child Psychology and Psychiatry.* 24(2) 247–259.

Janz, N. and Becker, M. (1984) The health belief model: a decade later. *Health Education Quarterly.* 11, 1–47.

Jay, S. (1988) Invasive medical procedures. Psychological intervention and assessment. In D. Routh (ed.) *Handbook of Pediatric Psychology.* New York: Guilford Press.

Jay, S., Ozolins, M., Elliott, C. and Caldwell, S. (1983) Assessment of children's distress during painful medical procedures. *Health Psychology.* 2, 133–147.

Jay, S., Elliott, C., Ozolins, M., Olson, R. and Pruitt, S. (1985) Behaviour management of children's distress during painful medical procedures. *Behaviour Research and Therapy.* 23(5) 513–520.

Jenkins, S., Bax, M. and Hart, H. (1980) Behaviour problems in preschool children. *Journal of Child Psychology and Psychiatry.* 25(1) 5–17.

John, A. and Bradford, R. (1991) Integrating family therapy into paediatric settings: a model. *Journal of Family Therapy.* 13, 207–223.

Johnson, M. (1982) Recognition of patients' worries by nurses and other patients. *British Journal of Clinical Psychology.* 21, 255–261.

Johnson, R. and Baldwin, D. (1968) Relationship of maternal anxiety to the behaviour of young children undergoing dental extraction. *Journal of Dental Research.* 47, 801–805.

Kanner, A., Coyne, J., Schaefer, C. and Lazarus, R. (1981) Comparisons of two modes of stress measurement: daily hassles and uplifts versus major life events. *Journal of Behavioural Medicine.* 4, 1–39.

Kanthor, H. (1974) Areas of responsibility in the health care of multiply handicapped children. *Pediatrics.* 54, 779–785.

Kaplan, R., Anderson, J. and Wu, A., Mathews, C., Kozin, F. and Orenstein, D. (1989) The quality of well-being scale: applications in AIDS, cystic fibrosis and arthritis. *Medical Care Supplement.* 27(3) 27–43.

Kasai, A. (1959) A new operation for 'non-correctable' biliary atresia: hepato-portoenterostomy. *Shijitsu.* 13, 733–739.

Katz, E., Kellerman, S. and Siegal, S. (1980) Behavioural distress in children undergoing medical procedures: developmental considerations. *Journal of Child Psychology and Psychiatry.* 21, 356–365.

Kavanagh, C. (1983) Psychological intervention with the severely burned child: report on an experimental comparison of two approaches and their effects on psychological sequelae. *Journal of American Academy of Child Psychology.* 22(2) 145–156.

Kazak, A. (1989) Families of chronically ill children: a systems and social-ecological model of adaptation and challenge. *Journal of Consulting and Clinical Psychology.* 57(1) 25–30.

Kellerman, J., Zeltzer, L., Ellenberg, L., Dash, J. and Rigler, D. (1980) Psychological effects of illness in adolescence. 1. Anxiety, self esteem and perception of control. *Journal of Pediatrics.* 97, 126–131.

Kennedy, J. (1970) Maternal reactions to the birth of a defective baby. *Social Casework.* 51, 411–416.

Kiernan, C. and Woodford, F. (eds) (1975) *Behaviour Modification with the Severely Retarded.* London: Associated Scientific Publishers.

Kings Fund Centre (1991) *Hospital at Home: The Coming Revolution.* London: Kings Fund Centre Communications Unit.

Klein, R. (1994) Anxiety disorders. In M. Rutter, E. Taylor and L. Hersov (eds) *Child and Adolescent Psychiatry: Modern Approaches.* Oxford: Blackwell.

Klein, S., Simmonds, R. and Anderson, C. (1984) Chronic kidney disease and transplantation in children and adolescence. In R. Blum (ed.) *Chronic Illness and Disabilities in Childhood and Adolescence.* New York: Grune and Stratton.

Kneher, C. and Bearn, A. (1956) Psychological impairment in Wilson's disease. *Journal of Nervous & Mental Diseases.* 124, 251–255.

Knowles, H. (1971) Diabetis Mellitus in childhood and adolescence. *Medical Clinics of North America.* 55, 1007.

Koocher, G. and O'Malley, J. (1981) *The Damocles Syndrome: Psychological Consequences of Surviving Childhood Cancer.* New York: McGraw-Hill.

Koocher, P., O'Malley, J., Cogan, J. and Foster, D. (1980) Psychological adjustment among pediatric cancer survivors. *Journal of Child Psychology and Psychiatry.* 21, 163–173.

Korsch, B. and Negrete, V. (1972) Doctor–patient communication. *Scientific American.* August, 66–73.

Korsch, B., Gozzi, E. and Francis, V. (1968) Gaps in doctor–patient communication. 1: Doctor–patient interaction and patient satisfaction. *Pediatrics.* 42, 855–871.

Korsch, B., Negrete, V. and Garcher, J. (1973) Kidney transplantation in children: psychosocial follow-up study on child and family. *Journal of Pediatrics.* 83, 399–408.

Korsch, B., Fine, R., Grushkin, G. and Negrete, V. (1971) Experiences with children and their families during extended haemodialysis and kidney transplantation. *Pediatric Clinics of North America.* 18, 625–637.

Kramer, H., Awiszus, D., Sterzel, U., Van Halteren, A. and Claben, R. (1989) Development of personality and intelligence in children with congenital heart disease. *Journal of Child Psychology and Psychiatry.* 30(2) 299–308.

Krantz, D., Baum, A. and Wideman, M. (1980) Assessment of preferences for self-treatment and information in health care. *Journal of Personality and Social Psychology.* 39(5) 977–990.

Krener, P. (1987) Psychiatric liaison to liver transplant recipients. *Clinical Pediatrics.* 26, 93–97.

Kroll, L. and Jacobs, B. (1995) Children coping with the death of a sibling. *Journal of the Royal Society of Medicine.* 88, 426–427.

La Greca, A. (1988) Adherence to prescribed medical regimens. In D. Routh (ed.) *Handbook of Pediatric Psychology.* New York: Guilford Press.

Lask, B. (1982) Physical illness and the family. In A. Bentovim, G. Barnes and A. Cooklin (eds) *Family Therapy. Vol. 2: Complementary Frameworks of Theory and Practice.* London: Grune and Stratton.

Lavigne, J. and Faier-Routman, J. (1982) Psychological adjustment to pediatric physical disorders: a meta-analytic review. *Journal of Pediatric Psychology.* 17(2) 133–158.

Lazarus, R. and Folkman, S. (1984) *Stress, Appraisal and Coping.* New York: Springer-Verlag.

Leff, J. and Vaughn, C. (1985) *Expressed Emotion in Families: Its Significance for Mental Illness.* New York: Guilford Press.

Leventhal, H., Nerenz, D. and Straus, A. (1982) Self regulation and the mechanisms for symptom appraisal. In D. Mechanic (ed.) *Symptoms, Illness Behavior and Help-seeking.* New York: Watson.

Lewis, C., Pantell, R. and Kieckhefer, G. (1989) Assessment of Children's Health Status: Field test of new approaches. *Medical Care.* 27(3) 54–65.

Ley, P. (1988) *Communicating with Patients: Improving Communication, Satisfaction and Compliance.* London: Chapman & Hall.

Linde, M., Rasof, B., Dunn, O. and Rabb, E. (1966) Attitudinal factors in congenital heart disease. *Pediatrics.* 38, 92–101.

Lipowski, Z. (1970) Physical illness, the individual and the coping process. *Psychiatry in Medicine.* 1, 91–98.

Lowit, I. (1973) Social and psychological consequences of chronic illness in children. *Developmental Medicine and Child Neurology.* 15, 71.

McAnarney, E., Pless, J., Satterwhite, B. and Friedman, S. (1974) Psychological problems of children with chronic juvenile arthritis. *Pediatrics.* 53, 523–528.

McClement, J., Howard, E. and Mowat, A. (1985) Results of surgical treatment for extra hepatic biliary atresia in the United Kingdom 1980–82. *British Medical Journal.* 290, 345–347.

MacLean, W., Perrin, J., Gortmaker, S. and Pierre, C. (1992) Psychological adjustment of children with asthma: effects of illness severity and recent stressful life events. *Journal of Pediatric Psychology.* 17(2) 159–172.

Maes, S., Leventhal, H. and Johnston, M. (eds) (1992) *International Review of Health. Vol. 1.* Chichester: John Wiley.

Magrab, P. and Jacobstein, D. (1984) Adolescents coping with renal disease and haemodialysis. *Dialysis and Transplantation.* 13, 151–155.

Maguire, P. (1984) Communication skills. In A. Steptoe and A. Matthews (eds) *Healthcare and Human Behaviour.* London: Academic Press.

Maguire, P. and Rutter, D. (1976) Training medical students to communicate. In A. Bennett (ed.) *Communication Between Doctors and Patients.* London: Oxford University Press.

Maguire, P. Fairbairn, S. and Fletcher, C. (1986a) Consultation skills of young doctors: 1. Benefits of feedback training in interviewing as students persist. *British Medical Journal.* 292, 1573–1576.

—— (1986b) Consultation skills of young doctors: 2. Most young doctors are bad at giving information. *British Medical Journal.* 292, 1576–1578.

Maguire, P., Julier, D., Hawton, K. and Bancroft, J., (1974) Psychiatric morbidity and referral on two general medical wards. *British Medical Journal.* 267(1) 268–270.

Main, M. (1973) *Exploration, Play and Cognitive Functioning as Related to Child–Mother Attachment.* Unpublished doctoral thesis. Johns Hopkins University.

Management Advisory Service Report to the NHS (1990) *National Review of Clinical Psychology Services. Report Digest.*

Manpower Planning Advisory Group (1990) *Report on the MPAG Project on Clinical Psychology.* London: Department of Health.

Mattsson, A. (1972) Long term physical illness in childhood: a challenge to psychosocial adaptation. *Pediatrics.* 50, 801–811.

Mattsson, A. and Gross, S. (1966) Adaptational and defensive behavior in young hemophiliacs and their parents. *American Journal of Psychiatry.* 122, 1349.

Mayou, R., Hawton, K. and Feldman, E. (1988) What happens to medical patients with psychiatric disorder? *Journal of Psychosomatic Research.* 32(4) 541–549.

Mechanic, D. (ed.) (1982) *Symptoms, Illness Behavior and Help-seeking.* New York: Watson.

Melamed, B. and Ridley-Johnson, R. (1988) Psychological preparation of families for hospitalisation. *Journal of Developmental and Behavioural Pediatrics.* 9, 96–102.

Melamed, B. and Seigel, L. (1975) Reduction of anxiety in children facing hospitalisation and surgery by use of filmed modelling. *Journal of Consulting and Clinical Psychology.* 43, 511–521.

Menzies Lyth, I. (1988) *Containing Anxiety in Institutions: Selected Essays.* London: Free Association Books.

Miles, C. and Carter, C. (1982) Sources of parental stress in paediatric intensive care units. *Child Health Care.* 11(2) 65–69.

Minuchin, S. and Fishman, H. (1981) *Family Therapy Techniques.* Cambridge MA: Harvard University Press.

Minuchin, S., Rosman, B. and Baker, L. (1978) *Psychosomatic Families: Anorexia Nervosa in Context.* Cambridge MA: Harvard University Press.

Minuchin, S., Baker, L., Rosman, B., Leibman, R., Milman, L. and Todd, T. (1975) A conceptual model of psychosomatic illness in children. *Archives of General Psychiatry.* 32, 1031–1038.

Moos, R. and Moos, B. (1981) *Family Environment Scale.* Palo Alto CA: Consulting Psychologists Press.

Moos, R. and Shaefer, J. (1984) *Coping with Physical Illness. 2. New Perspectives.* New York: Plenum.

Mowat, A. (1987) *Liver Disorders in Childhood.* London: Butterworth.

Mrazek, D. (1985) Child psychiatric consultant and liaison to paediatrics. In M. Rutter, E. Taylor, and L. Hersov (eds) *Child and Adolescent Psychiatry: Modern Approaches* (2nd edition). Oxford: Blackwell.

Mulhern, R., Wasserman, A., Friedman, A. and Fairclough, D. (1989) Social competence and behavioral adjustment of children who are long-term survivors of cancer. *Pediatrics.* 83, 18–25.

Mullins, L., Olsen, R., Reyes, S., Bernardy, D., Huszti, C. and Volk, R. (1991) Risk and resistance factors in the adaptation of mothers of children with cystic fibrosis. *Journal of Pediatric Psychology.* 16(6) 701–716.

Munson, S. (1986) Family orientated consultation in paediatrics. In L. Wynne, S. McDaniel and T. Webber (eds) *Systems Consultation: A New Perspective for Family Therapy.* London: Guilford Press.

Murray, J. and Callan, V. (1988) Predicting adjustment to perinatal death. *British Journal of Medical Psychology.* 61, 237–244.

Nelson, K. (1986) *Event Knowledge: Structure and Function in Development.* New York: Lawrence Erlbaum.

Nichols, K. (1985) Psychological care by nurses, paramedical and medical staff: essential developments for the general hospitals. *British Journal of Medical Psychology.* 58, 231–240.

Nitzberg, L., Pattern, J., Speilman, M. and Brown, R. (1985) In-patient hospital systemic consultation: providing team systemic consultation in in-patient settings where the team is part of the system. In D. Campbell and R. Draper (eds) *Applications of Systemic Family Therapy. The Milan Approach.* New York and London: Grune and Stratton.

Nuckolls, K. (1981) Nursing. In Select Panel for the Promotion of Child Health, *Better Health for our Children: A National Strategy. Vol. 4.* Department of Health and Human Services. Publication No. 79-55071. Washington DC: US Government Printing Office.

Nugent, G. (1987) Parental understanding of congenital hip dislocation. *Nursing Times.* 83, 28–31.

Olshansky, S. (1962) Parent response to having a mentally defective child. *Social Casework.* 43, 190–193.

Olson, D. (1986) Circumplex Model VII: validation studies and FACES III. *Family Process.* 25, 337–351.

Pantell, R., Stewart, T. and Dias, J. (1982) Physician communication with children and parents. *Pediatrics.* 70, 396–402.

Paradis, K., Freese, D. and Sharp, H. (1988) A pediatric perspective on liver transplantation. *Pediatric Clinics of North America.* 35, 409–433.

Penn, I., Bunch, D., Olenik, D. and Abouna, G. (1971) Psychiatric experience with patients receiving renal and hepatic transplants. *Seminars in Psychiatry.* 3, 133–144.

Perrin, E., Stein, R. and Drotar, D. (1991) Cautions in using the Child Behavior Checklist: observations based on research about children with a chronic illness. *Journal of Pediatric Psychology.* 16, 411–422.

Perrin, J. (1985) Special problems of chronic childhood illness in rural areas. In N. Hobbs and J. Perrin (eds) *Issues in the Care of Children with Chronic Illness.* London: Jossey-Bass.

Perrin, J. and MacLean, W. (1988) Children with chronic illness: the prevention of disfunction. *Pediatric Clinics of North America.* 35, 1325–1337.

Perrin, J., Maclean, W. E. and Perrin, E. (1989) Parental perceptions of health status and psychologic adjustmentment of children with asthma. *Pediatrics.* 83(1) 26–31.

Peterson, L. and Toler, S. (1986) An information seeking disposition in child surgery patients. *Health Psychology.* 5(4) 343–358.

Pett, S., Pelham, A., Tizard, J., Barnes, N., Vergani, G., Mowat, A., Williams, R., Rolles, K. and Calne, R. (1987) Paediatric liver transplantation: Cambridge/King's series, December 1983–August 1986. *Transplant Proceedings.* XIX, 3256–3260.

Pettle-Michaels, S. and Lansdown, R. (1986) Adjustment to the death of a sibling. *Archives of Disease in Childhood.* 61, 278–283.

Platt Report (1959) *The Welfare of Children in Hospital.* Ministry of Health-London: HMSO.

Pless, I. (1984) Clinical assessment: physical and psychological functioning. *Pediatric Clinics of North America.* 31(1) 33–46.

Pless, I. and Nolan, T. (1991) Revision, replication and neglect in research on maladjustment in chronic illness. *Journal of Child Psychology and Psychiatry.* 32, 347–365.

Pless, I. and Perrin, J. (1985) Issues common to a variety of illnesses. In N. Hobbs and J. Perrin (eds) *Issues in the Care of Children with Chronic Illness.* London: Jossey-Bass.

Pless, I. and Pinkerton, P. (1975) *Chronic Childhood Disorder – Promoting Patterns of Adjustment.* London: Henry Kimpton.

Pless, I. and Roghmann, K. (1971) Chronic illness and its consequences: observations based on three epidemiological surveys. *Journal of Pediatrics.* 79, 351–359.

Pless, I., Satterwhite, B. and Van Vechten, D. (1976) Chronic illness in childhood: a regional survey of care. *Pediatrics.* 58, 37–45.

Pot-Mees, C. (1989) *The Psychosocial Effects of Bone Marrow Transplantation in Children.* The Netherlands: Eburon.

Quine, L. and Rutter, D. (1994) First diagnosis of severe mental and physical disability: a study of doctor–patient communication. *Journal of Child Psychology and Psychiatry.* 35, 1273–1288.

Quinton, D. and Rutter, m. (1976) Early hospital admissions and later disturbances of behaviour: an attempted replication of Douglas' findings. *Developmental Medicine and Child Neurology.* 18, 447–459.

Raphael, B. (1984) *The Anatomy of Bereavement: A Handbook for the Caring Professions.* London: Unwin Hyman.

Reddihough, D., Landau, L., Jones, J. and Rickards, W. (1977) Family anxieties in childhood asthma. *Australian Paediatric Journal.* 13, 295–298.

Reiss, D. Gonzalez, S. and Kramer, N. (1986) Family process, chronic illness and death: on the weakness of strong bonds. *Archives of General Psychiatry.* 43, 795–804.

Richman, N. (1987) Is a behaviour checklist for preschool children useful? In P. Graham (ed.) *Epidemiological Approaches in Child Psychiatry.* London: Academic Press.

Rigden, S., Ward, G. and Turner, C. (1989) 20 year experience of renal transplantation in children. *Archives of Disease in Childhood.* 64(8) 1215.

Rizzoni, G., Broyer, M., Guest, G., Fine, R. and Holliday, M. (1986) Growth retardation in children with chronic renal disease: scope of the problem. *American Journal of Kidney Disease.* 7(4) 256–261.

Roberts, M. (1986) *Pediatric Psychology.* New York: Pergamon Press.

Roberts, M. and Wright, L. (1982) The role of the paediatric psychologist as consultant to paediatricians. In J. Tuma (ed.) *Handbook for the Practice of Pediatric Psychology.* New York: John Wiley.

—— (1987) The role of the paediatric psychologist as a consultant to paediatricians. In W. Doherty and M. Baird (eds) *Family Therapy and Family Medicine: Towards the Primary Care of Families.* New York and London: Guilford Press.

Robertson, J. (1958) *Young Children in Hospitals.* New York: Basic Books.

Robinson, D. (1968) Parents' satisfaction with in-hospital information about their young children. *Nursing Times.* 165–167.

Robinson, L. (1985) Double bind: a dilemma for parents of chronically ill children. *Paediatric Nursing.* March/April 112–115.

Rosenstock, I. (1974) Historical origins of the health belief model. *Health Education Monographs.* 2, 328.

Rosser, J. and Maguire, G. (1982) Dilemmas in general practice: the care of the cancer patient. *Social Science Medicine.* 16, 315–326.

Roth, H., Caron, H., Ort, R., Berger, D., Merrill, R., Albee, G. and Streeter, G. (1962) Patients' beliefs about peptic ulcer and its treatment. *Annals of International Medicine.* 56, 72–80.

Rothenberg, M. (1977) Child psychiatry and paediatrics. *Pediatrics.* 60, 649–650.

Routh, D. (ed.) (1988) *Handbook of Pediatric Psychology.* New York: Guilford Press.

Rutter, D., Quine, L. and Chesam, D. (1993) *Social Psychological Approaches to Health.* London: Harvester Wheatsheaf.

Rutter, M. (1985) Resilience in the face of adversity: protective factors and resistance to psychiatric disorder. *British Journal of Psychiatry.* 147, 598–61

Rutter, M., Taylor, E. and Hersov, L. (eds) (1994) *Child and Adolescent Psychiatry: Modern Approaches.* Oxford: Blackwell.

Rutter, M., Tizard, J. and Whitmore, K. (1970) *Education, Health and Behaviour*. London: Longman Press.

Sabbeth, B. and Laventhal, J. (1984) Marital adjustment to chronic childhood illness: a critique of the literature. *Pediatrics*. 73, 762–768.

Sainsbury, C., Gray, O., Cleary, J., Davies, M. and Rowlandson, A. (1986) Care by parents of their children in hospital. *Archives of Disease in Childhood*. 61, 612–615.

Salt, A., Noble-Jamieson, G., Barnes, N., Mowat, A., Rolles, K. and Jamieson, N. (1992) Liver transplantation in 100 children: Cambridge and King's College Hospital series. *British Medical Journal*. 304, 416–421.

Sarason, I., johnson, J. and Siegal, J. (1978) Assessing the impact of life changes: development of the Life Experiences Survey. *Journal of Consulting and Clinical Psychology*. 46, 932–946.

Sarason, I., Levine, H., Basham, R. and Sarason, B. (1983) Assessing social support: the social support questionnaire. *Journal of Personality and Social Psychology*. 44, 127–139.

Serrano, J., Verougstraete, C. and Ghislain, T. (1987) Psychological evaluation and support of paediatric patients and their parents. *Transplant Proceedings*. XIX 3358–3362.

Shaw, E. and Routh, D. (1982) Effect of mother presence on children's reaction to aversive procedures. *Journal of Pediatric Psychology*. 7(1) 33–42.

Simmons, R., Klein, S. and Simmons, R. (eds) (1988) *Gift of Life: The Social and Psychological Impact of Organ Transplantation*. New York: John Wiley.

Skuse, D. (1994) Feeding and sleep disorders. In M. Rutter, E. Taylor and L. Hersov (eds) *Child and Adolescent Psychiatry: Modern Approaches*. Oxford: Blackwell.

Slavin, L., O'Malley, J., Koocher, G. and Foster, D. (1982) Communication of the cancer diagnosis to pediatric patients: impact on long-term adjustment. *American Journal of Psychiatry*. 139, 179–183.

Spanier, G. (1976) Measuring dyadic adjustment: new scales for assessing the quality of marriage and similar dyads. *Journal of Marriage and the Family*. 38, 15–28.

Sparrow, S., Balla, D. and Cicchetti, D. (1984) *Vineland Adaptive Behavior Scales*. Circle Pines MN: American Guidance Service.

Spencer, R. and Behar, L. (1969) Adaptation in hemophiliac adolescence. *Psychosomatics*. 10, 304.

Springer, A. and Steele, M. (1980) Effects of physicians' early parental counseling on rearing Down's syndrome children. *American Journal of Mental Deficiency*. 85, 1–5.

Stabler, B. (1988) Pediatric consultation-liaison. In D. Routh (ed.) *Handbook of Pediatric Psychology*. New York: Guilford Press.

Stabler, B. and Mesibav, G. (1984) Role functions of pediatric and health psychologists in health care settings. *Professional Psychology: Research and Practice*. 15, 142–151.

Stacey, M., Deardon, R., Pill, R. and Robinson, D. (1971) *Hospitals, Children and their Families*. London: Routledge and Kegan Paul.

Stein, R. and Jessop, D. (1982) A non-categorical approach to chronic childhood illness. *Public Health Reports*. 97, 354–362.

—— (1985) Delivery of care to inner-city children with chronic conditions. In N. Hobbs and J. Perrin (eds) *Issues in the Care of Children with Chronic Illness*. London: Jossey-Bass.

Steinberg, D. (1989) *Interprofessional Consultation*. Oxford: Blackwell.

Steptoe, A. and Matthews, A. (eds) (1984) *Healthcare and Human Behaviour*. London: Academic Press.

Stevens, J. (1986) *Applied Multivariate Statistics for the Social Sciences*. London: Lawrence Erlbaum.

Stevenson, M. and Lamb, M. (1979) Effects of infants' sociability and caretaking environment on the infants' cognitive performance. *Child Development*. 50, 340–349.

Stewart, D., Stein, A., Forrest, G. and Clark, D. (1992) Psychosocial adjustment in siblings of children with chronic life-threatening illness: a research note. *Journal of Child Psychology and Psychiatry* 33, 779–784.

Stewart, S., Uauy, R., Waller, D., Kennard, B. and Andrews, W. (1987) Mental and motor development correlates in patients with end stage biliary atresia awaiting liver transplantation. *Pediatrics*. 79, 882–888.

—— (1988) Mental development and growth in children with chronic liver disease of early and late onset. *Pediatrics*. 82, 167–172.

Stewart S., Uauy R., Waller D., Kennard B., Benser, M. and Andrews, W. (1989) Mental and motor development, social competence and growth one year after successful pediatric liver transplantation. *Journal of Pediatrics*. 114, 574–581.

Stiles, W., Putnam, S., James, S. and Wolf, M. (1979) Dimensions of patient and physician roles in medical screening interviews. *Social Science and Medicine*. 13, 335–341.

Street, E. and Dryden, W. (1988) *Family Therapy in Britain*. Milton Keynes: Open University Press.

Svarstad, B. and Lipton, H. (1977) Informing parents about mental retardation: a study of professional communication and parental acceptance. *Social Science and Medicine*. 11, 645–651.

Tarter, R., Erb, S., Biller, P., Switala, J. and Van Thiel, D. (1988) The quality of life following liver transplantation: a preliminary report. Gastroenterol. *Clinics of North America*. 17, 207–217.

Tavormina, J., Kastner, L., Slatter, P. and Watt, S. (1976) Chronically ill children: a psychologically and emotionally deviant population? *Journal of Abnormal Child Psychology*. 4, 99–110.

Tew, B. and Laurence, K. (1973) Mothers, brothers and sisters of patients with spina bifida. *Developmental Medicine and Child Neurology*. 15, 69–76.

The National Health and Community Care Act, 1990 London: HMSO.

Thompson, J., Gustafson, K., Hamlett, K. and Spock, A. (1992a) Psychological adjustment of children with cystic fibrosis: the role of child cognitive processes and maternal adjustment. *Journal of Pediatrics*. 17(6) 741–755.

—— (1992b) Stress, coping, and family functioning in the psychological adjustment of mothers of children and adolescents. *Journal of Pediatric Psychology*. 17(5) 573–586.

Thompson, R. and Lamb, M. (1982) Stranger sociability and its relationship to temperament and social experience during the second year. *Infant Behaviour and Development*. 5, 277–287.

Treacher, A. (1984) Family therapy in mental hospitals. In A. Treacher and J. Carpenter (eds) *Using Family Therapy. A Guide for Practitioners in Different Professional Settings.* Oxford: Blackwell.

Tuma, J. (ed.) (1982) *Handbook for the Practice of Pediatric Psychology.* New York: John Wiley.

Valesco de Parra, M., Cortazar, S. and Covarrubias-Espinoza, G. (1973) The adaptive pattern of families with a leukaemic child. *Family Systems Medicine.* 1(4) 30–35.

Varni, J. and Wallander, J. (1988) Pediatric chronic disabilities: hemophilia and spina bifida as examples. In D. Routh (ed.) *Handbook of Pediatric Psychology.* New York: Guilford Press.

Vaughn, C. (1988) Expressed emotion in family relationships. *Journal of Child Psychology and Psychiatry.* 30, 13–22.

Veit, C. and Ware, J. (1983) The structure of psychological well-being in general populations. *Journal of Consulting and Clinical Psychology.* 51, 730–742.

Venham, L., Murray, P. and Gaulin-Kremer, E. (1979) Child rearing variables affecting the pre-school child's response to dental stress. *Journal of Dental Research.* 58(11) 2042–2045.

Vergani, G., Howard, E., Portman, B. and Mowat, A. (1989) Late referral for biliary atresia – missed opportunities for effective surgery. *The Lancet.* 25 February, 421–423.

Visintainer, M. and Wolfer, J. (1975) Psychological preparation for surgical pediatric patients: the effects on children's and parent's stress responses and adjustment. *Pediatrics.* 52, 187–202.

Waitzkin, H. (1989) A critical theory of medical discourse: ideology, social control, and the process of social context in medical encounters. *Journal of Health and Social Behaviour.* 30, 220–239.

Walker, C. (1988) Stress and coping in siblings of childhood cancer patients. *Nursing Research.* 37, 208–212.

Walker, D., Stein, R., Perrin, E. and Jessop, D. (1990) Assessing psychological adjustment of children with chronic illness. *Journal of Developmental and Behavioural Pediatrics.* 11, 116–121.

Walker, L. and Greene, J. (1991) The Functional Disability Inventory: measuring a neglected dimension of child health status. *Journal of Pediatric Psychology.* 16, 39–58.

Walker, L., Ford, M. and Donald, W. (1987) Cystic fibrosis and family stress: effects of age and severity of illness. *Pediatrics.* 79, 239–246.

Wallander, J., Feldman, W. and Varni, J. (1989a) Physical status and psychosocial adjustment in children with spina bifida. *Journal of Pediatric Psychology.* 14(1) 89–102.

Wallander, J., Pitt, L. and Mellins, C. (1990) Child functional independence and maternal psychosocial stress as risk factors threatening adaptation in mothers of physically or sensorially handicapped children. *Journal of Consulting and Clinical Psychology.* 58(6) 818–824.

Wallander, J., Varni, J., Babani, L., Banis, H. and Wilcox, K. (1988) Children with chronic physical disorders: maternal reports of their psychological adjustment. *Journal of Pediatric Psychology.* 13(2) 197–212.

Wallander, J.,Varni, J., Babani, L., Banis, H. and Wilcox, K. (1989b) Family resources as resistance factors for psychological maladjustment in chronically ill and handicapped children. *Journal of Pediatric Psychology.* 14(2) 157–173.

Wallander, J., Varni, J., Babani, L., Banis, H., DeHaan, C. and Wilcox, K. (1989c) Disability perimeters, chronic strain and adaptation of physically handicapped children and their mothers. *Journal of Pediatric Psychology.* 14(1) 23–42.

Wallander, J., Varni, J., Babani, L., DeHeen, C., Wilcox, K. and Banis, H. (1989d) The social environment and the adaptation of mothers of physically handicapped children. *Journal of Pediatric Psychology.* 14, 371–388.

Watts, F. (1984) Applicable research in the NHS. *Bulletin of The British Psychological Society* 34, 41–42.

—— (ed.) (1985) *New Perspectives in Clinical Psychology. Vol. 1.* Leicester: British Psychological Society Books.

Weichler, N. and Hakos, L. (1989) Information needs of primary care givers in pediatric liver transplantation. *Transplant Proceedings.* XXI, 3562.

Wells, R. and Schwebel, A. (1987) Chronically ill children and their mothers. *Journal of Development and Behavioural Pediatric Psychology.* 8(2) 83–89.

West, R. (1991) *Child Health Guide.* London: Hamlyn.

Wilkinson, G., Borsey, D., Leslie, P., Newton, R., Lind, C. and Ballinger, C. (1987) Psychiatric disorder in patients with diabetes mellitus attending a general hospital clinic. *Psychological Medicine.* 17, 515–517.

Will, D. and Wrate, R. (1985) *Integrated Family Therapy: A Problem-centred Psychodynamic Approach.* London: Tavistock.

Wilson, S. (1912) Progressive lenticular degeneration: a familial nervous disease associated with cirrhosis of the liver. *Brain.* 34, 295–509.

Wilson-Barnett, J. (1978) Patients' emotional responses to barium X-rays. *Journal of Advanced Nursing.* 3, 37–46.

Winefield, H. (1992) Doctor–patient communication: an interpersonal helping process. In S. Maes, H. Leventhal and M. Johnston (eds) *International Review of Health Psychology. Vol 1.* Chichester: John Wiley.

Wolfer, J. and Visintainer, M. (1975) Pediatric surgical patients' and parents' stress responses and adjustment. *Nursing Research.* 24(4) 244–255.

Woods, B. (1994) One articulation of the structural family therapy model: a biobehavioural family model of chronic illness in children. *Journal of Family Therapy.* 16, 53–71.

Wooley, H., Stein, A., Forrest, G. and Baum, D. (1989a) Imparting the diagnosis of life threatening illness in children. *British Medical Journal.* 298, 1623–1626.

—— (1989b) Staff stress and job satisfaction at a children's hospice. *Archives of Disease in Childhood.* 64, 114–118.

Worchel, F., Nolan, B.,Wilson,V., Purser, J., Copeland, D. and Pfefferbaum, B. (1988) Assessment of depression in children with cancer. *Journal of Pediatric Psychology.* 13, 101–112.

Wynne, L.,Weber, T. and McDaniels, S. (1986) The road from family therapy to systems consultation. In L. Wynne, S. McDaniels and T. Weber (eds) *Systems Consultation: A New Perspective for Family Therapy.* New York and London: Guilford Press.

Zabin, M. and Melamed, B. (1980) Relationship between parental discipline and children's ability to cope with stress. *Journal of Behavioural Assessment.* 2(1) 17–39.

Zastowny, T., Kerschenbaum, D. and Meng, A. (1986) Coping skills training for children: effects on distress before, during and after hospitalization for surgery. *Health Psychology.* 5(3) 231–247.

Zitelli, B., Malatack, J., Gartner, C., Urback, A., Williams, I., Miller, J. and Kirkpatrick, B. (1986) Evaluation of the pediatric patient for liver transplantation. *Pediatrics.* 78, 559–565.

Zitelli, B., Miller, J., Gartner, C., Malatack, J., Urbank, A., Belle, S., Williams, L., Kirkpatrick, B. and Starzl, T. (1988) Changes in life style after liver transplantation. *Pediatrics.* 82, 173–180.

Zitelli, B., Gartner, J., Malatack, A., Urbank, A., Miller, J., Williams, I., Kirkpatrick, B., Breinig, M. and Ho, M. (1987) Pediatric liver transplantation: patient evaluation and selection, infectious complications and life style after transplantation. *Transplant Proceedings.* XIX, 3309–3316.

Index